C000220376

HOME WATERS MTBs & MGBs
AT WAR
1939–1945

From the same author in the MTBs trilogy

Dog Boats at War
Mediterranean MTBs at War

The author, 1944.

HOME WATERS MTBs & MGBs AT WAR 1939–1945

LEONARD C. REYNOLDS

FOREWORD BY ADMIRAL OF THE FLEET SIR JULIAN OSWALD

SUTTON PUBLISHING

in association with
THE IMPERIAL WAR MUSEUM

First published in the United Kingdom in 2000 by
Sutton Publishing Limited · Phoenix Mill
Thrupp · Stroud · Gloucestershire · GL5 2BU
in association with the Imperial War Museum

British Library Cataloguing in Publication Data
A catalogue record for this book is available from the British Library

ISBN 0 7509 2518 3

Endpapers: Front: A 71ft Vosper 1939 Class MTB of the 4th Flotilla, spring 1943; Back: MTB 447 of the 35th Flotilla, 1944.

Typeset in 10/13 pt Sabon.
Typesetting and origination by
Sutton Publishing Limited.
Printed and bound in England by
J.H. Haynes & Co. Ltd, Sparkford.

CONTENTS

LIST OF MAPS

FOREWORD

BY ADMIRAL OF THE FLEET SIR JULIAN OSWALD GCB

The history of Royal Naval Coastal Forces in the twentieth century contains many puzzling enigmas. Why were the lessons of the First World War so largely neglected in the inter-war years? Why was it that only the willingness of certain specialist ship builders to invest heavily to keep development alive provided at least *some* basis on which to build when the Second World War loomed? Why did it take so long to equip MTBs/MGBs with seriously heavy armament? And perhaps most poignantly of all for the amazingly brave and dedicated officers and ratings involved, why was official recognition of their efforts so hard to win? This book and its companion volumes give the reader the essential background to these questions in the form of a carefully researched and fully factual account of MTB and MGB operations in the Second World War. But the questions remain!

Were these crews 'amazingly brave and dedicated'? The answer must be a resounding YES! How else *can* one describe a man like Lt Cdr Hichens who won two DSOs and three DSCs? This represents repeated valour of an exceptional order. It surprises me that only one VC was awarded to Coastal Forces personnel: one wonders how many citations were forwarded.

This book brings out well the nature of the operations undertaken by relatively small boats, often in bad weather, largely at night, and the all-too-frequent frustration of targets which never appeared, or turned away, and of weapons or engines which failed. But when action did ensue it was high drama, and how frighteningly quickly issues of life and death were resolved.

As a young cadet at BRNC Dartmouth just after the war I knew the then Lt Cdrs Dickens, Jermain and Hamilton-Meikle. They were of course our heroes – but they were very modest ones indeed! In 1980 I returned to the College as the Captain and had the pleasure of inviting the three French admirals then commanding at Brest, Cherbourg and Lorient to our Remembrance Day Service. All three had served in the Free French 23rd MTB Flotilla based on Dartmouth, and one had won a DSC. Their experiences had formed friendships which lasted for life, and this is clearly very much the case with all those who served in these boats.

To return to just one of my opening questions. Since the Second World War, RN Coastal Forces as such have faded away. The initial enthusiasm which led to the building of three new classes (Bold, Gay and Dark) waned, numbers declined and eventually only three target boats remained, acting as loyal opposition for ships Working-Up at Portland. Even these are now long gone.

And yet, does not the fact that the Navy's operational emphasis has swung away from blue water warfare in the deep Atlantic to so-called brown water or littoral operations in support of power projection, almost anywhere in the world, suggest that the possession of some fighting units smaller than a 4,000-ton frigate or a 6,000-ton destroyer might be desirable? Many other navies now have highly capable missile-armed coastal forces. Can we be sure that our helicopters, fixed wing aircraft, destroyers and frigates can protect our high-value carriers, tankers and amphibious ships? At times of great budgetary strain it is always difficult to argue persuasively for the reintroduction of a capability foregone. But as the books of this trilogy show all too clearly, we have paid the price of neglect before, and some effort – at the very least to refresh our minds on Coastal Forces capabilities and techniques and provide our fleet with the wherewithal to exercise and train against them – would seem prudent. It would also serve as a lasting tribute to the men of Coastal Forces whose bravery and sacrifice are so well depicted in these volumes.

AUTHOR'S NOTE

This book, the third instalment of the history of the operations of the Royal Navy's Motor Torpedo Boats and Motor Gun Boats in the Second World War, represents the final response to an invitation extended by the Imperial War Museum in 1986. That invitation resulted in a long period of research before writing began in 1994; by that time I had realized that the subject matter demanded more than the compilation of one book: a trilogy was required to do it justice. The decision on how the trilogy should be written rested ultimately not on the logic of chronology (although each section is careful in that respect) but on more practical reasons.

The 'long' boats – predominantly the D Class Fairmiles, colloquially the 'Dog Boats' – were not introduced until 1942. As a result, the records of their operations were far more complete, and this – added to the fact that I personally had served in them – provided the incentive to make *Dog Boats at War* the first of the trilogy.

Similarly, there were special reasons for choosing *Mediterranean MTBs at War* as the second volume. It described the operations of the 'short' boat flotillas in the Mediterranean, with an enormous contribution by my co-author Bert Cooper, who had previously researched and written individual histories of those flotillas at my request.

By far the largest number of 'short' boats carried on their operations in the English Channel and in the North Sea, without cessation from 1939 to 1945. This was the true cradle and focus of the MTB/MGB battle, the area where throughout 1940, 1941 and 1942 the tactics evolved, the boats gradually improved, and the early leaders created the ethos of Coastal Forces from the forgotten void of a reputation first established in the years between 1915 and 1919, but thereafter sadly neglected. The names Hichens, Pumphrey, Richards, Gould, Dickens, Horne, Arnold-Forster, Trelawny, Macdonald, Dixon and many others grace these pages with the proofs of their skill and gallantry.

I have no need to apologize for a repetition of the thanks offered in the two earlier volumes. I acknowledge with great gratitude the assistance of countless people, first in the research phase and then during the compilation of the text and the collection of illustrations. Without the encouragement of Dr Christopher Dowling and the staff of the Imperial War Museum this work would never have begun. The support of a research grant from the Sir James Caird Trust of the National Maritime Museum was timely and greatly appreciated. The years of research at the Naval Historical Branch through Dr David Brown and my early mentor Paul Melton gave me an invaluable framework, later filled in by an even longer association with the splendid facilities of the Public Record Office at Kew and its staff.

The archive resource I have built up since 1986 owes an enormous debt to the veterans of Coastal Forces, reached through the CFVA and the MTB/MGB Officers' Association, which I thankfully acknowledge. Douglas Hunt, Claude Holloway, Pieter Jansen,

Peter Bickmore and Wallis Randall have all been invariably helpful.

In the preparation of this book, I owe a great deal to Geoffrey Hudson and to Christopher Dreyer who between them command an unequalled overall knowledge of Coastal Forces. Both have read the text and made many helpful suggestions. The generosity of Captain W. Chatterton Dickson RN (Retd) – 'Seedie' – the compiler of *Seedie's List of Coastal Forces Awards*, in giving his permission for the reproduction of material in Appendix 2 is gratefully acknowledged. My friends Desmond Wilton as a reader, and Colin Daniel and Roger Battye as computer advisors, together with Brian McConkey who translated German documents, have been of great service throughout the whole enterprise.

It is not possible to mention individually every one of the officers and men of the short MTBs and MGBs in Home Waters who have at some time provided me with information. Many are referred to in the text, but in particular the following deserve special thanks even at the risk of omitting some, to whom I apologize: E. Archer, A. Banger DSM, C. Burford, C. Burke DSC, V.F. Clarkson DSC, D. Currie DSC, H.G. Curtis DSM, J.D. Dixon DSC, W. Donovan, R.Q. Drayson DSC, Cdr C.W.S. Dreyer DSO DSC RN (Retd), B. Hetherington, Capt. D. Jermain DSC RN (Retd), J. Lake, P. Magnus DSC, A.F. Moody, Lord Newborough DSC, J.P. Perkins DSC, A. Rowbery, F.J.R. Shadbolt MBE DSC, A.V. Simpson, E.J.W. Slater DSM, N. Taylor DSC and P.A.R. Thompson DSC.

Last, but by no means least, I record once again my gratitude to my wife Win. Not only has she typed and retyped every word of all three manuscripts, interpreting my scrawl as only she can, but she has dealt with correspondence over fifteen years and sustained and supported me in every way throughout that time.

All the conventions adopted in the two previous books are continued, and I hope the use of less formality with names than is common in historical works will be accepted as typical of the atmosphere of Coastal Forces in all but the serious business of fighting a war.

Notes from the text appear in two categories. In order to assist other researchers and readers wishing to refer to original texts, sources of information are usually given as footnotes. Longer and more complex notes are marked 'Appendix 1, Note *X*' and appear in Appendix 1 in numerical order. Abbreviations and terms used in the notes are listed and explained at the beginning of Appendix 1.

INTRODUCTION

It is perhaps helpful to clarify here the apparent anomaly in the title of this book. Having already described in *Dog Boats at War* the operations of the 'long' MTBs and MGBs – mainly the Fairmile C and D Classes and the Steam Gun Boats – this history concerns itself almost completely with the 'short' boat MTB and MGB flotillas which operated in the English Channel and the North Sea. The craft concerned were the British Power Boats, the Vospers, the Elcos and the Samuel Whites which made up the great majority of the flotillas based mainly at Dover, Ramsgate, Newhaven and Dartmouth in the south, and at Felixstowe and Lowestoft on the east coast.

One notable point of difference in the approach of this history in comparison with other accounts of MTB operations is the constant reference to flotillas. As with RAF squadrons and Army regiments – albeit on a much smaller scale – the flotilla was the focus through which a definable individuality and spirit could be engendered. The eight or twelve boats would wherever possible berth together, while the crews trained together and made up fighting units on patrol, and in harbour used to socialize together. The Senior Officer could stamp his 'style' upon his flotilla, and certainly the great heroes of Coastal Forces invariably led the most successful flotillas, noted for aggression, for skilful employment of tactical dispositions and for results.

The approach throughout is chronological, and there is no attempt (except in the final stages of the Channel war) to separate the operations of the two main areas, off the French coast and off the Dutch coast. The operational areas, so abruptly established in the summer of 1940 by the fall of the Low Countries and then France, did not change until the Channel ports fell to the Allies one by one by September 1944, following the invasion of Normandy, with the Belgian and southern Dutch coasts following some months later. By the end of the war, the crews of the boats were as familiar with those enemy coasts as they were with their native shores.

The Coastal Force bases were well equipped with facilities for repairs and maintenance, and in most cases for accommodation ashore to ease the problems of lack of space aboard the boats. Allegiance to a base was another binding factor, frequently nurtured by the personality of the CO of the Base and his concern for the personnel of the boats in his care. Often Commanders brought back from retirement, they were a special breed and were among those who could most influence the success and happiness of the flotillas allotted to them.

It was a long and hard war, with interminable periods of fruitless patrols in bad weather punctuated by bursts of high drama whenever the enemy was encountered. Often the sea was as ruthless a foe as the E-boats and the heavily armed convoy escorts. The 266 'short' MTBs and MGBs involved in this area fought 308 battles: 76 boats were lost and, even more grievously, 285 men died.

The story of their war in this third volume of the trilogy completes the picture of the endeavours of the MTBs and MGBs of all types and in all areas in the Second World War, so that they may take their rightful place in the records of the Royal Navy at war. It is dedicated to those who gave their lives for their country.

CHAPTER 1

1939–1940: THE LEGACY OF NEGLECT

In political and military matters – as in all aspects of life – judgements reached with the benefits of hindsight are not necessarily sound. But the views expressed in a report prepared for the Admiralty soon after the end of the Second World War[1] was firm in its condemnation of the woeful state of unpreparedness of the Royal Navy's Coastal Forces in 1939. Those views were shared by many serving at that time.

During the period 1916–1919 the Navy had developed a force of Coastal Motor Boats (CMBs) and Motor Launches (MLs) which proved extremely effective for operations in waters where larger ships could not venture, in the shallow and coastal areas of the 'Narrow Seas'. Even with these relatively primitive boats they had achieved considerable success, which for reasons of expendability and cost-effectiveness had been assessed as of great value.

Many of the young naval officers who had served in those boats, and whose decorations included VCs, DSOs and DSCs in considerable numbers, had gone on to enjoy successful careers in the Royal Navy. Twenty years later they were captains and commanders. They had watched as their branch of the Navy was disbanded in the years after the Armistice, with no attempt made to preserve the lessons learned. And they had watched as other navies had continued the research and development of these craft, so that in the early 1930s both Mussolini and Hitler were in a position to begin the production of highly efficient, fast torpedo-carrying boats – the MAS boats of

[1] *The Coastal Forces Monograph*, a report prepared in 1952 for the Admiralty, on the lessons learned in war.

MTB 102 displaying the first Oerlikon gun fitted in an MTB, for trials, 1938. (Collection G.M. Hudson)

The Thornycroft MTB 105 attaining 2,600 revolutions on trials, August 1940. She was much later used as a tender to HMS *Fidelity*. (Collection G.M. Hudson)

the Italian Navy[2] and the *Schnellboote* of the German Navy, known to the British as E-boats (enemy boats) rather than S-boats. From the start the German E-boats enjoyed the benefits of high-speed Daimler-Benz diesel engines which were to prove of immense value in their operations.

In contrast, when war was declared in 1939 the Royal Navy had twelve boats serving in Malta and six in Hong Kong (all developed through commercial initiatives and somewhat reluctantly supported by the Admiralty, and all taken up late in the 1930s). In home waters only a handful of boats were available to pit against the enemy. There had been virtually no Admiralty input into the development of engine or hull designs in the inter-war years, and apart from two experimental Vospers, the Thornycroft models of 1919 were now hastily revived and boats being built for other navies were requisitioned.

In compiling a history of MTB and MGB operations throughout the Second World War in three volumes it is very difficult to avoid repetition. *Mediterranean MTBs at War*, for example, tells in some detail the story of Hubert Scott-Paine, the inspiration behind the building of the British Power Boats which formed the 1st MTB Flotilla and later the majority of the Motor Gun Boats of Coastal Forces.[3] It also describes not only the political and commercial struggle for ascendancy in the production of the 'short' Motor Torpedo Boats which led to the preference for the

[2] MAS: originally 'Motoscafo Armato SVAN', after the yard in Venice which built them.

[3] See also Rance, *Fast Boats and Flying Boats*, 1989.

Vosper boats designed by Peter Du Cane, but also the part played by Thornycrofts in both world wars.

The fact that the 1st MTB Flotilla served first in Malta and then made a dramatic passage through the French rivers and canals at the end of 1939 so that the surviving boats could serve in home waters is a significant theme in these interwoven histories. In both *Dog Boats at War* and *Mediterranean MTBs at War* there are many references to the previous service of boats and crews in home waters – and indeed the reverse, when after two years or more in the Mediterranean officers and men returned to serve with distinction in flotillas operating from the east coast and Channel bases.

Seven boats of the 1st Flotilla (MTBs 03, 04 and 14–18) were deemed serviceable enough to be available for operations after returning from Malta; mostly from the second batch of British Power Boats rather than the original six deployed in the Mediterranean, they joined the mixed bag of experimental and requisitioned boats in January 1940. There was, at the time, very little support for them: no central organization, no dedicated bases yet commissioned and no specialized training facilities. It was indeed a legacy of neglect. During the inter-war years any progress in concept and design of such boats had been left to private enterprise, while the heritage of the harsh lessons learned in the North Sea, the Channel, the Baltic and the Black Sea in the years 1916–1919 had been sadly discarded.

Fortunately, this was the period of the Phoney War, when the enemy could take little advantage of this total unpreparedness. At

The quadruple Lewis guns of MTB 18 on a practice shoot off Felixstowe, February 1940. (Courtesy the late J.T. Mannooch)

least it provided an opportunity for bases to be formed at Gosport (HMS *Hornet*), Felixstowe (HMS *Beehive*) and Portland (HMS *Attack*), with others to follow shortly after at Lowestoft, Great Yarmouth, Dover and Fowey. At first, the men put in command of these bases were able to inject new urgency into the struggle to obtain specialist spares and supplies. Some, like Cdr R.H. McBean DSC RN at Felixstowe and Lt Cdr Dennis at Dover, were veterans of the CMBs of the First World War, and gradually others with that background were appointed, and were important in passing on some of the spirit and traditions of this branch of the Navy.

All the Senior Officers (SOs) of the early flotillas, and the great majority of the COs of the original boats, were of necessity young RN officers in their first commands, and their crews consisted of 'Regular Service' ratings. The officers of the 1st Flotilla, introduced into service in 1937, brought with them from the Mediterranean valuable experience from the intensive training, both as a flotilla and with the fleet, in the first months of the war. It soon became clear, however, that the RN lieutenants would very soon be replaced as COs by RNVR officers with some prewar training, and with an almost universal background of sailing and love of the sea. Indeed from as early as August 1939 they were being appointed as first lieutenants in the boats. Nevertheless, it was largely from the group of RN officers that the Flotilla Senior Officers were chosen to become the leaders in the expanding service throughout 1940 and 1941.

There is no doubt that the nature of these small fast boats with their young officers and close-knit crews led to a particular spirit and comradeship in MTBs from the outset. This camaraderie spread from the individual boats to the flotillas as they became more coherent, and it led to the emergence of certain leaders – usually the Senior Officers of flotillas, but sometimes other COs – who became well known not only in the service but also in due course to the public, as their exploits were publicized in the Press. Among the first to be thus recognized in these early days were Lt P.F.S. (Stewart) Gould RN, Lt D. (Denis) Jermain RN and Lt C.W. (Christopher) Dreyer RN, all of whom became legends and whose names appear frequently in these histories.

Soon after their arrival at Felixstowe, the boats of the 1st Flotilla were joined by three boats – one Vosper and two Thornycrofts: 22, 24 and 25 – which had been ordered in 1938, and formed the 4th Flotilla under Lt Cdr A.B. Cole. Meanwhile, MTBs 100 (a 60ft British Power Boat) and 102 (a prewar experimental Vosper) had formed the 3rd Training Flotilla based first at HMS *Vernon* and then at HMS *Hornet* from April 1940 when it was formally commissioned as the first specialized MTB base. This was marked by the official adoption of the term Coastal Forces.

In 1938, when the Admiralty feared that U-boats might pose a threat in the Narrow Seas, the first five Motor Anti-Submarine Boats (MA/SBs) were ordered from British Power Boats at Hythe. They were 60 ft in length and very similar to the boats of the 1st Flotilla except that instead of torpedoes they were equipped with Asdic and depth charges. The first batch was based at Portland, at HMS *Osprey*, while others were nearing completion.

The 'Twilight War', as Churchill dubbed it, ended abruptly early in April 1940 when the German Army invaded Denmark and almost immediately moved on to Norway with multi-pronged landings as far apart as Kristiansand in the south and Narvik in the north. The battle there reached its inevitable conclusion within a month, and was followed on 10 May by the invasion of the Low Countries. Despite the rapid response by the Allied armies, the

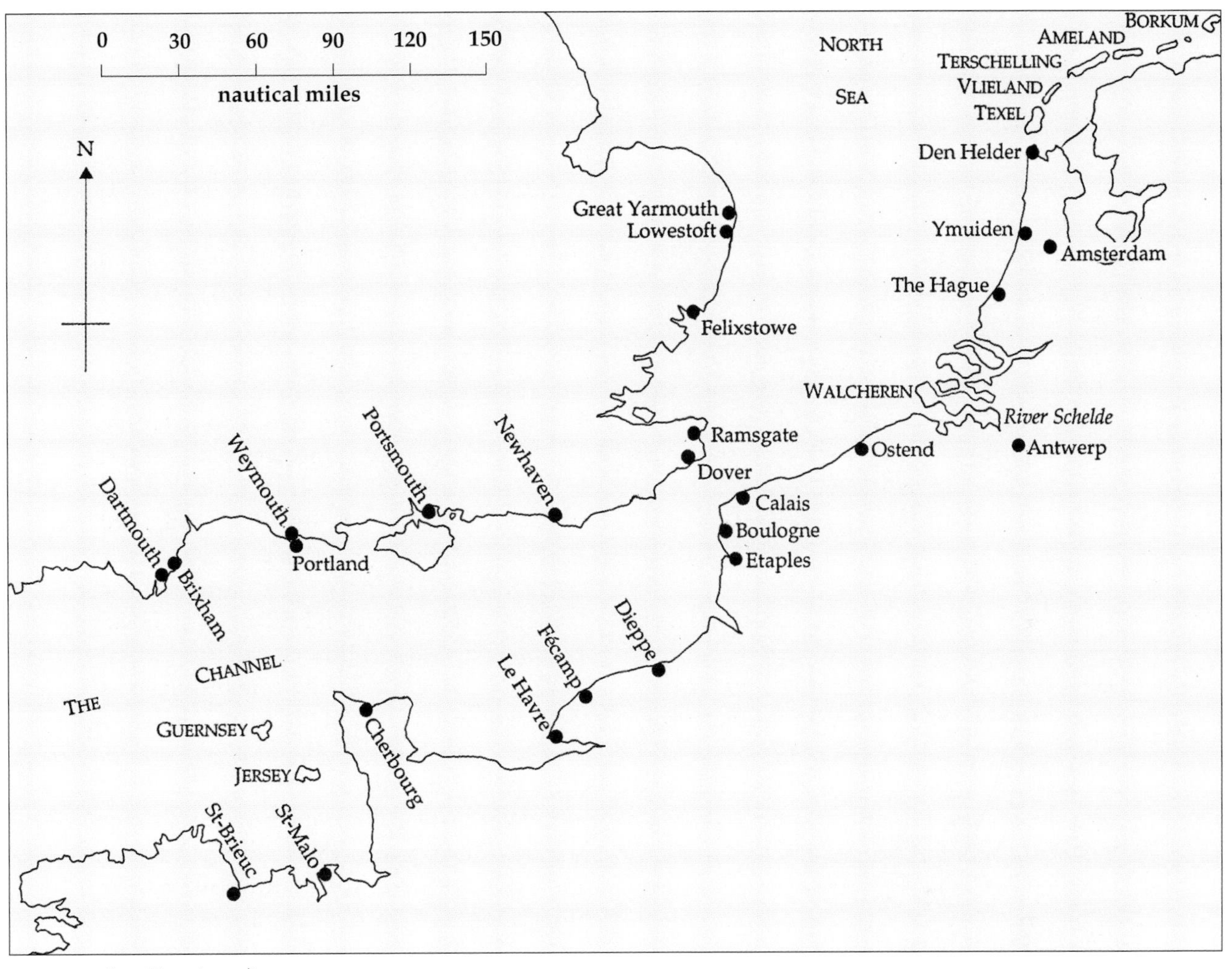

Home Waters (general).

enemy advance was relentless and expertly directed to take advantage of the weak points in the defences.[4]

At last an opportunity to join battle was presented to the Felixstowe boats. On 12 May MTBs 22 (Cole), 24 (Parkinson) and 25 (Litchfield) received orders to proceed to Ymuiden on the Dutch coast, where they were to await directions in a very rapidly changing situation.

[4] W.S. Churchill, *The Second World War, Vol. 1 The Gathering Storm.*

When issued, the operational orders were broad and varied: to bring back information on the current situation, and to prevent passage of enemy troops to the west by water. They might also be required to torpedo lock gates. They crossed the North Sea at 30 knots and were met by Rear Adm Vreede of the Royal Netherlands Navy and the British Liaison Officer, Cdr Goodenough. Soon after midnight, they were sent up the canal towards Amsterdam, withstood air attacks, passed through the lock into the Zuider Zee and moved northward to the

MTB 102 (CO, Lt C.W.S. Dreyer RN), a prewar experimental Vosper, in early 1940. (Collection G.M. Hudson)

MASBs 3 (P 67), 1 (P 00), 4 (P 39), 2 (P 21) and 5 (P 44) at Portland, August 1939. (Courtesy A. Henderson)

MTB 22, with 102 in the background flying the Admiralty flag, at the Fleet Review, off Weymouth, August 1939. (Collection G.M. Hudson)

town of Enkhuisen. There they covered the boats with camouflage netting while they awaited orders, but Intelligence soon reported that the lock they had passed through was now under attack, and that it was imperative that they evade capture at all costs. They left next morning prepared to fight their way out, but as they approached the lock at 1215 they found that the Dutch Army was still in control, although Amsterdam was being over-run. Along the canal fuel tanks were blazing and there was every indication that the end for Holland and Belgium could not be long delayed. The boats reached Ymuiden in the early evening, and left for Felixstowe at 2100. Once again they were attacked by aircraft and this time MTB 24's gunner, Able Seaman Stanley Aldridge, shot down a Heinkel 115, the first success against aircraft for Coastal Forces. Although nothing on the grand scale had been achieved, a great deal of experience had been gained very early in their operational existence, and the SO, Tony Cole, was well pleased with their performance.

As they returned to the base, the boats of the 1st Flotilla were setting out in various groups to carry out orders concerned with evacuation of key personnel from Dutch and Belgian ports. MTB 16 (Stewart Gould) went to the Hook of Holland and had the distinction of being the last ship to leave, with a small group of mainly service personnel, not long before Holland formally surrendered. The first Coastal Forces awards of the war were gazetted in July for the operations along the Dutch and Belgian coasts, when Lt Cdr Cole, Lt Gould, and

The Senior Officer of the 4th MTB Flotilla, Lt Cdr A.B. Cole RN (right) with two officers and two ratings from the unit, aboard MTB 22 after their foray to the Zuider Zee in May 1940. (Courtesy the late J.T. Mannooch)

AB Aldridge were all mentioned in despatches.[5]

A week later an attempt was made to block the entrance to the Bruges canal at Zeebrugge on the Belgian coast. The force was accompanied by MTBs 15 and 16 whose task was to bring off the crews of the blockships, but the expedition failed when both blockships grounded on mud-flats well outside the fairway. After thirty-six hours a second attempt was made, this time with MTBs 14 and 15 in support. MTB 15 (Lt Hilary Gamble) led the blockships right up to the lock gates – not without several mishaps – and the detonators settled both in the right position. Other boats of the flotilla were busy ferrying across VIPs who were trying to assess the constantly changing situation, despite suffering constant air attacks. (Appendix 1, Note 1)

After the Low Countries had fallen, the Germans swept through the gap at the end of the Maginot Line to reach the French ports, and immediately British attention switched to the plight of over 300,000 troops trapped on the beaches around and to the north of Dunkirk. Operation Dynamo, directed from Dover, was initiated almost at once to attempt the seemingly impossible task of rescuing this huge number of men, under constant attack from both artillery and the

[5] Article by Geoffrey Granville, in 1940 a sub-lieutenant RNVR, first lieutenant of MTB 24; awards from *Seedie's List of Coastal Forces Awards*.

air, on exposed and gently shelving beaches which could be approached only by very small craft. The recruitment of hundreds of tiny private vessels manned by young and old who immediately volunteered for this hazardous work has rightly been given a special place in the history of the war, as an appalling defeat was somehow averted by a miraculous feat of improvisation. The small boats travelled daily across the Strait of Dover and then made countless journeys between the beaches and the deeper water where destroyers waited to take on board the exhausted troops, many of them wounded.

All the MTBs were, of course, involved. The 1st Flotilla's boats were mainly deployed 2 or more miles off Dunkirk to ensure that E-boats should not interfere with the work at the beaches. The first of the available MA/SBs – 10 and 6 – were summoned from the boatyard at Hythe, barely finished and with totally untried crews. MA/SB 10, commanded by Lt R.G.H.G. Eyre RN, was also pressed into most unsuitable service as a tug holding ships against the mole in Dunkirk; by the end of the operation her hull had been damaged so severely that she was paid off.

MTB 102 of the Training Flotilla, commanded by Lt C. Dreyer, journeyed day after day to Dunkirk. She spent the first day ferrying troops off the beaches, then found herself acting frequently as Rear Adm Wake-Walker's flagship, delivering him hither and thither, and flying his flag – to his amusement the 'flag' was a traditional naval 'St George's flag' tea-towel suitably adorned with two red balls. By the end of the evacuation the crew was exhausted from lack of sleep, their labours having been interrupted only by one enforced day in harbour to repair and maintain 102's engines.

Many other boats performed heroic services, and one deserves a special mention. MTB 107 was a 40ft Thornycroft – very like the smallest CMBs of the First World War – and she was commanded by Lt (Jock) Cameron RNVR. At forty years old, and already an established KC, he was far older than the majority of MTB officers, and was affectionately known as 'Grandpa' to all. 107 performed heroically, and despite the disadvantage of having no astern gear, she spent the last night of the evacuation of Dunkirk bringing off the crews of blockships until Cameron realized that he had become the sole focus of enemy fire. His was the last warship to leave the stricken port. (Appendix 1, Note 2)

The completion of Operation Dynamo was formally announced on 4 June. It had been extended in order to bring more than 25,000 French troops across the Channel. Churchill made one of his greatest speeches in Parliament as he reported the details, and was careful to point out that 'this deliverance was not a victory . . . wars are not won by evacuations; but we shall fight on. We shall fight in France, and in the seas and oceans. We shall fight on the beaches, in the streets, in the fields, in the hills; we shall never surrender.'[6]

To the Royal Navy, and especially to the men of Coastal Forces, whose role was concerned principally with the Narrow Seas, the last few weeks had totally changed the strategic situation. The whole seaboard of Western Europe 'from Bergen to Bordeaux' was now in enemy hands, and all its ports and airfields were available to enemy forces. The prewar E-boat force (which already outnumbered the MTBs) was rapidly growing and would soon have many more bases from which to attack the Channel and North Sea convoys.

But vital time had been gained, and a mixture of boats began to assemble in the new bases. N 5 and N 6, the first of the Norwegian boats, had just been completed by Vospers and their Norwegian COs took them

[6] W.S. Churchill, *The Second World War, Vol. 2 Their Finest Hour.*

MTBs 18 (Lt J.T. Mannooch RN), 15 (Lt L.J.H. Gamble RN) and 16 (Lt P.F.S. Gould RN) of the 1st Flotilla off Felixstowe, February 1940. (Courtesy IWM – HU52784)

to join the 11th Flotilla at Dover during July 1940. They were joined by four more Vospers, 69 to 72, and began to operate in the Channel under the command of Lt King-Church RN. All these Vospers had Italian Isotta Fraschini engines which gave them a good turn of speed. They were used mainly as rescue boats, retrieving aircrew who had ditched and the crews of merchant vessels sunk by dive-bombers in the Strait of Dover. There were some inconclusive exchanges of fire with E-boats, but with the air battle raging over their heads and long-range coastal guns firing from the French coast, their work was never dull.

The MA/SBs were gathering at Portland but were clearly of little use in their projected role as anti-submarine boats and they too were also engaged mainly in air-sea rescue. Notes received from Vice Adm Sir A.A. Fitzroy-Talbot KBE CB DSO before he died throw some light on the evolution of the first MGBs from some of these MA/SBs during 1940. He was appointed – as a young lieutenant RN – to be SO of the 3rd MGB Flotilla, although whether his boats were still MA/SBs officially is unclear. Certainly there was no doubt in his mind that if they could not be used for anti-submarine work they should have some offensive role and were therefore properly gunboats.

Fitzroy-Talbot picked up his boats in Hythe, and after trials in the Solent soon proceeded to Fowey, where the Operations Room was established in an ice-cream parlour on the front! No one really knew much about the running or operation of these very fast craft, which were a mixed bag of 70ft and 63ft boats, commandeered from the French Navy which had originally ordered them. Several of his officers, particularly Lt A.C.B. Blomfield RN and Sub Lt Cornelius Burke RCNVR, were to feature prominently in operations later in the war.

During the autumn of 1940 this flotilla carried out offensive sweeps off Cherbourg and anti-E-boat patrols from Dartmouth, and even

MTB N 5, Royal Norwegian Navy, July 1940. (Collection G.M. Hudson)

The 3rd MASB Flotilla (later the 3rd MGBs) leaves Southampton for Fowey, with the SO, Lt A.A. Fitzroy-Talbot RN, leading in MASB 46, July 1940. (Collection G.M. Hudson)

tried its hand at detonating acoustic mines to clear Plymouth harbour. On one occasion the flotilla was sent to work with Lord Mountbatten, Captain (D), in HMS *Javelin*, escorting the battleship *Revenge*, while she bombarded the port of Cherbourg. The MGBs were sent in close to the breakwater as shells screamed overhead. It was very frightening, but the hope that E-boats would be flushed out came to nothing. The enemy evidently thought it was an air-raid, and when all the searchlights on the jetty started searching the skies, the flotilla was able to run at speed along the breakwater in line ahead picking them off and dowsing the lights one by one.

At *Beehive*, the 1st Flotilla had been joined by Lt Cdr Cole's 4th Flotilla, which had now been reinforced by the arrival of MTBs 29, 30, 31 and 32. The early patrols met with no enemy contacts, but on 13 August MTBs 18 (Lt J.T. Mannooch RN), 16 (Lt P.F.S. Gould RN) and 14 (Lt Hamilton-Hill) encountered a group of enemy ships off the Dutch coast. Believing them to be E-boats, Mannooch decided to ram. Too late he realized that his target was a far more robust minesweeper, and 18 lost her bow but hardly damaged the enemy. Gould also attacked but was mauled. Hamilton-Hill was busy going to the aid of 18 when the first real opportunity of torpedoing enemy ships was lost as several armed trawlers steamed by. It was miraculous that none of the MTBs was sunk.

The long-awaited first successful torpedo attack by MTBs followed shortly after. On 8 September MTBs 15 (Eardley-Wilmot) and

The CO, Lt J.T. Mannooch, with members of the crew, inspects damage to the bow of MTB 18 after ramming an enemy minesweeper off the Dutch coast on 17 August 1940 in one of the earliest MTB actions of the war. (Courtesy the late J.T. Mannooch)

17 (Faulkner) of the 1st Flotilla at *Beehive* entered the anchorage off Ostend, which destroyers and aircraft had already attacked, and made torpedo runs on the twenty merchant vessels gathered there. The official report credits them with one certain sinking – an ammunition ship which blew up – and one probable.

The next success fell to the 4th Flotilla on 11 October, during a special operation from Dover. Cole's MTB 22 led 31 (Lt D. Jermain) and 32 (Lt N. Poland) in support of the monitor HMS *Erebus* which was bombarding Calais. They sighted a group of trawlers and attacked with torpedoes. One was sunk at once and a second crippled, so Jermain – who in exercises had become the main exponent of depth-charge attacks – went in close under her bow and finished her off with two charges. Thirty-four prisoners were taken and delivered to Dover.[7]

Denis Jermain, who later became the distinguished SO of the 10th Flotilla in the Mediterranean, was involved in two more successful actions in the next month, which did a great deal to boost the morale of the MTB crews after their lack of targets for so long. On 30 November Jermain in MTB 31 took over as leader of a patrol when Cole had to return to base with engine trouble. His companion was Lt Corsar RNVR in MTB 30. To their surprise, they came across a line of merchant ships anchored off the Schelde

[7] Actions on 13 August, 8 September, and 11 October 1940: summaries in list of CF Actions held at NHB.

Lt Denis Jermain RN (second from left, front row), CO of MTB 31, with the crew on return from sinking a merchant ship with depth charges in the Schelde estuary, 30 November 1940. (Courtesy D. Jermain)

estuary. As they moved in to attack, they were sighted and came under heavy fire. Jermain got his first torpedo away, and it ran accurately at the target but failed to hit – presumably passing harmlessly under its hull. Meanwhile 30 was badly hit and her steering and torpedo firing gear were disabled; for a time she was out of control, circling wildly and losing touch with 31. As soon as she could be brought under control she disengaged and set course for base, unable to take part in the action.

Meanwhile Jermain fired his second torpedo but suffered a frustrating misfire. But true to form he could not bear to leave the merchant ships at anchor without attacking and made another depth charge attack, although still under heavy fire. He made two runs at the biggest of the ships, and planted his depth charges expertly very close to her hull, resulting in highly satisfactory explosions and great spouts of water from beneath her. Jermain did not hang around to observe the results, but Intelligence picked up a plain language distress call from the target, identifying her as a 6,000-ton vessel.[8]

This success was followed a week later, on 7 December, by another patrol by the 4th Flotilla off Flushing. MTB 32 (Lt R. Ellis RN) led, followed by 29 (Lt C.A. James) and 31 (Jermain). After several hours' patrolling,

[8] ROP by Lt D. Jermain held by the author.

MASB 41, a 63ft British Power Boat, June 1940. (Collection G.M. Hudson)

they suddenly encountered, at 100 yards range, a large merchant ship at anchor. After adjusting range and firing angle, Ellis and James each fired one torpedo and both hit. As they disengaged, they were confronted by a flak trawler whose gunners, fortunately, had not yet learned to fire low. As a bonus, a torpedo from Jermain's boat sank the trawler. The MTBs suffered no damage and no casualties. The merchant ship was later found to be the *Santos*, and her loss was confirmed.[9]

An interesting sidelight on this successful operation reveals that Ellis's first lieutenant was Sub Lt D.G.H. Wright RNVR – the first junior RNVR officer to be acknowledged in this history – whose name will continue to appear in these pages right through to the end of the war.

During the last few months of 1940 the use of mines by both the British and the Germans had been dramatically increasing, and bringing the inevitable consequences in the sinking of ships and the loss of hundreds of lives. The early appearance of magnetic mines, against which a method of sweeping had to be devised, and later of acoustic mines provided unpleasant work for the MTBs, which were frequently involved in an experimental method of detonating the mines – by passing over them at high speed, in the belief that they would be far enough away from the resulting explosion to avoid damage. They were also pressed into service as minelayers off the Dutch coast, which was a very unpopular occupation for all concerned.

Sadly, the boats suffered grievously from mines. During September and October 1940 three of the most active boats of the 1st Flotilla fell victim to them, when in rapid succession MTBs 15, 16 and 17 were sunk on patrol or on passage. They represented a high proportion of the available force of MTBs at this time.

But at least by the end of 1940 the handful of boats in the early flotillas had made a start in taking the war to the enemy. And things were at last moving in Admiralty circles to provide more support for their operations.

9 Summary of actions at NHB.

CHAPTER 2

1941: GRADUAL PROGRESS AND THE FIRST MGBS

From the start of the war the total lack of any overall responsibility for Coastal Forces in the corridors of power had proved a great weakness. It was finally addressed in November 1940 by the appointment of a flag officer and staff to coordinate the developments which were already taking place more or less at random. Rear Adm Piers Kekewich was designated RACF (Rear Admiral Coastal Forces) and his Chief of Staff was Capt A.W.S. Agar VC DSO RN, whose VC had been won in 1919 when his CMB sank a Russian cruiser near Kronstadt.[1] They had a team of specialists in all the branches of the naval service and set up their headquarters first in HMS *St Christopher*, then at Portland and finally in North London.

Unfortunately RACF could have little influence in the field of operations, which remained entirely the province of commanders-in-chief. This was unquestionably a potential problem, as it became increasingly obvious that very few of the C-in-Cs (or their Staff Operations Officers) had a clear idea of the capabilities of the craft and the most effective way in which they could be used. But at least the central organization created a new link between the Admiralty and the Commands, which extended to the Mediterranean and the Far East, and work could begin on developing the stronger understanding that was necessary.

[1] Capt A. Agar VC DSO, *Baltic Episode*.

A major task for the new department was to pull together the strands of the construction programme which had been growing rather like Topsy for the first eighteen months of the war. Mistakes had been made, and time lost through lack of planning and inadequate knowledge of the requirements of the various types of boat. One example was the introduction of the Motor Anti-Submarine Boats (MA/SBs), which were Hubert Scott-Paine's first development from his British Power Boat design used in the MTBs of the 1st and 2nd Flotillas. In practice, they had quickly proved to be of little use in anti-submarine warfare, and the German conquest of the Low Countries and France had already shown that there were other, far more valuable, potential uses for them.

After June 1940 the enemy had immediately taken over the newly captured Belgian, Dutch and Channel ports, using them as bases for escort vessels and for the rapidly increasing force of E- and R-boats. The E-boats (actually *Schnellboote*) and R-boats (*Raumboote*) were the equivalent of the British MTBs and MLs; although their origins also lay in the First World War, their development in the inter-war years had been very different. The Versailles treaty was intended to make Germany militarily impotent, but in naval terms the reduction of the size and strength of the German Navy had some unanticipated results. It certainly led to

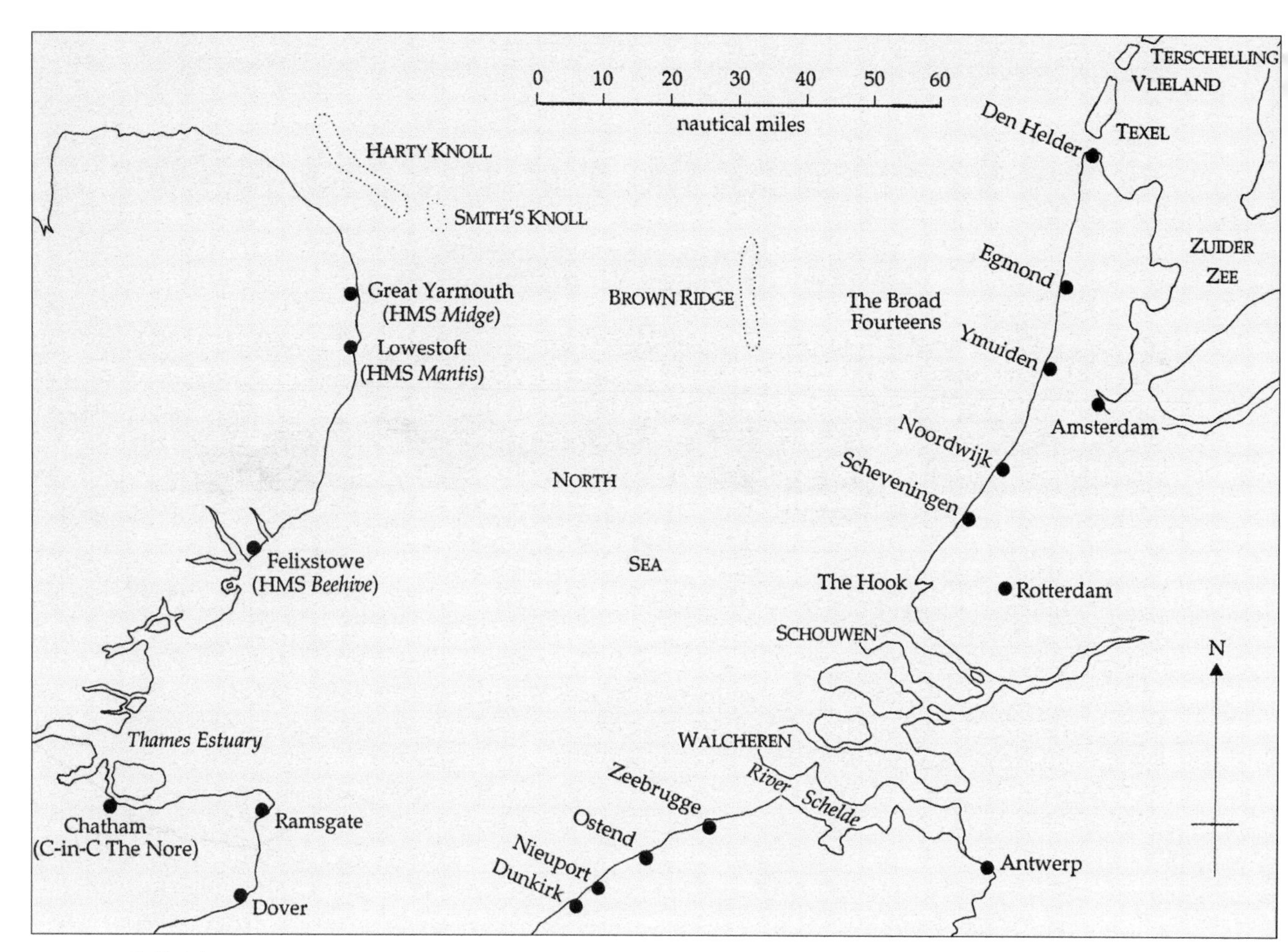

The North Sea.

an early search for ways to circumvent the restrictions and in 1923 the Germans began to examine designs for fast boats capable of carrying torpedoes. From the start the Kriegsmarine laid down three basic requirements for the design of these boats: with the North Sea in mind, they had to have a hull strong enough to enable them to operate in bad weather if so required; to have engines with a high power/weight ratio to give a superior speed to that of their adversaries, without vulnerability of fuel; and to present a low profile to assist undetected approach.[2]

[2] M.J. Whitley, *German Coastal Forces of WW2*.

To satisfy these demands took the E-boat designers many years, but the mere fact that these criteria had been established so early, and were successfully achieved well before the Second World War began, gave the German Navy a major advantage. The E-boat had Daimler-Benz diesel engines which gave its low, sleek 110ft hull a speed of over 40 knots. Some designs which were discarded were turned to advantage as R-boats, using the slower MAN diesel engines. Some were larger and more heavily armed than the E-boats, and they were used primarily for escort work but also as shallow-water minesweepers and minelayers – a very similar

MGB 46 (originally the Dutch TM 51) of the 3rd MGB Flotilla, commanded by Lt Cdr A.A. Fitzroy-Talbot, the SO, February 1941. (Collection G.M. Hudson)

role to that of the Royal Navy's MLs. They were often encountered by Coastal Forces boats, and were so difficult to differentiate from E-boats at slow speeds that escorts were often described in action reports as 'E/R-boats'.

The German position was in marked contrast to the situation in Coastal Forces. Ironically an end-of-war reflective think-tank in the Admiralty, preparing a report on the lessons of 1939–45 and the needs of the future, produced the same three main criteria that the German Navy had established in the 1920s. The report[3] bemoaned the lack of any unified planning in the prewar period which had led to the 'legacy of neglect' described in Chapter 1.

[3] *The Coastal Forces Monograph*, Admiralty, 1952.

There was clearly a need to counter the threat of the raiding E-boats with fast manoeuvrable boats which could engage them in shallow waters and were provided with a heavier gun armament than was possible with the MTBs.

This need was addressed by converting many of the British Power Boat MA/SBs to operate as Motor Gun Boats – a term first authorised and used in January 1941. Those already built varied in length from 63 ft to 75 ft, but were mostly 70 ft long. Their top speed varied depending upon the engines which powered them, and in due course the slower ones were retained as MA/SBs (although used for air-sea rescue duties) while those capable of 35–40 knots became MGBs and were assigned, as they became available, to form five MGB Flotillas. Their conversion

FLOTILLA	MGBS	CLASSES	ENGINES	BASES
2nd	6–13	BPB 70ft	Napier Sealions replaced by Packards	Dover
3rd	40–48	BPB 63ft (6) BPB 70ft (1) White 75ft (2)	Rolls-Royce Merlins Rolls-Royce Merlins Isotta Fraschini	Fowey, Dartmouth, Dover
4th	50–57	BPB 70ft	Rolls-Royce Merlins	Portland
5th	14–21	BPB 70ft	Napier Sealions replaced by Packards	Lowestoft
6th	58–65, 67	BPB 70ft	Rolls-Royce Merlins	Felixstowe[4]

from MA/SBs took time, but from April 1941 they began to appear with increasing frequency in the lists of recorded actions. More MGB flotillas (the 1st, 7th, 8th, 9th and 10th) were added during 1942 and 1943.

Quite apart from this development of MGBs, the programme for new flotillas of MTBs had already been set in train and began to show results by the end of 1941. But throughout 1941 the MTBs in the Channel and the North Sea were basically the same ill-equipped boats which had seen action in 1940. These vulnerable craft patrolled whenever the weather did not prevent them from going to sea to search for the enemy. They rarely found them, largely because they had no RDF (radar) at this time and communications with the better-equipped shore bases were still rudimentary at this stage. The earliest boats had little armament other than a variety of machine-guns, but by 1941 all the MTBs were equipped with twin 0.5in guns in a powered turret. In short, they were wooden boats containing thousands of gallons of 100 octane petrol, fast but with little striking power unless their torpedoes could be fired.

However, 1941 did see the first changes in the personnel of the boats. Until this point in the war the sight of an RNVR Commanding Officer was very rare indeed, and certainly all the Senior Officers of the flotillas wore the straight rings of the Royal Navy career officers. Gradually during 1941 the percentage of RNVR COs increased as those with the highest seniority – and often with periods of prewar training under their belts – received their commands. Most were experienced yachtsmen, some with an acknowledged pedigree in dinghy racing. In any case, the more senior RN lieutenants were often required in destroyers.

Similarly the crews, which had previously been made up entirely of career ratings, now began to receive a number of Reserve and Hostilities Only (HO) men, the products of the recent establishment of the Coastal Forces Training Base at Fort William, HMS *St Christopher*. There, under the watchful eye of Cdr A.E.P. Welman DSO DSC RN, and using the sheltered waters of Loch Linnhe for instruction afloat, every young officer and newly trained rating received a brief overview of the specific skills related to service in Coastal Force boats. Cdr Welman, with his background of distinguished service in the CMBs of the First World War, was an inspirational leader. Officers completing this course were appointed as first lieutenants (or Spare Officers) to the flotillas of MTBs and

[4] Courtesy G.M. Hudson.

Lt H.L. ('Harpy') Lloyd RN (left), CO of MTB 34, SO of the 4th MTB Flotilla, with his First Lieutenant, Sub Lt J. Neill, Felixstowe 1941. (Courtesy the late J.T. Mannooch)

MLs. Fortunately for the COs of the boats, the 'active service' coxswains (usually petty officers) were retained, to ensure that the new arrivals among the ratings had professional and experienced guidance under which they rapidly became members of the team.

It is not really surprising that no actions are recorded in the bad weather of the first three months of 1941, although during March the E-boats made five attacks on east coast convoys. In the first of these, on 7/8 March, five E-boats attacked a northbound convoy of nine ships, and sank three of them; two others had to be beached, and the destroyer escort claimed only to have damaged one E-boat. On the other four occasions the attacks were beaten off by destroyers, but the need to strengthen the escorts – which were of necessity thinly spread – by the addition of MGBs able to chase and engage the E-boats had already been clearly demonstrated.

Fortunately, the first of the new MGB flotillas was now available and ready for operations. The 6th Flotilla, whose boats had been taken over from the French and were originally designated MA/SBs, was composed of nine 70ft British Power Boats. They had begun to assemble in Fowey in the previous November and moved to Felixstowe in mid-March. Their three Rolls-Royce Merlin engines delivered a maximum speed of 40 knots, and their original armament included one 20mm Oerlikon in MGBs 58–60, or four 0.303in Brownings in aircraft turrets in MGBs 61–65 and 67 (due to Oerlikons no longer being available), in addition to two twin 0.303in Lewis machine-guns. The flotilla's first SO was Lt Peter Howes RN. No fewer than seven of the boats

MY *Sister Ann*, accommodation ship for officers, Fowey. (Courtesy A.H. Lewis)

MGB 58 of the 6th MGB Flotilla, 1941. (Collection G.M. Hudson)

were originally commanded by RN lieutenants – Howes, Griffiths, Richards, Shaw, Whitehead, Nigel Dixon and Johnson, and the only RNVR CO at first was Lt Robert Peverell Hichens, who in prewar days had been a Cornish solicitor, a champion dinghy sailor and a racing driver in his Aston Martin. He had already earned a DSC when serving in a minesweeper at Dunkirk: sent ashore to help organize the movement of troops from the beaches to the boats lying off, he saved several hundred men by his ingenuity in rigging a life-line to an anchored yacht.

Hichens was to become the most renowned of all the Coastal Force leaders, not only for his gallantry and determination to attack the enemy, but also for his tactical wisdom and influence, which developed the concepts of MTB and MGB operations from their amateur beginnings to a refined sophistication and led to great successes against the enemy.

It says much for the spirit of this flotilla that so many of its officers became notable leaders, particularly G.D.K. (Dicky) Richards and David Shaw, but also, much later, several of the younger RNVR and RCNVR sub-lieutenants – Corny Burke, Ronnie Barge, John Dudley Dixon, Francis Head and Derek Leaf.

When they first reached Felixstowe, their arrival caused some difficulties for the Operations Officers as no one quite knew how best to use these fast, aggressive boats. They were sent out with destroyers, but their captains complained that the MGBs were noisy and attracted attention so that the destroyers were unable to lie stopped on radar watch. Eventually they were allowed to roam to seaward of the convoys, stopping to listen for the rumble of diesel engines and hoping that they could catch the E-boats either on their approach or on their way home.

It nearly worked on 18 April. At dawn 60, 64 and 59 were on their way back to Felixstowe when an E-boat appeared on the opposite course. Strangely it made no attempt to avoid them. It closed to 75 yards and there was a spirited exchange of fire but the E-boat escaped. It was followed by a second, which made smoke and could not be brought to further close action. It was a frustrating first brush with the enemy but as both Hichens and Richards were there some lessons for the future were obviously learned. A week later 61 and 59 chased two E-boats after a raid and again exchanged fire, with minor damage to each side.[5]

It was the same again in mid-June when 58, 59 and 65 chased five E-boats virtually to the harbour entrance at Ymuiden, maintaining maximum speed for nearly an hour, which would have appalled the engineers at the base. The Rolls-Royce Merlins coped magnificently – but once again the flotilla could not bring the enemy to a decisive conclusion. Their one consolation was that clearly the E-boats did not want any confrontation, and psychologically that put the MGBs in the stronger position. But they still had not proved themselves.[6]

In August 1941 Lt Howes left the flotilla, and Robert Hichens was promoted to lieutenant commander and became the SO. He was the first RNVR officer to be so honoured, and in the next eighteen months he became a legend. But 'Hitch', as he was known throughout Coastal Forces, had to wait until November before the 6th MGB Flotilla at last claimed its first victory. The patrol began most inauspiciously when the third boat of the unit returned to harbour with engine trouble leaving only 64 (the SO's boat) and 67 (Lt L.G.R. Campbell) to continue. Disaster struck again when one of 64's engines packed up, greatly reducing her speed, and leaving her no chance of carrying out the original plan of lying in wait off Ymuiden, the E-boats' base.

Instead Hichens decided to lie stopped in a position some 20 miles to seaward of the convoy route, on the most likely course of the E-boats' return. They waited, with ears strained for the tell-tale noise of engines, for three hours or more and by 0500 were beginning to believe that once again they had miscalculated. Suddenly they heard the E-boats coming, and started up their engines. Almost at once they came across a group of five E-boats, obviously gathering at a rendezvous point before setting off eastward. The enemy was taken by surprise and at once the two MGBs closed and set about the superior enemy numbers at very close range, attacking with depth charges and guns. The E-boats' reply was erratic and inaccurate, showing an apparent lack of preparedness, but one shell put 64's Oerlikon – her main strike weapon – out of action and Hichens was left with only two twin 0.5in Vickers guns as his main armament. In contrast, 67 was undamaged. The two boats set off in pursuit, aware that with reduced speed their only hope was to find that one of the E-boats had been disabled.

They came across one, but it was still under way and increased speed to escape. But Hichens persevered, and eventually the sharp hearing of PO Henry Curtis, his coxswain, detected the presence of boats. They closed, and to their delight found an abandoned E-boat, which had obviously suffered damage in the battle and apparently also from a collision. It seemed that Curtis had heard another E-boat engaged in taking off the

[5] Summary from list of recorded actions.

[6] CFI 4.

Lt Cdr R.P. Hichens on the bridge of MGB 64 flying the Nazi ensign taken from S 41 on 20 November 1941. (Courtesy IWM – A 7632)

crew. The stricken E-boat, S 41, had clearly been scuttled and was about to sink. It would have been a great prize to be able to tow her home, but she sank almost at once so the MGBs had to be content to return to harbour flying the E-boat's ensign beneath the White Ensign.[7]

While the MGBs were making their first impressions from the east coast bases, activity in the Channel continued. This was a different sort of warfare, as here the term 'the Narrow Seas' was truly apt. Indeed, so narrow was the Strait of Dover that even in harbour the crews felt part of the action, and from the SO's office in the Lord Warden Hotel the French coast was clearly visible in good weather. Shells from the heavy guns on the French coast could reach Dover, and if visibility was sufficient, the convoys distributing the cargoes so necessary to Britain's survival could also be straddled. Both sides now had some degree of radar use. The British system developed rapidly to give more and more effective coverage of movement on the far shore, while the German version was of less certain quality, but was believed to be improving from a slower start.

In Dover the early MTBs of the 11th Flotilla, and later the 5th and 6th MTB Flotillas, were slowly building up. There was a mixture of types, of varying reliability and

[7] Account by Henry Curtis DSM.

The plaque with the original 'Hornet' badge, which was displayed on many early MTBs. (Courtesy Sir John Moore)

speeds, and several of them were manned by Norwegian crews. Patrols were commonly made up of those boats which were in good running order, irrespective of flotilla. The first Senior Officer of the 11th was Lt Kenneth Cradock-Hartopp RN, while Lt Cdr J.C. Cole RN led the first boats of the 5th until he was killed when MTB 41 was mined in February 1941. He was succeeded by Lt Hilary Gamble RN, one of the Mediterranean 1st Flotilla COs.

Gamble and Lt John Eardley-Wilmot RN, the new SO of the 11th, brought some stability to the organization of the MTB activities at Dover, but the problems inherent in operating such diverse boats continued for a long time. The first boats at Dover had been Vospers – the Norwegian MTBs N 5 and N 6, both of which had sunk by mid-1941, and 70 and 71 – with occasional appearances there of the experimental MTBs 100 and 102.

The RACF began to produce monthly 'Coastal Forces Information Bulletins' (CFIs) in March 1941 and the first issue, CFI 1, included references to the 'old 11th' and the 'new 11th'! The 'new' was to be composed of MTBs 49–56, eight 72ft Thornycroft boats, being built at Hampton-on-Thames and Woolston. The command of MTB 49, the first to be completed in April 1941, was given to Cradock-Hartopp. He tells how Roger Thornycroft acted as Thames pilot to take 49 down to Long Reach for trials, but he 'ran her aground opposite the Houses of Parliament, where at least the MPs could see what an MTB looked like'.

In September 1941 Lt Nigel Pumphrey RN arrived at Dover as SO of the 6th MTB Flotilla. The build-up of even more boats – his were Vospers – and his appointment as 'SO MTBs Dover' to coordinate the work of all three flotillas brought further complications. He commented that the 5th and 6th Flotillas were so mixed up in 1941–2 as to be virtually integrated. Not many of the boats seemed to be serviceable at any one time owing to action damage and breakdowns, and as six boats were required each night, three at immediate notice and three on standby, boats of any of the three flotillas could be called upon.

The main problem for the leader of a mixed unit arose from the range of boats used. The 11th had the 72ft Thornycroft boats, which had been ordered immediately war broke out in September 1939, with a maximum speed of 29 knots; the 5th had Samuel Whites with very sound hulls, but a variety of engines – some had Packards (replacing the Isotta Fraschinis, which soon became unavailable), while others had 24-knot Hall Scott engines – none of which

An early Vosper MTB fires both torpedoes on trials, 1941. (Courtesy D. Jermain)

were truly compatible with their hulls; and the 6th had Vospers of assorted ages. It was remarkable in the circumstances that they managed to achieve any successes, though they were few and far between during this period.

Also in Dover Command but based normally at Ramsgate were two flotillas of MGBs, the 2nd led by Lt G.D.K. (Dicky) Richards, and the 3rd now under the command of Lt P.F.S. (Stewart) Gould. Their boats were almost all British Power Boats but, just like the MTBs, they were of different lengths, vintages and engines, although most were re-engined successfully with three 1250bhp Packards. The 2nd Flotilla boats were numbered between 6 and 13, and those of the 3rd, which had begun life in Fowey, between 40 and 48. When Polish crews took over some of the boats, the numbers were changed: 48 as S 1, 44 as S 2, and 45 as S 3. The Polish COs, famous for their aggression and 'style', had largely unpronouncable surnames but were known universally as 'Whisky' (Lt E. Wcislicki – S 2), 'Soda' (Lt Dabrowski – S 1) and 'Andrew' (Lt Jarakovski – S 3).

The operations from Dover were not like those in the North Sea, where boats were sent to patrol a section of the enemy coast. In the

MTB 54 (Lt Per Danielsen RNorN), manned by Norwegian personnel, approaches harbour with MTB 56 astern. (Collection G.M. Hudson)

Channel the boats were specifically vectored towards targets picked up off the French coast by British shore-based radar. The MGBs sent their immediate notice and standby units to Dover from Ramsgate as required, and these could be deployed either separately or with the MTBs.

During June and July 1941 assorted boats had inconclusive brushes with the enemy, and there was also some minelaying off Boulogne. It was not until 8 September that Dover Command was able to report a truly successful action involving many of the leaders who had either already established their reputations or were to go on to earn them. The patrol was led by the Senior Officer of the MTBs, Lt Cdr E.N. (Nigel) Pumphrey RN, in 35, with 218, whose CO was a Canadian, C.E. (Chuck) Bonnell, both of the 6th Flotilla, and 54 of the 11th, which had a Norwegian CO (Per Danielsen) and crew. In a separate unit but vectored to the same area were two MGBs, 43 and 52, with Stewart Gould as SO and Lt W.G.B. (Barry) Leith in command of 52.[8]

Pumphrey's and Gould's reports of proceedings vividly tell the story of this gallant action, which has already been reported in other books but which had so many lessons for the future that it must be analysed as a significant point in the development of Coastal Forces tactics. Many things went wrong, but the leadership and determination of Pumphrey and Gould, the skill of Danielsen and the magnificent courage, resourcefulness and ability of the crews overcame the damage, the casualties and the limited resources of power and armament of the boats of this time.

Pumphrey reveals that because his boats had been out for the previous five nights, they were not at immediate notice. When a unit

[8] MO 14924; ADM 199/676.

was urgently called for, his crews had to be recalled from 'entertainments' ashore; this paucity of choice reflects the unreliability of the majority of boats as they gathered at Dover. Radar had detected an enemy convoy leaving Boulogne northbound, consisting of two heavily laden merchant ships escorted by trawlers and E- or R-boats. There was time to intercept them off Cap Blanc Nez. Pumphrey knew that Stewart Gould's MGBs were already in the area and was certain they would make contact and play their part in any action. Danielsen's 54 could not leave with the unit, but was ordered to follow when ready. It was flat calm, moonless but not very dark, and the convoy was sighted at 4,000 yards.

The MTBs crept in as quietly as possible on one engine and surprisingly got right in, passing between two of the escorting E/R-boats before starting up the wing engines when the range was about 1,000 yards. At 800 yards Pumphrey fired his torpedoes at the rearmost merchantman and disengaged astern of her. One torpedo struck – the clear evidence was an explosion from the ship and the underwater percussion. Following up, Bonnell in 218 fired his torpedoes at an M Class minesweeper – the largest of the escorts – but they missed, so he took on the E/R-boats in a gun attack, scoring seven hits and actually seeing them firing at each other as he got away and returned to base.

Pumphrey withdrew to check for damage and discovered that his starboard torpedo had misfired and that he had suffered some hits, but none was vital. Danielsen in 54 now arrived and joined up, and they set course to overtake the remaining target, trying to get well ahead to launch another attack. The manoeuvre nearly failed as the convoy had increased speed and was nowhere to be seen, but Danielsen sighted them and the two boats gave chase again. As they closed, the position of Gould's MGB was revealed by an exchange of tracer further astern.

Gould's report reveals that he had mistaken the E/R-boats of the inshore screen for the MTBs. He challenged them and received some accurate fire in reply which wounded both his Lewis gunners. But he began a series of depth charge and gun attacks first on the E/R-boats – probably sinking one – and then on a trawler, before finding the way clear, albeit through countless streams of wild and inaccurate tracer, to attack the remaining merchantman. Having thoroughly demoralised the enemy, Gould then withdrew. Meanwhile Leith's MGB 52 had suffered severe damage, losing one engine, and was making water fast. She took six hours to regain harbour, eventually being towed in by a trawler.

By now the efforts of the MGBs had enabled the two MTBs to make a torpedo attack on the remaining merchantman. Danielsen, in the faster boat, fired first, then disengaged, leaving space for Pumphrey to run in through smoke. As he did so, he nearly ran into four E-boats; ignoring their heavy fire, he got his torpedo away only to see the target disintegrate as Danielsen's torpedo struck. 35 was now attracting heavy fire from E-boats and a trawler. Both wing engines were stopped, and the stern was hit by a 3in shell which blew off a rudder and made steering impossible. A big fire broke out in the fuel tank space midships, and there was petrol swilling in the bilges. Under power from the centre engine, 35 was circling out of control. All looked lost. Pumphrey describes how his 0.5in gunner, AB Carruthers, was firing so accurately at the trawler and at the leader of the four E-boats that both ceased fire; presumably believing 35 to be in a sinking state, they left her to her fate.

Every man aboard performed miracles of competence and persistence. Each one – the flotilla's spare CO who happened to be aboard, the first lieutenant, the coxswain, the motor mechanic, the stokers and the seamen

– played his part. Determined to get 35 back to harbour, they dowsed the fire, rigged emergency steering, got a second engine going and gave first aid to the wounded (including Pumphrey himself, and the telegraphist and torpedoman who both carried on with their duties without complaint).

Their success provided a tremendous boost to the morale of the Dover flotillas. There were valuable indications of the effectiveness of intelligent cooperation between MTBs and MGBs; the importance of training, which enabled crew members to adapt to unexpected situations, had been strongly reinforced; most of all, there had been a clear demonstration of how aggressive attacking, even against seemingly impossible odds, could have a demoralising effect on an enemy force. Several awards resulted from this action, and all were totally deserved: Pumphrey won the DSC, and there were DSMs for AB Carruthers and POMM Gordon, and 'Mentions' for the First Lieutenant Sub Lt Sheldrick and coxswain PO Hadley. Danielsen in MTB 54 also received the DSC.[9]

Gould's MGBs were again in action three days later on 11/12 September, engaging three trawlers after an abortive MTB attack. His unit came under heavy fire from the greatly superior armament of these much larger escorts, which they fought for twenty minutes. In his report Gould singled out for praise AB L.D. Lanfear of MGB 43 who had already distinguished himself in the earlier action as the after gunner. On this occasion, after being instrumental in damaging the target, Lanfear was seriously wounded but in Gould's words, 'he displayed gallantry and devotion to duty of the very highest order. He had multiple injuries and was in great pain and unable to stand, but seized a stripped Lewis gun and directed rapid and accurate fire at the enemy until he finally collapsed from the effects of these wounds.' Small wonder that Lanfear was honoured with the exceptional award of the CGM (Conspicuous Gallantry Medal). It was promulgated in the same issue of the *London Gazette* as awards to Gould (DSC), and AB Tate (DSM).[10]

This book, as has been made clear, is specifically concerned with the 'short' MTBs and MGBs, but it would be wrong to give the impression that they were the only Coastal Forces boats involved in these waters. For almost a year the A and B Class Fairmile Motor Launches (MLs) had been playing their part. The A Class boats, fore-runners of the 'long' C and D Class MGBs, were already building up a reputation as fearless minelayers from Dover. The Bs, round-bottomed yachtlike MLs which were wonderful sea-going craft, were engaged in a multitude of tasks including convoy escort, minesweeping and anti-submarine work. In September 1941 the earliest C Class Motor Gun Boats are recorded in action for the first time when MGBs 323 and 313, operating from Yarmouth as a convoy anti-E-boat screen, engaged a group of E-boats moving in to attack, taking advantage of aircraft flares illuminating the enemy. They were nowhere near fast enough to press home their attack, but they certainly made their presence felt. There were only twenty-four of them in all, but they were to prove invaluable, operating mostly from east coast bases, but also from Dover.[11]

Similarly, particularly because Lt Per Danielsen of the Royal Norwegian Navy has already been mentioned, it would be wrong to omit any reference to the remarkable feat of seamanship carried out in Norwegian waters by MTB 56 (now under his command) of the

[9] *Seedie's List of Coastal Forces Awards.*

[10] MO 14946; ADM 199/676; *Seedie's List of Coastal Forces Awards.*

[11] CFI 8.

11th Flotilla, a Dover-based boat. The Norwegian Command had called for a special operation and Lt Danielsen and his largely Norwegian crew took MTB 56 to Scapa Flow on 1 October; she was towed towards Norway by the Norwegian destroyer *Draug*. The tow was slipped after 120 miles, leaving 140 miles for 56 to cross. Making her approach, she safely negotiated an entry through the intricate pattern of islands into the Inner Leads, a few miles south of Bergen. Then, after a brief period of hiding under camouflage deep in a fjord, she emerged to intercept a convoy consisting of a tanker escorted by two minesweepers. She penetrated the escort screen and fired two torpedoes; both struck, and 56's crew watched as the M/T *Borgny* sank, denying the enemy 3,500 tons of aviation fuel. Then 56, at the limit of her fuel, safely rejoined the *Draug* before returning to Lerwick and later to Dover. It was a remarkable achievement for a 72ft boat, and set a pattern which later in the year led to the formation of a flotilla of D Class Fairmile MTBs at Lerwick carrying out similar operations. On board MTB 56 was Leading Telegraphist E.J.W. Slater, whose splendid description of the operation reveals the problems and the extreme tension of the approach and the attack, and displays the highest respect for Lt Danielsen and the Norwegian crew. Danielsen received a Bar to his DSC and several of the crew also gained British awards.[12]

The Norwegian-manned MTB 56. The CO, on the far left, is Lt Prebensen RNorN. (Collection G.M. Hudson)

Pumphrey and Gould had to wait till 3/4 November before they could notch up another success, and once again it was only a success because the MTBs and MGBs worked together. Pumphrey's unit – MTBs 38, 218 (Bonnell) and 220 (Cornish) – would never have been able to penetrate the screen and torpedo a 5,000-ton merchant ship without the extraordinary gallantry of the two MGBs, 43 (Gould) and 42 (Lt M.G. Fowke RN), which engaged the heavy escort, attracting considerable fire. They first took on an M Class minesweeper, and then found themselves engaged at short range by a T Class Torpedo Boat (a small destroyer) of 600 tons, armed with 4in guns and a multitude of smaller weapons. They inflicted many hits, but in the process both were badly damaged. 42 limped away on one engine, and 43 was nearly rammed by the Torpedo Boat. All Gould's guns had been knocked out of action, and there were many casualties, but he managed to escape – almost from the entrance to Boulogne harbour. 43 was in a parlous state and would not have got back to base without a tow summoned by a vigilant fighter pilot who spotted them soon after dawn and realized their plight.[13]

12 V-Adm Gundersen; L/Tel E.J.W. Slater; *Seedie's List of Coastal Forces Awards*.

13 MO 17933; ADM 199/676.

During November the other two MGB flotillas, the 5th and the 7th, were beginning to operate from Lowestoft and had one or two brushes with the enemy's E-boats. As yet, however, they did not have the experience (or the good fortune) to do more than turn back E-boat raids. But in the Channel, the three MTB flotillas at Dover continued to put together useful patrols, well supported by the two MGB flotillas at Ramsgate, although enemy action was steadily reducing their numbers as they required repairs. Not all their patrols were successful, and not all the torpedoes hit, but the crews invariably had to withstand damage and casualties, and try to get their boats back to harbour. A notable incident took place on the night of 3/4 December. MTB 218 (Lt H.P. Granlund) was holed below the water-line by a large shell; despite the heroic efforts of Leading Telegraphist Phillips to plug the hole (and to keep the plug in place), the water rose above deck level. Granlund turned 218 round and continued astern, finally reaching Dover five-and-a-half hours after the shell hit, with the hull almost totally submerged. It was a great feat of seamanship and fortitude.[14]

The last recorded action of 1941 took place on 19/20 December when Hichens led a unit of his 6th Flotilla from Felixstowe in what is described as a 'long but inconclusive skirmish, in bad visibility', with three E-boats. Having intercepted the enemy boats, the three MGBs (65, 63 and 67) tried everything to disable them – close-range gun attacks and even depth-charge attacks – but the pitch darkness prevented them from keeping the pressure on, and in the end the E-boats got away, certainly damaged though not in a sinking condition.

There was no doubt that from a hopelessly inadequate start considerable progress had been made in terms of new flotillas with more boats and the development of a coordinated organization. The MGBs had begun to make their mark, and tactics were beginning to evolve from best practice and greater experience in these difficult high-speed light-craft operations. The MTBs still needed to be more powerful and more strongly armed, but at least the flow of Packard engines for hulls designed to receive them was increasing. The building programme for the new boats was well under way after the inevitable delay between design and production, and the arrival of new classes of boat in 1942, including the new breed of D Class Fairmiles, the SGBs and the British Power Boat 71ft 6in MGBs, gave the prospect of a more flexible force able to operate in all weathers.

Certainly the quality of the leadership in the boats had been proved beyond doubt and this was bolstered by the steadfastness of the crews, who found in the fellowship of their small boats a great team spirit that was much to their liking. That spirit is demonstrated by the way in which Rear Adm Piers Kekewich (RACF) showed a very personal interest in the young officers and men of his command. He took the time to send a hand-written note to every new commanding officer when he joined his boat, wishing him and his crew every success. It was a gesture much appreciated by the hundreds of lieutenants and sub-lieutenants who joined the Coastal Forces family.

At a time when there seemed to be constant bad news, much of it concerning ship losses, from the Far East and the Mediterranean, and when the tide of war seemed to be running against the Allies, the public began to look forward to the growing number of reports in the press describing close-range battles fought around the very coasts of Britain. They began 'Last night our Light Coastal Forces . . .', and they were to increase during 1942, creating new heroes and providing some much-needed cheer on the home front.

[14] CFI 10; MO 19342; ADM 199/676.

CHAPTER 3

JANUARY TO MARCH 1942

The year 1941 had seen the first signs of the establishment of some organizational order in Coastal Forces, and the arrival of the first new boats and some of the equipment which had been ordered late in 1939. Unfortunately, much of the new building in the 1939 programme had perforce been based on prewar models, and the development of new hull designs and of weapon technology was understandably slow. In 1940 the greater urgency brought by the downfall of the Low Countries, France and Norway had led to a larger building programme and a greater concentration on the perceived needs of a totally new situation.

Many of the boats produced in mid-1941 were therefore still lacking in speed and in effective armament, but despite these drawbacks they were pressed into service for many months to make up the numbers required for the increasing patrols.

Manpower for the boats as the force expanded was also a difficult matter. The Navy was still adjusting to the change from its traditional training methods to a more rapid through-put, which clearly meant a diminution in experience, seamanship and technical skills among the crews, which had to be overcome before confidence and inbred automatic response could be gained. The very small number of RN officers who before the war had learned to sail in small wooden boats with temperamental engines had been invaluable to the early flotillas. Their successors – even those who wore the straight rings of the RN career officer – had to learn those lessons in a harsher war-time environment, and much more quickly, too. Many of the older RNVR officers had years of experience of the sea, but that did not automatically endow them with the skills of warfare.

High among those skills, and absolutely crucial in a typical MTB/MGB action, where two groups of opposing craft met together in darkness, attacked, and then split up again to return to base, was the ability to comprehend and assess relative positions, courses and speeds. This was an extremely difficult skill to develop, and was probably the most significant factor of all in identifying the most successful Senior Officers of units.

In Coastal Forces warfare several factors governed the frequency of actions with the enemy. The weather was important. Patrols went out on almost every night when weather allowed: winds of Force 5 or more were not only hazardous to the fragile hulls of the 'short' boats, but more significantly did not permit a stable platform for a gun or torpedo attack. Another factor was the availability of a sufficient force of serviceable boats, and the actual presence of enemy ships to attack was a third. Even when all these conditions were satisfied and patrols could be mounted, the search for targets was not always successful even in these 'narrow' seas. In the Dover Strait, where radar covered the entire width of the Channel, boats could be vectored on to any enemy force detected, and there was a high percentage of contact. Elsewhere, operational orders were based either on Intelligence (including, we now know, the decoding of enemy signals) or on the need to

Several 55-ft Thornycroft MTBs (ex-12th MTB Flotilla) in the sheds at Haslar Gun Boat Yard. (Collection G.M. Hudson)

monitor regularly the normal enemy convoy routes. In the latter case, the skills of detection and successful tracking had to be learned. Persistence and determination to 'seek out and destroy' were naturally not evenly distributed among all those who led units, but were invariably shown by those officers who began to accumulate impressive records.

Any set of statistics can only be of real value when they have a basis of common factors: the following comparison of the number of enemy engagements in 1940 and 1941 is therefore simply an indication of growing opportunity, together with an ability to take advantage of it. There were eleven actions by the 'short' boats in home waters in the second half of 1940; in 1941 there were twenty, around half of them involving MGBs. In 1942 the figure increased to 62, with (as yet) very few other actions by the 'long' boats – the Fairmile Cs and Ds, and the SGBs.

It is surprising that in the first ten weeks of 1942 not a single action is recorded for the MTB and MGB flotillas on the east coast, whereas the Dover Command boats were frequently in touch with the enemy. The main factors were probably the weather, a shortage of targets and problems of non-availability at Felixstowe and Lowestoft. In his book *We Fought Them in Gunboats*, Hichens later commented that the ratio of fruitless patrols to actions was frustratingly high, despite his aggression and determination to find and engage the enemy if they were at sea.

The Dover boats also had the advantage of shore-based radar to find the enemy for them, and their first engagement of the year came on 16/17 January. It fell to a mixed unit of MGBs from the 2nd and 3rd Flotillas, led by Lt Dicky Richards RN in his MGB 8, with S 3, a Polish boat commanded by 'Bruno', and MGB 43. The report indicates that they surprised two large armed barges and damaged both with gunfire, before making a daring depth charge attack under the bow of the leading barge which left it crippled. Return fire was heavy. The *London Gazette* of 3 March 1942 records the award of the Conspicuous Gallantry Medal to AB Joseph Booth of MGB 8, but sadly – as is so often the case in naval awards – there is no citation to explain the exceptional nature of his bravery.[1]

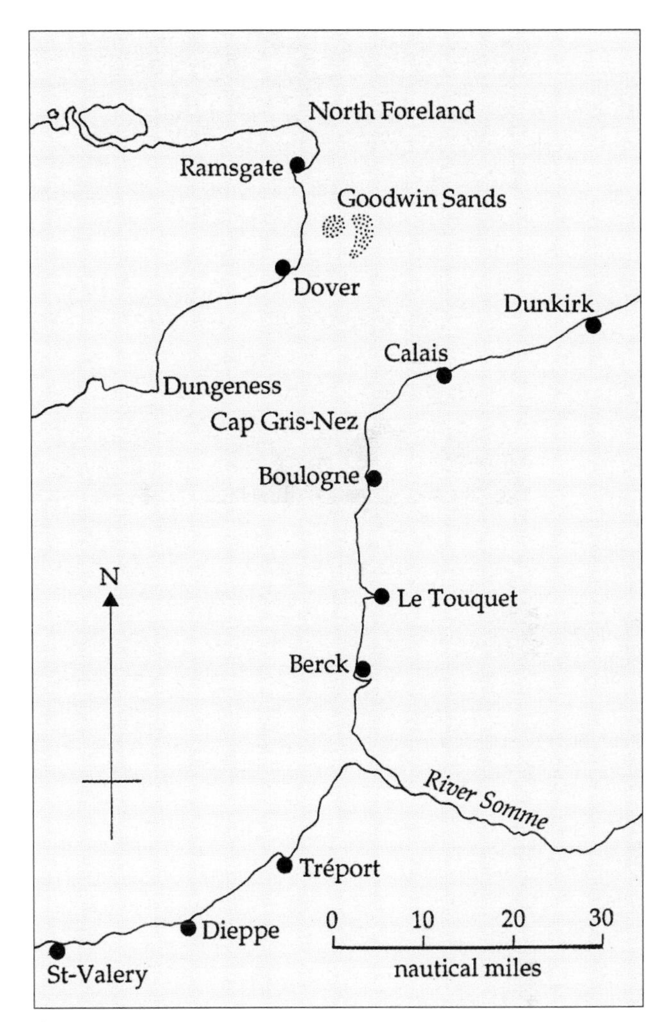

The Dover Strait.

On the very next night it was the turn of the 5th MTB Flotilla at Dover, who were vectored with a unit of C Class MGBs to the French coast north of Boulogne. The Cs intercepted a convoy protected by heavily armed escorts, and then broke off to allow the MTBs to attack. Again Pumphrey was the SO, and his boat (38) fired both torpedoes but failed to hit; as he disengaged under heavy fire the third boat in the unit, MTB 47, became separated and was never seen again by the other two. News was later received that she had been sunk off Cap Gris-Nez and that the CO, Lt W.I.C. Ewart RNVR and eleven of his crew had been picked up and were prisoners-of-war.

It was not until after the war that more details of the fate of MTB 47 were obtained from two sources. Lt Ewart made his report on his return from imprisonment in the notorious Colditz Castle. He described how 47, already out of touch with the rest of his unit, closed with the enemy but was heavily attacked by an escort firing guns of 37mm and 20mm calibre. Almost at once 47 was hit in the engine room on the waterline and she quickly became uncontrollable, veering towards the enemy and being repeatedly hit. Ewart, seriously wounded in the eye and leg, ordered 'abandon ship' but remained on board with a stoker to ensure that the boat was set alight and could not fall into enemy hands. The two of them then jumped into a rubber dinghy and were picked up, joining the rest of the crew.

The second account is from a letter sent to the Naval Historical Branch in 1987 and it provides a most unusual opportunity of

[1] CFI 11; ADM 199/676; *Seedie's List of Coastal Forces Awards*.

learning in detail from the captain of an enemy ship the background to the composition of the convoy and each phase of the attack. Adolf Schmidt was the CO of a Siebel Ferry (SF110) manned by German Air Force personnel as an anti-aircraft flak ship, armed with one 37mm, two quadruple 20mm and two single 20mm guns. Siebel Ferries were ungainly craft built in two sections and joined by a lower section holding the engine. Strangely on this operation SF110 was pressed into service as the rear escort to the convoy although she was being towed by a tug. She took no part in the early attack by the MGBs or in the unsuccessful torpedo attack by Pumphrey, and it was completely by chance that MTB 47, creeping along to get into position for an attack, found herself suddenly confronted by this heavily armed if unmanoeuvrable escort, at a range of about 25 metres. The broadside from SF110's nine 20mm guns was devastating (the 37mm could not depress sufficiently to join in) and in a very short time some 950 explosive and incendiary shells had done their work, and 47 was on fire and doomed. Schmidt later saw Lt Ewart and his crew in Boulogne, on board the rescue ship, and in his letter, some forty-five years later, asked to be put in touch with Lt Ewart. The two armed trawlers were indeed heavily armed, with 88mm, 37mm and 20mm guns in profusion. Ewart (DSC) and Stoker Maurice Beason (DSM) were decorated in 1945 when the facts were learned, for 'preventing the boat from falling into enemy hands when damaged and stopped off the enemy coast'.[2]

On 12 February the nation's morale suffered a major blow. The battle cruisers *Scharnhorst* and *Gneisenau* and the heavy cruiser *Prinz Eugen* broke out from their base at Brest and made a successful passage through the Dover Strait to return to Germany. The hazardous enterprise was brilliantly planned and meticulously executed, the ships being protected by a massive escort of destroyers, Torpedo Boats and E- and R-boats, together with a fighter screen, as they passed through the narrowest section of the Strait. That the ships got away seems at first glance to represent a failure by the forces sent in to attack – the torpedo-bombers of the Fleet Air Arm and the MTBs at Dover, but this view takes no account of their extreme gallantry in the face of insurmountable odds. It was recognized later that the faults lay not only in errors of communication and judgement, but also in the fundamental lack of preparation for war which led to a situation where the courage of the men involved was not matched by the boats and the aircraft provided for their attack.

It fell to Lt Cdr Nigel Pumphrey, SO MTBs at Dover, to lead the MTB challenge. The urgent order to sail was received so late in the morning (at 1135) that his boats were at four hours' notice, ready to respond to a call for a patrol that night. When the Chief of Staff told him the enemy were already off Boulogne, Pumphrey realized that even if he could muster a force to leave at once it would be almost impossible to achieve an interception. The maximum speed of his boats was 24 knots – but the enemy convoy was steaming away at 27 knots – and Pumphrey knew that his five available boats would need to maintain maximum revolutions for a long period just to get within range. He also knew that it would be a miracle if they could all do so without breakdowns, and he wasn't sure if all five could in fact sail virtually immediately. However, by good fortune none of the boats was immobilised by engine maintenance procedures, and none of the crews had been

[2] CFI 11; MO 1260; ADM 199/680; report from Adolf Schmidt at NHB; *Seedie's List of Coastal Forces Awards.*

The engine-room of a 70ft Vosper MTB, 1941. (Courtesy Vosper Ltd.)

despatched on stores parties or other duties. Twenty minutes later, in a heady atmosphere of excitement at the most unusual noon start to an operation, Pumphrey described (with heavy irony) how the boats 'screamed out of Dover at 24 knots'.

The boats involved were MTBs 221 (which Pumphrey took over, as her own CO was on duty elsewhere), 219 (Mark Arnold-Forster), 45 (Hilary Gamble), 44 (the Australian R.F (Dick) Saunders) and 48 (the Canadian C.A. (Tony) Law). Pumphrey's fears were well founded: 44 lost an engine but struggled on astern, and station-keeping at top speed was difficult. But at least they reached a point where they could exchange gunfire (ineffectively) with the E-boat screen, and eventually they sighted the capital ships a further 2 miles beyond. The Messerschmitts and the E-boats both maintained an impassive reluctance to leave station, and concentrated on keeping the MTBs at a distance. Pumphrey decided to brave the E-boat screen to get as close as he could before firing torpedoes, although there was little chance of getting in to a reasonable range. The four boats (with 44 still in pursuit astern) got into line abreast and began their gallant but hopeless attack, which was not helped by a further engine failure in 221. They got in to 4,000 yards, fired and then disengaged, eyes glued towards the targets. They saw one of the huge ships turn towards them and the other two away, and knew that this meant there was no chance of a hit, although Saunders in 44 fired at the closing ship. Suddenly a German destroyer came charging towards them, engaging heavily but inaccurately.

MTB 48 (Lt C.A. Law RCNVR) of the 5th MTB Flotilla at Dover, 1942. (Collection G.M. Hudson)

Things looked very grave, but once again fate – in the person of Stewart Gould in MGB 43 with 41 astern – intervened. Obliged to leave harbour later than the MTBs, the MGBs had much greater speed, and arrived at a very opportune moment. Both steered straight for the destroyer, firing their single Oerlikons, and to everyone's astonishment it turned away and rejoined the inner screen.

There was frustration all round, with criticisms voiced about their slow boats and their small numbers. Lt Cdr Esmonde, the leader of the six obsolete Swordfish torpedo-bombers which attacked through a tremendous hail of anti-aircraft fire, was brought down and died; the next two of his flight got in close enough to release their torpedoes but were then shot down: five of the survivors were picked up by the MTBs. The three Swordfish of the second flight went in to attack but were all shot down.

Lt Cdr Esmonde was subsequently awarded a posthumous VC, while Pumphrey received the DSO, Gould a bar to his DSC, and Saunders the DSC for their parts in the engagement. (Appendix 1, Note 3)

There was no respite for the Dover boats, which were sent out night after night as the shore radar detected possible targets on the far shore. On 14/15 February a mixed group of MTBs, MGBs and C Class boats, operating in coordinated but separate units, intercepted a *Sperrbrecher* (a large 'mine destructor') and some other enemy vessels, and Pumphrey, Gamble and Cornish attacked. Despite heavy fire they got in to 500 yards and 44 then fired her torpedoes, but missed. Each of the other units tried to press home attacks with gunfire but heavy fire beat them off.[3]

[3] CFI 13; Summary of Actions.

After several fruitless attempts at interceptions, it was two weeks before another group of units from the 5th and 6th MTBs together with the 3rd MGBs had a successful night. On 1/2 March two units were vectored to intercept a heavily defended convoy, consisting of two 4,000–5,000-ton tankers escorted by an M Class minesweeper and several armed trawlers. The MTBs, 45 (Gamble), 221 (Paul Gibson, a Free French officer) and 219 (Mark Arnold-Forster), took advantage of a diversionary attack by Gould's MGBs 43 and 41 and penetrated the screen, enabling Gamble to torpedo one of the tankers. With the aid of the MGBs they were able to disengage without damage or casualties. Later it was realized that the tanker had in fact not sunk, so Pumphrey's unit was despatched to finish her off. There was dense fog, and the tanker's escort was positioned to ward off another attack. Pumphrey tried hard to get through, but in the ensuing battle 38 was damaged and four of her crew – including Pumphrey himself – were wounded.[4]

Two nights later it was the turn of the 4th MTB Flotilla, which had not featured in any of the actions so far described. Their 72ft Vospers had – at this stage – Isotta Fraschini engines which gave a good turn of speed. The SO, in MTB 34, was Lt H.P. (Harpy) Lloyd RN, who had been a CO in the prewar 1st MTB Flotilla, and his unit was composed of 30 (Lt John Weeden) and 31 (Sub Lt Robert Varvill). The latter was one of the group of RNVR midshipmen who had joined the MTBs

[4] MO 3510; ADM 199/782.

The crew of MTB 48 on return to Dover after the daylight attack on the *Scharnhorst* and *Gneisenau* in the Dover Strait on 12 February 1942. (Collection G.M. Hudson)

MTB 34, a 1939 Vosper of the 4th MTB Flotilla. (Courtesy V.F. Clarkson)

in 1939 and he went on to be a distinguished SO in the Mediterranean, in action right to the end of the war. They were despatched from Dover to attack a convoy off Cap Gris-Nez – another heavily escorted tanker – and their plan was to follow the tactics which Pumphrey and Gamble had been implementing successfully: to get to a position about 3 miles off the coast and then to make a silent approach, hoping to penetrate the screen. The enemy was sighted at 21.17, and the boats moved in to attack. At about 600 yards 34 fired but no hits were observed. 30 followed suit but with no certain outcome. 31 was unfortunately baulked as 30 disengaged across his bow. But the enemy had now been alerted and the boats came under a hail of fire, with 31 suffering grievously. Three of her crew were killed and the CO and the coxswain were seriously wounded. The boat was already on fire and her engines stopped, but her momentum enabled her to get away from the action. The first lieutenant – New Zealander Sub Lt G.J. Macdonald – took charge of the survivors in a Carley float, but when 31 remained afloat he went back on board with some of the crew to try to restore order.

Meanwhile MGBs 43 (Gould) and 41 (Roger King) from the 3rd MGB Flotilla had, as arranged, been attacking the rear of the convoy which was now seen to include two merchant ships as well as the tanker. One of them was stopped, probably damaged. The MTBs got so close to the coast – within a mile

– that they were heavily engaged by the shore batteries. The E-boats of the escort screen were also challenged in a series of exchanges, but neither boat received any damage.

Two C Class MGBs were sent from Dover to give what aid they could to 31, and they arrived in time to help Macdonald and the wounded, and to tow the stricken boat back to Dover. It was a difficult tow, and when they finally entered harbour 31's stern was at least two feet under water.[5]

There had been no actions to report from the east coast flotillas since the New Year, which does not mean that they had been inactive. In the early part of its commission, the 7th MGB Flotilla based at Lowestoft had spent much of its time on unpopular anti-E-boat patrols beyond the east coast convoy route. However, as the C Class MGBs began to take over that task, the 'short' MGBs were used more often for the greatly preferred duty of hunting the E-boats as they returned to their bases.

Commanded by Lt J. Bremer Horne RN, the flotilla had fast 70ft US Elco boats and had worked hard but fruitlessly for months. On 14/15 March they finally got a chance to chalk up a success in the battle with the E-boats. Horne in MGB 88 had with him Lt S.G. (Tim) Bennett RCNVR in 87 and Sub Lt P.A.R. Thompson – another Canadian – in 91. The patrol lay stopped about 20 miles from the Dutch coast, and there began a long, uncomfortable wait, only relieved by occasional adjustments of position to bring them nearer to Ymuiden. They waited until nearly dawn, and were about to depart when suddenly a single E-boat (S 111) appeared, heading straight for them. It was subjected to immediate and concerted fire from all three boats, positioned on each quarter. At once the CO tried the normal E-boat tactic of avoidance and flight (in order to live for another day when more valuable targets for the torpedoes might be available), but the Elcos could match her speed and refused to let her escape, pumping shells relentlessly into her until she stopped. The MGB crews watched as some of the E-boat's crew jumped overboard and others made gestures of surrender. 87 went alongside with a boarding party armed and ready, while 88 and 91 picked up survivors. The eight crew who surrendered included five wounded. A White Ensign was hoisted and, although the E-boat was making water, Bremer Horne decided to try to get her back to Lowestoft. He took her in tow and set off back to harbour.

It soon became apparent that S 111 had been able to send a signal to Ymuiden, as from the east came four E-boats obviously intent on preventing the capture. Unfortunately, after a long period of fast running in the chase, 91 suffered a fault in her centre engine gearing and her speed dropped to 20 knots. Horne slipped the tow regretfully, made sure S 111 was sinking and set off for home, unaware that 91 was now at the mercy of the fresh E-boats. She was badly hit – Peter Thompson next day counted 120 shell holes – and only escaped by the timely discovery of a fog bank which provided sufficient cover for a get-away, preceded by some gallant and accurate Oerlikon fire which deterred the enemy.

There were seven wounded, including one of the prisoners, and 91 eventually reached Lowestoft at 15.30 that afternoon. The CO paid particular tribute to his most elderly engine room rating John Richards (known as 'Father' at the great age of thirty!), who despite being wounded spent hours holding two fuel lines together to enable the engines to keep going.[6]

[5] CFI 13; MO 3510; ADM 199/782.

[6] CFI 14; MO 4268; ADM 199/680; accounts by P.A.R. Thompson and A.V. Simpson.

The German E-boat (S 111) captured by the 7th MGB Flotilla off Ymuiden on 14/15 March 1942, wearing the White Ensign. (Courtesy P. Garnier)

This was the 7th Flotilla's first real success against the E-boats, and it did a great deal for morale at Lowestoft. It was followed shortly afterwards by the first action for the 5th MGB Flotilla, also based at Lowestoft, whose boats had originally been ordered from British Power Boats as 70ft MA/SBs with two Napier Sealion engines, but on conversion to MGBs they were given three Packards. Their refits had been completed by the end of 1941, and they had only recently become operational.

On 26/27 March a unit consisting of MGBs 14 (Lt J.D. Maitland RCNVR), 15 (Sub Lt M.G. Bowyer) and 18 (Lt E.F. Smyth) set out for a patrol off Ymuiden. Douglas Maitland from Vancouver was to become a highly renowned SO of a Dog Boat Flotilla in the Mediterranean, but this was his first operation as Senior Officer of a unit. Both Bowyer and Smyth were also later destined to serve in the Mediterranean.[7] The three MGBs intercepted an armed trawler, taking its crew by surprise as they first raked it with gunfire at 100 yards, and then made two depth charge attacks. The trawler sank without having fired in reply. In forwarding the reports, the base CO commended Maitland's leadership, indicating that he had injected punch and snap into the attack, virtues which had earlier been missing in operations by the 5th Flotilla.[8]

The end of the first quarter of this year of burgeoning progress, already marked by a string of successful operations despite the still inadequate resources, was marked by the historic St Nazaire raid. If nothing earlier had brought home to the British people the existence of Coastal Forces, this gallant enterprise did so with great impact. The main glory was earned by the stalwart crews who took their fifteen small wooden MLs – slow and poorly armed but utterly reliable boats – into the cauldron of the heavily defended

[7] *Dog Boats at War.*

[8] CFI 14; MO 4756; ADM 199/782.

S 111 in tow by MGB 88 (Lt J.B. Horne RN, SO of the 7th MGB Flotilla), 15 March 1942. (Courtesy P. Garnier)

MGBs 14 (Lt J.D. Maitland RCNVR) and 15 (Sub-Lt M.G. Bowyer) of the 5th MGB Flotilla, 1942. (Courtesy the late J.D. Maitland)

St Nazaire harbour deep in the Loire estuary to deliver their commandos.

The story of the raid, in which the ancient destroyer HMS *Campbeltown*, carrying a huge explosive charge, was to ram the gates of the Normandie Dock – the most important dry dock available to the German Navy for its capital ships – and so render it unusable, has been told so often that it need not be repeated here. The role of the MLs, only three of which returned to Falmouth, is also well documented and is acknowledged here as a wonderful display of heroism and sacrifice which brought huge credit to Coastal Forces, but again it is not the province of this book. The story of C Class MGB 314, which led the raid as headquarters ship, aboard which Cdr Ryder played his distinguished part, totally justifying his award of the Victoria Cross, has already been briefly described in *Dog Boats at War*. The posthumous VC awarded to Able Seaman William Savage, 314's forward gunner, acknowledged not only his own extreme gallantry but also that of countless other unnamed men of Coastal Forces, and it too deserves a special mention here.

The story of MTB 74 demands special attention, however. She was commanded by Sub Lt R.C.M.V. (Micky) Wynn RNVR, who became Lord Newborough after the war. His personal help in recording the incident accurately has made it possible to amplify many earlier accounts. Wynn had distinguished himself (and brought himself to the attention of senior Admiralty officials) as a civilian at Dunkirk. When he was commissioned in the RNVR, he served at HMS *Hornet*, and while there he conceived (he says after a very hilarious guest night) a very foolhardy plan to enter Brest harbour in some tiny craft and attempt to sink the *Scharnhorst* and *Gneisenau* by placing a charge beneath them.

To his great surprise, the idea was received with interest by Their Lordships, and eventually he was given a free hand to take the plan further and was sent down to Plymouth to report to the C-in-C. At first, he had planned to use a very small craft, but information on the fortifications at Brest had persuaded him that he should be given an MTB under construction and modify it for this special operation. So it was that MTB 74 was selected and Wynn was appointed her CO. He was to work in absolute secrecy, was responsible only to one branch of the Admiralty, and not even RACF knew anything about the arrangement – although he showed a proper curiosity as to why one of this batch of Vospers somehow disappeared.

The usual upper deck equipment was removed and the bridge cut down to a minimum; there was no armament other than the paratroop machine-guns, and the torpedo tubes were mounted on the fo'c'sle. The 'torpedoes' she carried were actually Mark X depth charges, each filled with 2,000lb of Amatol. Sadly, all these initial preparations and numerous rehearsals from their base came to naught when the two intended victims left Brest on their run up the Channel. Wynn was told the whole enterprise was off. It was an enormous disappointment after weeks of hard work.

Instead, 74 was sent to Dover and soon new orders came through that she would be used for 'pin-pricking raids on enemy harbours'. Then, suddenly, Wynn was ordered to report to Cdr Ryder, who was planning the major raid on St Nazaire. After examining 74's suitability for the task he had in mind, Ryder wrote her into the plans and sent her to Falmouth. There were last-minute problems with the fitting of more appropriate fuses for the charges, and even worse when Cdr Ryder came out on a trial run and one of the engines failed. He was prepared to eliminate 74 from the operation, but Wynn persuaded him that she could be ready.

In fact a replacement Packard engine was found and, despite the total lack of facilities at Falmouth for an engine change, Chief Motor Mechanic (MM) W.H. Lovegrove set about the task with improvised lifting gear. Assisted only by his stokers and the upper deck crew, he accomplished the change successfully in just twenty-three hours – a remarkable feat.

During the passage to the mouth of the Loire estuary, 74 was towed by HMS *Atherstone* and it was dusk on 27 March before the tow was released after thirty-four hours of tension. 74 was the last ship in the line and her precise role was to be determined only when the dock was reached. She would use her charges either to destroy the dock gates if *Campbeltown* failed to complete her blocking operation, or to torpedo the 'Old Entrance' into the outer Bassin de St Nazaire, just south of the Normandie Dock.

The passage up river, with the privileged view from the rear of the attacking force, became increasingly subject to intermittent fire from the port and from gun emplacements on the west side; fortunately MGB 314's bluffing tactics in sending confusing messages delayed the battle until they were so close that it was necessary for *Campbeltown*, MGB 314 and the MLs to open fire. It was at this early stage that 74 was first hit: a shell entered the engine room, putting the centre engine out of action and severely wounding the redoubtable CMM Lovegrove. Disregarding his pain, he set to work to effect a repair, with blood streaming from his leg.

The tiny MTB followed MGB 314 to the jetty outside the Old Entrance and waited while Cdr Ryder went to see if *Campbeltown* was firmly in position blocking the dock. When he returned he ordered Wynn to fire his torpedoes at the gates of the Old Entrance, and that task was rapidly completed. Having no main armament and carrying no troops she had no further part to play, and so was ordered to leave and make her way back down river, carrying twenty-six wounded survivors from *Campbeltown* and the MLs. Lovegrove was able to report that the centre engine was repaired, and 74 set off for home.

Sighting a Carley float with two survivors aboard, Wynn decided to stop to pick them up. Almost at once a coastal battery scored a direct hit on the stationary MTB. Wynn was blown into the wheel-house by the tremendous force of the explosion, and almost lost consciousness; he was wounded so badly that he lost an eye. As the crew abandoned ship it was Lovegrove who fought his way through the flames looking for his CO; he got him on deck, then pulled him into the water and swam with him to a Carley float. Surprisingly few of the crew were wounded, but after twelve hours in the water six of them – including the coxswain and Sub Lt O'Connor – died from exhaustion. They were finally picked up by a German gunboat and the four survivors taken prisoner.

Totally irrepressible, Micky Wynn, having regained his strength, was given a first-class artificial eye and sent back to the prison camp from the hospital. The very next day he escaped. He was recaptured, served his time in the 'cooler', and was eventually sent to Colditz, labelled a trouble-maker. He was finally exchanged early in 1945. In making his report on 74's part in the St Nazaire raid, he made sure that CMM Lovegrove was awarded the highly coveted Conspicuous Gallantry Medal (CGM). Wynn himself received the DSC.[9]

The first three months of 1942 had seen a slow development in Coastal Forces' strength, but the pace of the build-up, in terms of numbers and improved armaments, still lagged far behind the hopes of the keen young men who awaited high-quality boats impatiently. They were to see signs of better things in the months to come.

[9] Notes from Lord Newborough; Ryder, *The Attack on St Nazaire*; *Seedie's List of Coastal Forces Awards*.

CHAPTER 4

APRIL TO JUNE 1942

The first, and very significant, indication of the improvements in the boats so eagerly awaited came early in April, when MGB 74 made its appearance at Felixstowe. Robert Hichens, who had been leading the 6th MGB Flotilla of 70ft British Power Boats so successfully since September 1941, had for months been well aware of the progress in the building programme of the new design, and had used his considerable influence to ensure that the first batch would be allocated to replace the ageing boats in his 6th Flotilla. The new boats had been ordered in November 1940 when the need for a new model of MGB, more powerful than the converted MA/SBs of 1940–1, had been realized.

Designed by the renowned George Selman, the new boats were slightly larger, at 71ft 6in in length, and altogether more robust. (Appendix 1, Note 4) They carried a 2-pounder Pom-Pom forward, and a twin Oerlikon aft of the bridge, both in power-operated turrets – a great advance on the machine-guns previously available. Lt George Bailey was the first of the flotilla to receive a new boat, and the rest of Hitch's flotilla, once they had seen 74, found it hard to wait their turn, so impressed were they with what they saw of her performance and the many new features in her design. It had been decided that the new boats would form the 8th MGB Flotilla, while the surviving boats of the 6th Flotilla would continue to operate, in due course, as a separate unit.

Selman's design, in the next three years, was to provide a high proportion of the 'short' MGBs and MTBs which were to alter the balance of the 'Battle of the Narrow Seas'. Together with the later breed of Vosper MTBs and the 200 Fairmile 115ft-long Dog Boats, they were to establish a totally new force of far more effective craft which revolutionized operations for the rest of the war. It was not, however, a rapid process: 74 arrived three months ahead of the rest of the 8th Flotilla, and it was 1943 before the new Vospers and the Dog Boats appeared in large numbers.

Robert Hichens selected the COs for his new flotilla largely from the 'band of brothers' he had been nurturing for months. The 8th Flotilla was of such significance that it warrants a full note of its details:

MGB	COMPLETED	FIRST CO	FIRST ACTION	FATE
74	14.2.42	Lt G.E. Bailey	6/7.6.42	Sunk 27.7.44 as MTB 412
75	8.5.42	Lt T.E. Ladner	14/15.7.42	MTB 413
76	14.5.42	Lt L.G.R. Campbell	20/21.6.42	Sunk 6.10.42
77	8.6.42	Lt Cdr R.P. Hichens	14/15.7.42	MTB 414
78	8.6.42	Lt G.F. Duncan	1/2.8.42	Sunk 3.10.42
79	24.7.42	Lt D. James	27/28.2.43	Sunk 28.2.43
80	27.6.42	Lt R.A. Carr	1/2.8.42	MTB 415
81	11.7.42	Sub Lt J.A. Cowley	13/14.8.42	MTB 416[1]

1 Ships' cards, NHB; author's records.

The 6th MGB Flotilla leaves for patrol, 1942. (Courtesy IWM – A4265)

The first action of the month took place on 11/12 April when three MTBs of the 5/6th Flotillas from Dover intercepted a convoy close to the enemy coast. MTBs 44 and 45 were Samuel White boats, and 221 was a 72ft Vosper. The attack was pressed home to very close range. 44 fired one torpedo at 200 yards but it did not hit, and the return fire at that range was impossible to avoid. The CO was killed and the coxswain wounded.[2]

Hichens records that his 6th Flotilla at Felixstowe had been called upon to patrol

[2] CFI 15.

An MTB turning sharply at speed. (Courtesy R.D. Fletcher)

night after night, seeking the enemy by every stratagem they had developed. In these early days the main method of detecting the enemy was to place the boats in the probable path of the E-boats returning from their attacks on the Allied east coast convoys; there they would lie stopped, with engines cut, and the crews would listen for the sound of approaching engines. Unsurprisingly, the men were feeling the strain, and the base Medical Officer suggested that the drug Benzedrine would help to keep them alert – even if it had side-effects and could only be a short-term measure.

In April a new face appeared at Felixstowe. The bearded Lt P.G.C. Dickens RN had recently been appointed as Senior Officer of the 21st Flotilla. When he first arrived, he was very aware that this was a new type of war of which he had no experience whatsoever, despite a long period in HMS *Cotswold* on east coast convoy escort duty, where he had met Hichens on one occasion. (Appendix 1, Note 5)

Dickens brought with him from HMS *Bee* two of his new flotilla of Vospers, MTB 232 (Lt Ian Trelawny) and 233 (Lt J. Fraser), and they joined up with 241 (Sub Lt G.J. Macdonald RNZNVR). Dickens was awaiting the completion of his own boat, 237, but it was not ready, and at first he was forced to ride in one of the others, and he spent some time watching how the boats handled, and trying out some of his own ideas. It was a useful experience, but when 237 seemed to be delayed again his patience ran out and he shamelessly took over the next boat to finish trials, which was 234. She had been allocated long before to Lt J.P. Perkins, who had already been standing by her for weeks. 'Polly' Perkins was reallocated to 230, which was assigned to the 22nd Flotilla, not yet formed but to be based at Lowestoft; he was to become a major asset to Peter Dickens in the near future, with 230 being a reliable boat, always available when few of the 21st were serviceable, and Perkins himself proved to be an aggressive and highly accurate torpedo marksman. However, the 21st Flotilla was not really in any shape to join operations until June, when Dickens returned from working-up 234 at HMS *Bee*.

On 21 April, after Intelligence had revealed that a flotilla of E-boats was now operating from Ostend, Hichens tried a new ploy. He took four boats of his flotilla, leaving base much earlier than usual in order to arrive off the port by dusk, with the intention of catching any E-boats just setting out on patrol. He split the unit into two to give more chance of interception, and both divisions (Hichens with Carr, and Duncan with Cowley 5 miles further west) lay stopped, listening for the first sounds of movement out of Ostend. They did not have long to wait. First came the rumble of engines, and Duncan was told to join up, and then a few minutes later, as eyes were glued to glasses, they were suddenly in sight: four E-boats, possibly six, in line ahead. Hichens' relationship with his coxswain, PO Henry Curtis, was one of absolute confidence and trust – he had already proved himself to the hilt – and only a murmur was necessary to alter course or pass information. Hichens in 64 rapidly overtook the last E-boat in line, which was already firing, and was closing all the time as they ran on in close station up the line on a parallel course. They saw their shells burst on the E-boat's hull, and in no time they were up to the next in line, switching their attack to her and leaving 'Bussy' Carr to finish off the first target. By this time though, 64 had been severely hit. The starboard gun had been silenced and two of its crew lay wounded, but others sprang forward to reload. On the bridge with Hichens was George Bailey, one of the senior COs, who had just arrived back with the first 71ft 6in boat, and was out as a passenger. Slightly wounded, and with blood streaming down his face, he seized the bridge Lewis gun and poured rounds into the third of the E-boats, which was already turning away. Relentlessly 64 swept up the line – there *were* six E-boats – and as they headed towards the leader, she too broke off and turned away. The first objective had been achieved: the E-boats had at least temporarily been diverted from their course towards their patrol area.

In the general confusion, Hichens' next move was to call the four MGBs together, and try to establish what the E-boats' next move would be. MGB 64 had suffered grievously: five of the crew of ten were wounded, mostly seriously; the starboard gun was shattered; and the hull was holed in at least thirteen places. But luckily none of the holes was vital – most were forward and above the waterline. Francis Head, the first lieutenant, was already administering morphia to the wounded. Very soon Hichens was joined by the three other boats and they lay silent, trying to work out the course the E-boats would take: westward to continue their patrol, or southward to return to Ostend? A murmur of distant engines to the south solved the puzzle – they were turning for home.

At once, Hichens shouted 'we'll chase them in – we might pick up a straggler'. However, mist came down and the engine sounds abruptly ceased: the E-boats had reached harbour. But still Hichens would not give up. He ordered Bailey to take 64 back to base to get medical attention for the wounded as fast as possible, then he transferred to 65 (Duncan) and the three remaining MGBs waited outside Ostend, off the harbour entrance, in case the E-boats should regroup and try again. But they stayed in harbour, their intention of attacking an east coast convoy totally thwarted.

There were two results of this gallant action: Hichens was awarded his first DSO,

MTB 65 of the 6th MGB Flotilla, commanded by Lt G. Duncan, one of Hichens' 'Band of Brothers', 1942. (Collection G.M. Hudson)

and, much more important to him, the E-boats stopped operating from Ostend.[3]

It was extremely frustrating for the MTB and MGB crews that just when the weather was improving and hopes for more enemy contacts were high, there were only two major actions during May 1942, even though patrols were mounted almost every night. As ever, these periods of lack of contacts resulted from a variety of causes, but at this time it seems that the enemy was not sending its ships to sea as frequently as had been the case.

On 11/12 May a unit of three MGBs, two of them from the 3rd Flotilla, left Ramsgate to intercept a force of enemy Torpedo Boats off the French coast. The composition of this unit reflects the international nature of the 3rd Flotilla normally led by Lt Stewart Gould. In the lead was Lt Roger King RN in MGB 41. A regular officer in the French Navy in 1940, he escaped to England on the fall of France and spent the rest of the war in Coastal Forces, and King was the nom-de-plume given him by the Admiralty. Next in line was MGB 46, commanded by Lt Schreuder of the Royal Netherlands Navy. This boat had an extraordinary history. Ordered by the Netherlands Admiralty in 1938 from the British Power Boat Yard at Hythe, by 28 August 1939 she was so near to completion that she was on trials in Southampton Water with the Dutch liaison officer on board. Lt Cdr Otto de Booy RNethN (later a renowned submarine officer), realizing that war was inevitable and

[3] MO 50770; MO 50890; ADM 199/784; *Seedie's List of Coastal Forces Awards*; Hichens, *We Fought Them in Gunboats*.

that the boat might never be allowed to leave Britain, boldly decided to act on his own initiative. He 'extended his trials in a south-easterly direction' and to everyone's surprise, the boat ended up in a Dutch port! She was commissioned as TM 51 on 6 November 1939 and under the command of Lt Jan van Stavaren, saw her first action on 10 May 1940 at Rotterdam when attacking German troops who were attempting to capture the strategically important Willemsbrug (bridge). And her rollercoaster story did not end there. On the capitulation of the Netherlands, she at once escaped to Britain, arriving at *Hornet* on 15 May 1940, and was handed over to the Royal Navy. With commendable courtesy, in due course she was handed back to Dutch personnel, and joined the 3rd MGB Flotilla first at Fowey and then at Dover.

The unit was completed by MGB 67 (Lt 'Boffin' Campbell) of Hichens' 6th Flotilla, which happened to be in Ramsgate when the call-out came.

Sadly, the only official record of the action is contained in the 'summary of actions', and, considering the implications of the tremendous difference in fire-power between the three MGBs (three Oerlikons, several 0.5in Vickers and Lewis guns), and the four Torpedo Boats (3in, 37mm and 20mm guns), the stated results are most remarkable: 'Four Torpedo Boats severely damaged, one small craft shot up, and hits on one E-boat.'

Forty-eight hours later came a very gallant battle in the Channel when three boats of the 5/6th MTB Flotillas at Dover were sent to intercept a very important convoy. The MTBs had been gaining the upper hand in attacks on lightly escorted merchant ships, but on this occasion one of the enemy's armed merchant raiders, *Stier*, was to be passed through the Strait to reach Boulogne, and it was given a massive escort of four Mowe Class Torpedo Boats, eight M Class minesweepers and ten E/R-boats. The fire-power of this force should have been able to keep the MTBs at bay easily, but the determination of the Senior Officer, Lt E.A.E. Cornish in 220, supported by Sub Lt Barry Easton in 221 and Mark Arnold-Forster in 219, enabled the boats to get close enough to make an attack.

Sadly, the SO's boat was severely damaged and Lt Cornish himself was killed after he had got his torpedoes away and secured one hit on a major escort, but the official record is extraordinarily lacking in detail. Whether 220 was hit by large shells – or even rammed – is not known. Easton in 221 also penetrated the escort screen by using smoke, and secured a second hit; 219 and the two MGBs of the 2nd Flotilla did their best to get in but were driven off. Fortunately post-war Intelligence reports from Kriegsmarine records reveal that two Torpedo Boats – *Iltis* and *See Adler* – were sunk, although *Stier* successfully reached Boulogne.[4]

Although May had been disappointingly unproductive for the MTBs, the onset of better weather in June led to a series of actions in each area. It also heralded the introduction to operations not only of the first 71ft 6in MGBs but also of the newly arrived 21st MTB Flotilla at Felixstowe, which under SO Lt Peter Dickens RN later built a reputation of efficiency and gallantry.

On the night of 6/7 June there was another success against the enemy Torpedo Boats when MTBs of the 4th Flotilla, led by Lt H.L. (Harpy) Lloyd in 30, followed by 70 (Lt T. Neill), pushed their attack home although illuminated and heavily shelled. Both boats were damaged but Neill scored a hit on one of the Torpedo Boats and sank it. Two other boats were involved: MTB 72 and 241 of the 21st Flotilla, commanded by

[4] CFI 15; Battle Summary NHB 32; NID 1.8.45; M2305/45; Summary in Actions List.

Sub Lt G.J. Macdonald, a very young New Zealander who was destined to become one of the great Coastal Forces leaders, attacked E-boats and a large barge at close range under heavy fire.

Activity at Dover continued unabated, and on 14/15 June a bruising battle was fought by three boats of the newly arrived 9th MTB Flotilla. This flotilla of Vospers, commanded by Lt C. Philpotts RN, consisted initially of four boats manned entirely by officers and men of the Royal Netherlands Navy, and four more with Royal Navy crews. On this night the unit was led by Lt G.L. Cotton in 201, followed by 203 (Lt E.H. Larive RNethN) and 229 (Lt A. McDougall). Their task was to attack a large tanker which had already escaped destruction twice, but was obviously of importance to the enemy. Intelligence had established that this tanker would sail, heavily escorted, eastward through the Strait from Boulogne.

In order to give the MTBs every chance, a force of five MGBs from Ramsgate, led by the SO of the 2nd Flotilla, Lt G.D.K. Richards RN, was despatched in advance to lay mines ahead of the convoy. However, detected by searchlights and starshell, they were subjected to very heavy fire from both the shore and the leading escorts, and MGB 46 was seriously damaged by fire from Vp 1806.[5] Some of the escorts turned into Calais, but the remainder continued towards Dunkirk. Richards and his boats had no chance of laying mines accurately.

Cotton and his MTBs were in position to attack by 02.00, but as 201 turned in to attack, all the escorts opened fire and Cotton was faced with a wall of shells and tracer. With

[5] Vp: *Vorpostenboote*: enemy auxiliary escort vessels of wide variety, some large.

A.B. Ducker of MTB 24 (CO K. Horlock) in his 0.5-in turret, at Dover, 1942. The High Commissioner for New Zealand, visiting the Base, looks on. (Courtesy D. Newman)

MTB 204 of the 9th MTB Flotilla at Dover, manned by personnel of the Royal Netherlands Navy, 1942. It was a Samuel White built to Vosper design with Packard engines. (Collection G.M. Hudson)

Larive in very close station astern, he roared in to penetrate the screen, but had extreme difficulty in deciding which of the shapes ahead was his main target. He got one torpedo away, and then 201 received a devastating burst of fire which virtually immobilized everyone on the bridge: Cotton was wounded, together with the first lieutenant, the coxswain, the telegraphist, and a bridge messenger. The signalman was killed. The Canadian spare officer, Sub Lt I.D. Moore, took the wheel, and the second torpedo was fired. One engine had been hit and was out of action, and there were casualties in the engine room.

Larive – still close astern – then fired his torpedoes, and everyone was sure that at least one hit was obtained, although from which boat no one was sure – and it did not seem to matter. Still under fire and trying to disengage, 201 came to rest some distance from the escort screen, but with two trawlers still firing at her. Cotton ordered the crew to 'abandon ship', ditched the confidential books and gathered the crew in a raft. However, 201 did not sink, and when the trawlers finally left, Cotton reboarded, hoping it might be possible to get her back to Dover. He succeeded in getting under way on the auxiliary engine, and they crept painfully towards base. All but two of the crew had been wounded, and by this time three had died and two more were seriously in need of medical attention. Despite the efforts to keep baling and pumping, the boat was making water rapidly. At 0745 two RAF Air Sea Rescue boats arrived. One took off the badly wounded while the other attempted to tow the stricken boat. Sadly, at 0848, 201 turned over and sank. It was an unhappy end to a gallant and determined action.

By the nature of war, the news that would have brought some consolation to Cotton and his crew could not come rapidly: they discovered

Visit by the High Commissioner for New Zealand to the Base at Dover (HMS *Wasp*). He meets crew of MTB 24 of 5th MTB Flotilla (CO K. Horlock, First Lieutenant Sub Lt D. Newman). (Courtesy D. Newman)

that the tanker had reached Dunkirk, but not whether it was damaged. After the war enemy records revealed that there *had* been a successful torpedo hit on the ocean-going tug *Cherbourgois V*. The awards announced in August included DSCs for Cotton and Larive, a Conspicuous Gallantry Medal for Stoker Robert Spinks, who had kept the engine room working even though badly wounded, and despite the deaths of his motor mechanic and the leading stoker. There was also a DSM for 201's coxswain Leading Seaman A.E. Collins.[6]

The significance of an operation on 20/21 June lay more in the composition of the force involved rather than in the results they achieved. Hichens led four MGBs, three of his 6th Flotilla, and, most importantly, MGB 76, the second of the two 71ft 6in British Power Boats which had arrived at Felixstowe to form the 8th Flotilla, which Hitch would eventually take over. 76 was commanded by Lt L.G.R. (Boffin) Campbell and this was the first time he had taken her out on patrol and sighted the enemy.

Also out for the first time in earnest was Peter Dickens, the new SO of the 21st MTB Flotilla, who had just arrived from working up his own MTB 234 at HMS *Bee*, the training base at Weymouth which was now operating at full pressure and was already having a profound effect on the efficiency of newly commissioned boats and crews. On this night Dickens was out in MTB 241 with Macdonald, and he was already worried about unreliable

[6] CFI 18; MO 8887; ADM 1/12369; BS NHB 43; *Seedie's List of Coastal Forces Awards.*

boats: not one of the other three boats was ready for operations, and he was obliged to 'borrow' MTB 72 (Gardner) of the 4th Flotilla as his second boat. He had already discovered that the lovely Vosper hulls of his new boats were originally designed to be powered by Isotta Fraschini engines, but were now running with Packards – excellent engines, but in his view they were lying on 'a wrong-sized bed at an uncomfortable angle' – which led all too often to failures and frustration. In fact, the MTBs never made an interception and had to be content with a brief brush with E-boats. The MGBs, however, tore into a convoy escorted by armed trawlers – never easy adversaries – and were much impressed with the performance of 76's heavier armament. One trawler was severely damaged, and experience was gained all round.[7]

On the following night (21/22 June) one of the Polish boats of the 3rd MGB Flotilla fought a most unusual lone action in the Dover Strait. Lt E. Wcislicki ('Whisky') had set out in S 2 to patrol with S 3, but the latter had developed engine trouble and had to return to Ramsgate. In a typically aggressive response, 'Whisky' decided to maintain a lone patrol off the Varne knowing that Intelligence had anticipated E-boat activity there – either mine-laying or perhaps an attack on the coastal convoy. Dover Command sent a signal to recall S 2, but it was apparently not received – although some doubt was later cast on that by the Command, who made a reference to 'a blind eye' when passing on Whisky's report. Nevertheless, at 0105, S 2 sighted six E-boats, and immediately attacked, opening fire at 200–300 yards, almost certainly damaging his first target. Return fire was heavy but fortunately not very accurate, although the boat received several hits from cannon shells. Having expended almost all his ready-use ammunition, Whisky withdrew to reload and left the enemy boats firing at one another.[8] He later joined up with some C Class MGBs and discovered that the enemy had not continued across the Channel.

Mention of the 'long' C Class gunboats provides an opportunity to refer briefly to their valuable activities. In fact these heavily armed (but slower) boats were very soon (within three weeks) to be joined by the first of the new D Class Fairmile MGBs and MTBs (the Dog Boats) which were to make a huge impact in Coastal Forces warfare from the start of 1943. At this early stage it was expected that the 30-knot Dog Boats would be too slow to bring the E-boats to action, but that their heavier armament would be formidable in tackling slower and larger targets. As they were being built in groups of gunboats and Torpedo Boats, which would have different roles, it remained to be seen how they would be deployed. The fact that many of the 'short' boats could match the E-boats for speed was still a major factor. The Steam Gun Boats – only seven of them – had also been operating for some months; even larger, steel-hulled and with rather vulnerable steam engines, they brought a new dimension to the attack force.[9]

On 29/30 June a unit from the 21st MTB Flotilla under Peter Dickens operated with a unit of MGBs from the 8th and 6th Flotillas under Robert Hichens, which included both 77 and 76, the two new available British Power Boats. The patrol was not eventful, but interestingly Hichens comments in his report that he considered the Vospers to be very noisy at high revs. There is no reciprocal comment from Dickens, which might have been very interesting.[10]

[7] ADM 199/680; BS NHB 50; Dickens, *Night Action*.

[8] CFI 17; ADM 199/680.

[9] *Dog Boats at War*.

[10] MO 9272; ADM 199/784.

MGB 89, a 70ft Elco of the 7th MGB Flotilla based at Lowestoft, 1942. (Courtesy M.G. Bowyer)

The second quarter of 1942 was brought to a close by a spirited action off Texel on the last night of June. Three US Elcos (70ft MGBs) of the 7th MGB Flotilla from Lowestoft were patrolling off the Texel, which was a long haul for the boats as it was so far north. The group was led by a Canadian, Lt P.A.R. Thompson DSC, in MGB 83, followed by 86 (M.T.C. Sadler) and 91 (E.W.D. Leaf). The 7th had spent most of its time in the past months on anti-E-boat patrols beyond the east coast convoy route, and this was one of its first truly offensive missions.

They were rather taken aback when the targets presented to them were several merchant vessels, with barrage balloons above and several escorts. These were hardly suitable gunboat targets, and for once they wished they had torpedoes. But each MGB had depth charges, and if the opportunity presented itself, they could try a depth charge attack – a tactic that required them to pass dangerously close under the bows of a large ship. Suddenly there *was* such an opportunity, and after a good deal of gunfire from each side the MGBs raced through a gap in the convoy and Derek Leaf found himself almost colliding with his target. When he 'pulled the string which released the depth charges' only one dropped, but it was *very* close to the stem towering above his boat as she squeezed through. The Oerlikon gunner saw the explosion, level with the foremast, and there was every hope and expectation that it had done some damage. There were five wounded and some damage, particularly to 83, but all the boats returned safely in time for breakfast.[11]

[11] MO 9678; ADM 199/782; CFI 18.

CHAPTER 5

JULY TO SEPTEMBER 1942

In all Commands the system for ordering operational patrols followed a similar pattern. The C-in-C's staff would receive Intelligence (mostly by this time from intercepted and decoded radio signals) and would decide on the required action. The orders would be passed to the SOO (Staff Officer, Operations) at the relevant base, who would consult with the SOs of flotillas and decide which boats were available to make up the units required. He would then write the appropriate sailing orders ('Being in all respects ready for sea you are to proceed . . .'). This would be followed by a briefing meeting for COs with the SOO if there were any complex Intelligence factors, or the SO would simply hand out orders.

Reference has already been made to the strange way in which at certain periods, even when patrols were out each night, there was no contact with the enemy. In many ways the strain and subsequent anti-climax of a fruitless night peering through binoculars or lying stopped, listening for the engines of enemy craft were more stressful than the hectic bursts of fierce action. The latter at least kept everyone so busy – whatever happened – that with the adrenalin flowing they brought some emotional satisfaction rather than frustration.

July 1942 brought one of those periods. The records show that despite reasonable sea conditions a combination of factors meant that the enemy were challenged only on three occasions. Peter Dickens complained that his boats were constantly breaking down and becoming unserviceable because of their incompatible engines, resulting in shaft bearings running hot. He could not conceal his bitterness that 'Authority' (whoever that was) had again failed to provide a fighting force with effective weapons.

Hichens' new boats were successively coming into service, and he was to pick up his own MGB 77 and carry out a brief working-up at HMS *Bee* at the beginning of the month. By 10 July he had gathered the first four boats together at Felixstowe, and declared that the 8th MGB Flotilla was formed. Straightaway came a new challenge. Intelligence had revealed a new concentration of E-boats in the Channel ports, and Hichens was ordered to take his flotilla to Dartmouth. This move resulted in a productive period of operations and cemented the reputations of both Robert Hichens and his flotilla of 71ft 6in boats with their increased fire-power and tremendous reliability and performance.

A West Country man by birth and upbringing, and totally at home in these new waters, Hichens arrived on the 13th and on the 14/15 July set out to patrol off the Channel Islands, leading in his own MGB 77 and followed by 78 (Duncan), 76 (Campbell) and 75 (Lt T.E. Ladner RCNVR). Tom Ladner was the only CO in the new flotilla who had not been with Hichens in the 6th, and he was something of an unknown factor. 78 had to return with a minor defect, but soon the other three were lying stopped 12 miles north of Alderney in a sea which was getting increasingly rough. Hichens soon decided that E-boats were unlikely to be out in these conditions, but somehow he had a feeling that something might come along. He moved closer to the north coast of Alderney,

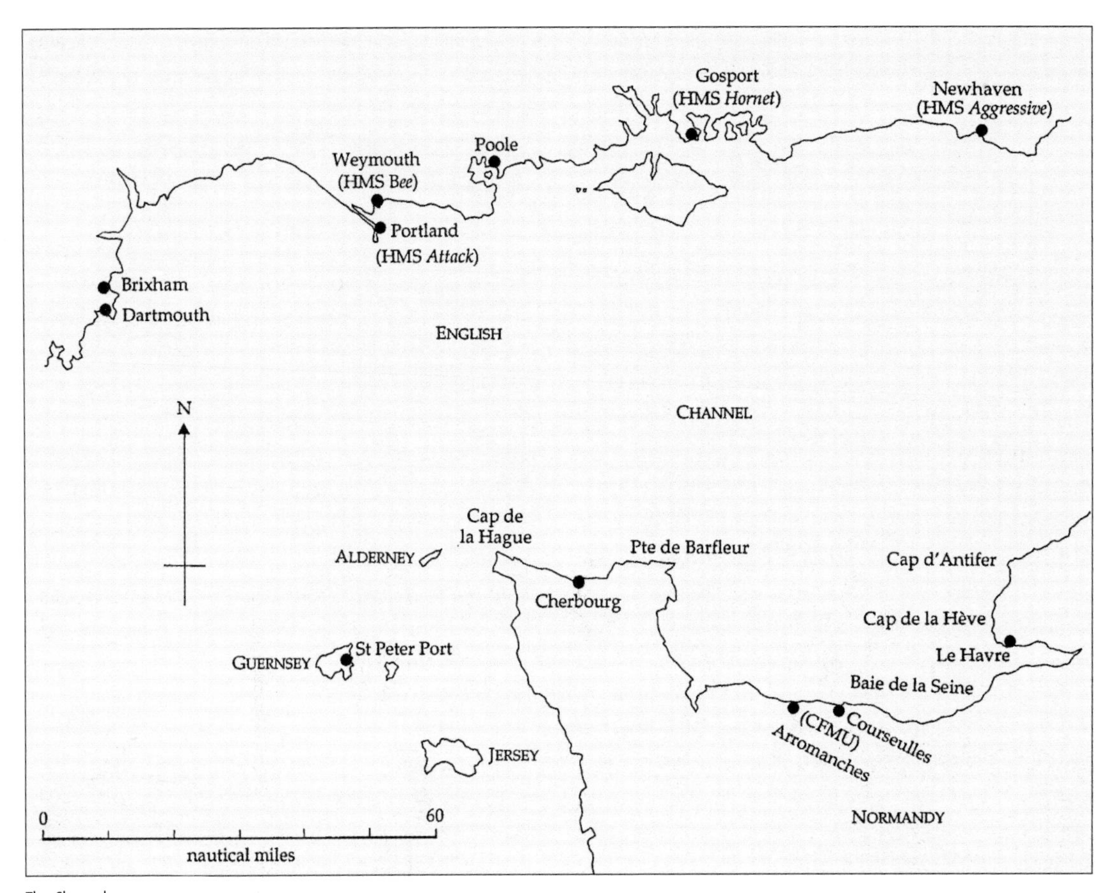

The Channel.

moving at only 12 knots to reduce the noise. Suddenly a light was reported to starboard. They closed and two dim dark blobs showed . . . two large trawlers steering west at about 8 knots. It was decision time for Hichens: should he increase speed and risk being heard but gain the benefits of getting ahead? He chose to speed up, and moved abreast within 200 yards of the nearer trawler before it challenged and he gave the order to open fire.

The three boats in close formation poured out their broadsides – now so much more effective than in the past – and the target was hit hard, and was so surprised that it hardly fired in return. As he raced past, Hichens realized that the trawlers were the rear escort for a small tanker just ahead. He made an instant decision to depth charge her, and turned in across her bow. It was a move they had practised – after all, without torpedoes the depth charge was their most lethal weapon for sinking a larger target. This was the time for the coxswain to take charge – with the wheel in his hands he had the best chance of steering as close across the bow as was possible. Henry Curtis rose to the challenge, running 77 past just 10 feet from the tanker's sharp, overhanging stem, and as they passed, First Lt Head released the depth charge. The guns still roared out, the shells bursting on the tanker's hull – but at the same time 77 was hit by a hail of larger shells from the disengaged trawler astern. But at least the depth charge had done its work. There was a shudder as the boat shook to an underwater explosion, but now there were more urgent things to worry about near at hand. Fire spurted from the wheelhouse and ammunition was exploding. Hichens left the bridge and set about extinguishing the fire with all the help he could get. Among those who joined him was AB John Barnes: along with five others, he had been wounded in that burst of fire – but he left his turret and painfully followed his CO below where the flames were threatening the ready-use ammunition lockers. The men worked until the fire was out and the danger had passed. Hichens then returned to the bridge and found that Curtis, calm and competent as ever, left on his own on the bridge, had steered northward and disengaged in a wide sweep to get the boat out of trouble.

Hichens took stock. The tanker was stopped, on fire and surrounded by smoke; he felt she was almost certainly doomed. His boat was very badly damaged, but her engines were intact. He called up the other boats and fixed a rendezvous. What grieved him most was the realization that his crew had once again borne the brunt of the attack: one killed, two severely wounded and three others needing hospital attention.

77 needed several weeks for repairs, but this operation had a number of repercussions, some of them far-reaching. The first was the discussion – initiated by the deep-thinking Hichens himself – on the implications for MGBs faced with a torpedo target when operating alone. There was certainly a case for bringing down an MTB flotilla to provide a two-pronged attack force. And was there

Lt Cdr R.P. Hichens DSO* DSC**, SO 8th MGB Flotilla, briefing his COs for an operation, 1942. (Courtesy IWM – A12908)

not a case, now that the gunboats were stronger, for putting torpedo tubes on them? This idea was much debated in the months ahead, before it was totally adopted over a year later. More immediately, there was a Bar to his DSO for Hichens and for AB John Barnes the exceptional award of the Conspicuous Gallantry Medal – for his sterling efforts in fire-fighting despite being wounded.[1]

The 8th continued to patrol right through the moon period, seeking the E-boats which now had bases in both Cherbourg and Guernsey, but not finding them.

The rest of the month was mainly the province of the 'long' boats: two C boats and 601, the first Dog Boat in commission, fought a bruising battle from Dover, and the Steam Gun Boats sank a trawler off Barfleur. The only action by the 'short' boats was in the Nore, when on 28/29 July a double unit from the 4th MTBs and the 6th MGBs from Felixstowe met a convoy escorted by E-boats off Ostend. Both units were 'under new management'. The 6th MGBs had been handed over to George Bailey, the Senior Officer of the old team, and now leading a new set of COs in their famous boats. They naturally regarded themselves as the 'second division' but were determined to prove themselves. Bailey, now a lieutenant commander, led in 67, with 63 (Boissard) in support. The 4th were led by D.G.H. (Jake) Wright in MTB 32, with MTB 69 (M.A. Pryor) in company. When the convoy was sighted, the MGBs took on the E-boats of the escort, while Wright in 32 was able to close with a merchant vessel and scored a torpedo hit. His boat received some damage and casualties. Soon after, Bailey decided to launch a depth charge attack on a trawler – very similar to Hichens' attack two weeks earlier; he had similar results both in terms of success and in the severe damage and multiple casualties suffered. Bailey's boat was badly holed forward, and was set on fire. There was another parallel with the earlier action: George Bailey was awarded the DSO, and Jake Wright a DSC, while both their crews were honoured with several DSMs.[2]

The month closed with another 'combined' operation from Lowestoft on 31 July. The patrol consisted of boats of the 5th MGBs and three MTBs of the 4th and 11th Flotillas. They sighted a convoy and Dyer, leading the MGBs, created a diversion, making two runs with all guns firing, but the MTBs lost bearing and failed to make contact.

August was a much more profitable month with a record seventeen actions listed. It began with another first-class action by Hichens and the 8th Flotilla against E-boats off Cherbourg. The SO was aboard MGB 80 (Carr), followed by 76 (Campbell), 78 (Duncan) and 75 (Ladner), and after many fruitless patrols they set off in their usual hopeful – but resigned – attitude. They ran into a dense fog belt and wondered whether it was worth continuing the patrol. Suddenly, reports began to come through of two groups of E-boats aiming for the Channel convoy route from Cherbourg. Then Hichens heard they had turned back. He thought through the various possibilities and decided to press on at top speed through the fog to reach their base before they could return there. It required great skill on the part of his COs, who were following blind, but he had confidence in them and they covered the 65 miles to a position off Cherbourg without hitch, passing out of the fog into a still, clear

[1] CFI 18; MO 10078; ADM 199/782; *Seedie's List of Coastal Forces Awards.*

[2] MO 10737; ADM 199/782; *Seedie's List of Coastal Forces Awards.*

night. When they stopped and cut engines, they immediately heard the distinctive subdued rumble of E-boat engines from the harbour entrance, and realized at once that at least one of the groups had beaten them back to Cherbourg.

Hichens was nothing if not determined and persistent, and decided he would wait 'on the doorstep' in case the second group had not yet returned. They did not have long to wait. They started up and moved closer to the breakwater, as the E-boats, totally oblivious, came closer and closer. Hichens disregarded a 600-ton Torpedo Boat lying half a mile away, reasoning that her CO would assume they were E-boats waiting to enter harbour. At last it was time to open fire: all four MGBs raced up the line, pouring their concentrated fire into each E-boat in turn, with virtually no return fire at all. They had achieved complete surprise. They circled round and repeated the attack, their fire engulfing each of the enemy. Gradually, the shore batteries and two Torpedo Boats began to take a hand: starshell burst overhead, and shells and tracer intensified. It was time to go. From a distance they saw two great pillars of fire, and considered they could safely claim two E-boats destroyed and two severely damaged. It had been an exemplary attack, in conception, in development and in execution.[3]

The need for an MTB flotilla to join Hichens in Dartmouth has already been mentioned: the orders had now been given, and Peter Dickens had set off from Felixstowe with the available boats of his 21st Flotilla. By 6 August they had staged at HMS *Hornet*, the base at Gosport, and while there they were despatched to patrol off Cape Barfleur where Intelligence had learned that the sea-going tug *Oceanie* was to move from Cherbourg to Le Havre, heavily escorted.

[3] CFI 18 and 19; MO 10773; ADM 199/680.

A gunner in the 0.5in Vickers turret exercises his guns on MTB 96. (Courtesy R.D. Fletcher)

Dickens' unit consisted of three boats. He chose to ride in 237, newly arrived and with Lt Guy Fison in command. Astern were two stalwarts of the 21st, Ian Trelawny in 232 and Jim Macdonald the New Zealander in 241. As Peter Dickens confesses in his book *Night Action*, he was feeling very insecure at this time as he struggled to learn the ropes of leading a flotilla of MTBs without any previous experience. He refers to this action as 'The Second Battle of Barfleur'.

When they reached a position close to the expected route of the convoy they slowed, using auxiliary engines for silent running, and eased down into the Baie de la Seine. Macdonald was the first to sight the enemy to

A 71ft Vosper 1939 Class MTB of the 4th Flotilla, spring 1943. (Courtesy IWM – HU73784)

starboard, and Dickens ordered the attack. Almost at once 237 was hit and lost power and steering, but managed to fire her torpedoes at the first target that presented itself. As they attempted to disengage a 37mm shell hit the wheelhouse, but after a torrid few seconds they were through, and setting a course for home with hand-steering aft. 232 was also heavily attacked and hit: Trelawny was badly wounded, two engines were knocked out and the steering was lost. The first lieutenant took over and tried to sustain the attack but quickly realized that he simply did not have the wherewithal to do so, and disengaged. Macdonald in 241 was miraculously not hit and pressed home a gun attack, although he did not find a torpedo target worthy of the name. He did find 237 drifting helplessly and on fire, and stood by while her crew fought the blaze. Disappearing briefly to investigate a possible enemy ship, Macdonald returned just in time as 237's fire gained the upper hand and there was an explosion in the petrol compartment. Clearly she was doomed, but 241 was able to take off her crew; she took a long time to sink. Dickens felt that his first action with the 21st had been inglorious: he had lost a boat, several men had been wounded and Trelawny's injuries took him out of action for months and he was lost to the flotilla. But – once again – experience had been gained and it was not long before Dickens began to put together some significant successes.[4]

The German Navy was in fact very busy on the night of 6/7 August. In addition to the heavy escort provided for the *Oceanie* further west, they were also aiming to pass the

[4] CFI 18; Dickens, *Night Action*.

4,000-ton *Schwabenland* (described in one report as a seaplane tender) through the Dover Strait, with an escort of fifteen ships ranging from M Class minesweepers to flak ships and R-boats. It was obviously regarded as a very important convoy. The Dover Command threw four units into the fray. Leading the first was the new SO MTBs (Dover), Lt Christopher Dreyer RN, just returned to Coastal Forces after a spell in destroyers and on courses. His boats were slow Samuel Whites with Hall Scott engines. He embarked in MTB 44 (V.F. Clarkson), with 45 (Hay) and 48 in support, and his plan was to cross the Channel ahead of the convoy and attack from an inshore position. Three C Class MGBs – 330 (SO), 324 and 331, were to create a diversion from seaward so that the inshore torpedo attack would have a better chance of making an undetected approach. It was not to be. With the shore batteries firing starshell and the convoy on high alert, Dreyer's boats came under very heavy fire at short range as he made his final approach. 44 was hit in the engine room by a 40mm shell; all three engines were put out of action and all the crew there wounded. Dreyer later discovered that 45, the second boat in line, had also been hit and the CO, Sub Lt W. Hay, had been killed. The MGBs made a spirited gun attack on the main target but their small calibre guns could make no impression on this large ship.

With no engines, 44 was totally disabled, and there was no alternative but to abandon ship and destroy her unless help arrived very soon. Preparations were made and the Carley float launched. Dreyer decided that with petrol in the bilges she had to be despatched, so fired a Very pistol into the engine room and for his pains was blown off the ship; when he came round he found himself being towed to the float. Meanwhile Sidebottom, the SO of the C boats, whose boat had also been badly damaged, was searching for 44, knowing she was in trouble. He made a run along the course of the action, and on his way back close inshore suddenly sighted the Carley float and was able to pick up all the crew very close to the French shore. MGB 324 then towed MTB 45 back to Dover.

The other two units made their very gallant attacks later when the convoy was east of Calais. The three MTBs (221, 35 and 38, led by Lt H.P. Granlund), made approach after approach but were beaten off by a wall of fire. Lt B. Easton in 38 was particularly persistent, returning twice more after being severely damaged in his first attack.

The *Schwabenland* had got through, but she and her escorts had been constantly attacked and there was no doubt about the determination and gallantry of all the MTBs and MGBs involved. Casualties were heavy: in all, two men were killed and seventeen wounded. They needed more fire-power, and the search continued for tactical counter-measures to the imbalance created by the superior weight of numbers and the size of escorts. Meanwhile the C Class boats and the first two Dog Boats in commission had already appeared on the scene, and more were to come.[5]

Attempts by the 2nd and 3rd MGB Flotillas from Ramsgate to lay mines close inshore along the French coast to catch enemy convoys were repelled twice in the next few nights by vigilant shore batteries which put up starshells to locate them and then used their heavy calibre guns to drive them off.

Further west, four boats of Hichens' 8th MGBs carried out an unobserved attack off Guernsey on two armed trawlers on 13/14 August. They achieved complete surprise and by concentrating their fire, shot

[5] CFI 18 and 19; C.W.S. Dreyer; V.F. Clarkson; ROP held by Author.

up one trawler very severely before tackling the other. As the enemy gunners recovered from the shock, their return fire became more and more accurate. Hichens reasoned that the odds had now changed, and that if he persevered he could inflict only minor damage – and run the risk of losing one of his precious new gunboats. He consequently disengaged, and then learned to his distress that 'Bussy' Carr in MGB 80 had been badly wounded. A bullet passed right through him, puncturing his lungs. Despite thick fog, they got him to hospital in time to save his life, but it had been a near thing.[6]

A major action on 16/17 August from Dover has already been partly described in *Dog Boats at War*, as it featured MGB 609, the second Dog in commission, together with a unit of C Class MGBs which sank an R-boat by ramming. But two 'short' MGBs of the 2nd Flotilla were also much involved in this fierce battle. The German authorities, much concerned by the attacks on their convoys by Coastal Forces boats, had taken to laying a defensive minefield in mid-Channel. They sent over twenty E- and R-boats early in the evening in an attempt to achieve surprise on a dull dark day. However, they were picked up by the Dover Plot and the two groups of MGBs were hastily ordered out to interrupt their lay.

The two 2nd Flotilla boats were delayed briefly by a defect but then the inestimable G.D.K. (Dicky) Richards in MGB 10 set off with MGB 6 (Lt R.M. Barge) at high speed. They arrived on the scene just as the 'long'

[6] CFI 19; Hichens, *We Fought Them in Gunboats*.

MGB 50 off Weymouth, 1942. (Courtesy E. Read)

boats began their attack on the enemy's rear, and so Richards chose to attack those in the lead. Concentrating on the first in line, they used their far greater speed to roar past for a first devastating run, before swinging round to deliver their next broadside from the other side. They repeated the manoeuvre, and in no time the R-boat was stopped and on fire. Richards decided to attempt a capture: he went alongside and sent over a boarding party. His plan was thwarted by an explosion which was clearly going to sink the vessel. Instead, fifteen prisoners were taken and they were back in harbour by 2330 – a most unusual hour![7]

On the following night – 17/18 August – new tactics were tried in an effort to overcome the problems created by the heavy escorts of the German convoys. This time six MTBs drawn from three of the Dover flotillas – the 5th, 6th and 9th – were carefully briefed on a completely new disposition. It had never been tried before. The boats were to have more independence: each boat was given its own position, spread out along the Channel off Dunkirk. When a convoy passed, they were to attack the most appropriate target – quite a difficult strategy to defend against. The Senior Officer on this occasion was Lt C.L.G. Philpotts RN, who was aboard MTB 204 commanded by Willie de Looze, one of the star Dutch COs in his flotilla.

At first things seemed to go very well. A convoy appeared, and the plan was put into operation. 204 attacked the first escort and scored a torpedo hit; several others got in close and 38 (Nicholson) was thought to have been successful. But three boats were badly hit: 43 (Butler) was sunk, but all the crew were picked up. 218 (Ball) was hit in the engine room, though she tried another attack, despite being waterlogged. Sadly, when lying disabled, she hit a mine and sank in the explosion. Ball and four of his crew were killed but the remaining six were picked up by Mark Arnold-Forster as they swam about, with mines on the surface all around them. 38 was hit on the bridge and Nicholson killed after his determined attack. It was obvious that the demands of close-range attacks were bound to lead to losses and casualties, but Dover was felt to be suffering more than its fair share, and had led the way in aggression in this violent August.[8]

After Peter Dickens' first major battle off Barfleur, he arrived at Dartmouth keen to exchange ideas on tactics with Hichens before they began operating together. The various methods of coordinating MTB/MGB attacks on convoys had been tried out for many months and Dickens was sure that overall direction from one leader was the answer to success. He found Hichens – the master tactician – a willing partner in the discussions, and his experience both at Dover and along the east coast was invaluable. On 18/19 August they set out – with Hichens directing – to patrol off Alderney, hoping to put their ideas into practice. Sadly they found no convoy, and their hopes were dashed when the 21st was recalled to Felixstowe.

Dickens' frustration didn't end there. Staging once again at HMS *Hornet*, he found another opportunity to try out his ideas. In company with a group of gunboats he had never met before, he set off for Cherbourg and sighted the enemy. They were small craft – possibly E-boats – but when the attack began, and Dickens sent in the MGBs, they turned away, misunderstanding his intentions. The 21st carried on back to Felixstowe, only to discover that an operation was planned which would require them to move on up to Lowestoft.

[7] CFI 19; Battle summary 64 at NHB; Bray, *One Young Man's War*.

[8] CFI 18; Summary of Actions.

MGBs 8 and 10 of the 2nd MGB Flotilla based at Ramsgate, 1942. (Courtesy P. Garnier)

The last fling of August in the Channel involved another attack on a large formation of minelaying R-boats, this time by four MGBs of the 2nd and 3rd Flotillas from Ramsgate, led by N.K. Cale in MGB 6. Engaging the enemy soon after dawn on 24 August, they severely damaged one R-boat and disrupted the lay, which was the main objective in view of the disparity in numbers involved. Sadly Lt Cale was killed.

One drawback to writing a history of the 'short' boats only is that it is liable to lose some perspective and overlook the contributions of other craft. The other less powerful boats of Coastal Forces, the MLs and HDMLs, rarely won the limelight but were highly respected for their tremendous efforts in every sphere of operations. Nowhere is this comment more apposite than in the Dieppe Raid two days later, when four SGBs, twelve C Class MGBs and thirteen MLs represented Coastal Forces in very difficult circumstances. (Appendix 1, Note 6)

There were several actions at the end of the month, two of which illustrate very clearly the problems involved in working-up newly formed or reorganized flotillas. On 24/25 August a combined unit of 4th MTBs and 6th MGBs from Felixstowe attacked four armed trawlers off the Dutch coast. The 4th was 'Harpy' Lloyd's flotilla, and the earliest boats had Isotta Fraschini engines, giving them a top speed of 42 knots; the 6th, Hichens' old flotilla, was now led by Lt John Colville with a new set of COs. Although regarded, in the words of one of its officers, as the 'second eleven', the 6th was bursting to give a good account of itself. The plan of attack was the standard MGB diversion on the opposite side of the convoy, but on this occasion it nearly met with problems. 'Harpy' Lloyd, a very experienced SO, was reputed to possess the sharpest eyes in Coastal Forces and had been nicknamed 'Cats' Eyes'. A.F. Moody, one of 34's able seamen, remembers that on this night the SO was certain he'd seen ships further inshore, and so he sent the MGBs to investigate. They initially reported 'no trace' but when he insisted, they persevered and found the trawlers. The diversionary attack was started, enabling 34 and her companion (72) to get into a position close enough to fire their torpedoes at two of the large trawlers. Both claimed hits – 34's definite and the other possible – but there is nothing on record to confirm the results.[9]

The incident on 28/29 August was totally inconclusive but is of interest mainly because it provides the first mention of the 22nd Flotilla, working from Lowestoft (HMS *Mantis*). The first SO of the 22nd was Lt Denis Long RN who was out in MTB 230 on this night. The patrol had been scraped together, with two boats from the 22nd (MTBs 230 and 87) and two MGBs, 21 of the 5th and 88 of the 7th. A series of problems in 230 led to her return and the SO transferred to MTB 87, which was eventually alone when Long sighted an enemy surface vessel. He attacked but was beaten off by heavy fire, suffering two hits from 37mm shells which disabled the steering gear, put the W/T out of action and caused flooding. 87 struggled back to Lowestoft with great difficulty. It was a stern first test for the new SO.

September began quietly. Although countless patrols were mounted from Felixstowe, Lowestoft and Dover, the first encounter with the enemy took place off Dieppe on the night of the 7th. This was one of the first occasions when an attack on a convoy was assisted by the RAF, coordinated by Dover Command, who dropped flares which illuminated the targets and blinded the enemy, allowing the boats to approach undetected. Four boats from the 5/6th MTB Flotillas (25, 48, 219 and 221) were able to fire their torpedoes as two C Class MGBs created a diversion, but sadly none of the five torpedoes could be claimed as a hit. 221 followed up with a depth charge attack, and the gunboats severely mauled one of the escorts. The COs were self-critical of their lack of accuracy, although misses were not always the result of poor aiming, as quick evasive action by the enemy and faulty running of torpedoes often contributed.[10]

The E-boat flotillas were very active at this time, sending large groups out on many nights to attack the east coast convoys. Indeed on 10/11 September four separate engagements with the enemy are recorded in the North Sea – an unprecedented rate in Coastal Forces at this time. In the first of these, Lt Bremer Horne led three of his Lowestoft gunboats to intercept twelve E-boats working in groups of three in the mid-North Sea. He successfully caught one unit as it retired, scoring several hits, and then chased the other nine towards their base, maintaining contact for nearly an hour and damaging two E-boats.[11]

Further east, off Ymuiden, four C Class MGBs caught the returning E/R-boats – eleven of them – at first light, having been alerted by Horne's signals. In a fierce attack, which the E-boats resisted staunchly, several E-boats were mauled, and one of the Cs was unluckily hit in the engine room and disabled.

Off the Hook, just to the south of all this activity, MLs had begun to lay mines earlier in the night but after being engaged by armed trawlers they had to abandon the lay. Hichens, back from the West Country, had units of the 8th and 6th MGBs from

[9] CFI 18; MO 12076; ADM 199/782; A.F. Moody.

[10] CFI 19.

[11] CFI 19; MO 12495; ADM 199/784.

The CO, Lt F.N. Thompson (right), and First Lieutenant, Sub Lt P. Garnier, of MGB 89 of the 7th MGB Flotilla. (Courtesy P. Garnier)

Felixstowe nearby but could make no contact with the trawlers.

The most significant success of the night took place further north off Terschelling, and it featured Lt Peter Dickens in MTB 234, his own boat, together with Lt John Perkins in 230 from the 22nd Flotilla, and a unit of MGBs of the 7th Flotilla led by Lt Derek Leaf. Dickens had by now settled into MTB operations, after six weeks of what he felt had been a very necessary learning curve. The 21st had recently returned from the West Country, and Dickens was very anxious, after his set-back off Barfleur a month earlier, to make his mark at Lowestoft and to secure for Commander Barnard, the Base CO at *Mantis*, a little glory to set against the tremendous reputation established by Hichens' MGBs at HMS *Beehive* at Felixstowe. This patrol was to be a truly combined operation: Dickens was commanding all the MTBs and MGBs as a single unit – still unusual at this time.

Reliability among the MTBs at Lowestoft was still poor, and only the two that sailed were serviceable. The Operations Officer who dubbed them 'flying bedpans' was justified in his choice of words. But Dickens was pleased to have John (Polly) Perkins with him – he was an experienced and highly regarded commander. They were expecting a convoy to pass the Texel at about 01.30, and an RAF bombing attack was to be made in advance of the MTBs.

Reaching a point some miles off the coast in good time, Dickens gradually closed the coast. Sighting enemy ships which he identified as merchant ships of about 2,000 tons, he despatched Leaf and the MGBs as planned to create the diversion. This they did with great effect as the MTBs moved to attack. Perkins fired one torpedo which he thought might have hit, then Dickens fired two, the second of which certainly did hit. The gunboats' diversion was so effective that their gunfire helped to disable the two targets. The assessments made at the time were that one 2,000-ton ship had been sunk, another damaged and possibly sunk and three escorts had been damaged. Cdr Barnard at *Mantis*, C-in-C Nore, and Admiralty all added complimentary comments about the aggression shown and the faultless planning and execution of the two-pronged attack. Morale was greatly boosted: Dickens at last believed that success was possible even in the 'flying bedpans', and he was full of praise for the part played by Derek Leaf and the MGBs.

However, this action provides a fascinating insight into the differences between the perceptions of participating boats and the results as reported officially, and the actual facts as revealed years later by enemy reports. When Peter Dickens wrote his book *Night Action* in 1974, he revealed that the two targets, far from being large merchantmen, were actually two auxiliary patrol vessels, the ex-trawlers Vp 1234 and 1239. 1239 was indeed hit by 234's torpedo, but her crew was rescued and the sinking ship towed into Terschelling. Dickens was a very humble, self-critical man who was in any case to prove himself time after time.[12]

The last action of any note in September came on the 14th and once again involved four boats of the 8th Flotilla led by Hichens in 77, with 75 (Ladner), 76 (Campbell) and 81 (Cowley). Their objective was to intercept a small convoy off the Hook. It was escorted by four flak trawlers, which were beginning to build a fearsome reputation as convoy escorts. Hichens felt that given luck and favourable conditions he might be able to harm the main targets and to cause the trawlers trouble and perhaps put one or two out of action. Both these aims were accomplished to some extent. Using their speed and getting in close, the MGBs severely damaged two small merchantmen and registered several hits on the trawlers at the cost of very minor damage and casualties.[13]

In his book *We Fought Them in Gunboats*, Hichens mentions that after this he was told he was due to have a spell ashore – he certainly deserved it – to join the Training Staff at HMS *Bee*, the working-up base at Weymouth, where he could pass on his experience and tactical genius to other SOs and COs. He resisted this transfer vigorously, as he felt he could be of far greater service developing tactics on active service and leading the 8th Flotilla on to more successes. He wrote what was clearly a very effective 'Solicitor's letter' explaining how unsuitable he was for a teaching job, and the danger – as he saw it – passed.

[12] CFI 19; MO 12574; ADM 199/782; Dickens, *Night Action*.

[13] CFI 19; MO 12983; ADM 199/782.

CHAPTER 6

OCTOBER TO DECEMBER 1942

Although there were indications that new boats were on the way, they were still not ready. However, they were expected to have improved reliability and performance, and would be formed into new flotillas which would be well prepared for operations after a highly professional working-up period at HMS *Bee*.

A new development came at Dover when the enemy laid a massive minefield down the centre of the Channel. This halted operations for a period but as soon as ways through and round the minefield were organized, patrols resumed. These were generally fruitless, but the boats were kept busy laying mines off the enemy coast – a dangerous and unpopular task. With practice, the crews reached a high level of accuracy in their navigation, which was very important so that Allied ships knew the precise limits of their own fields. Long before the sophisticated navigational aids such as GEE and QH became available, a system known as 'taut-wire measuring' was used; in conjunction with careful use of the echo sounder, this was very accurate. The leading boat carried a reel of light wire with a lead weight attached to the end. This was dropped at a known position, and then the wire was paid out as the boat followed on a precise course and speed within a 5-mile arc. The success of the lay, of course, depended on a lack of interference from the enemy.

Christopher Dreyer was now Senior Officer MTBs at Dover. With many of his boats unserviceable and his own boat under repair, he was forced to rely mainly on the 9th MTB Flotilla, led by Christopher Philpotts, with its mixed Dutch and British-manned boats.

On the east coast, the Lowestoft boats began with an action-packed battle off Terschelling on 1 October. Once again they adopted the tactic of a combined attack on a convoy by MTBs and MGBs working together; the plan was talked through beforehand, although not practised. The group was led by Peter Dickens in MTB 234, supported by three MTBs from three different flotillas. Two were forced to turn back, and this account concerns only 230 (John Perkins) of the 22nd Flotilla. The gunboats were also a mixed bunch: 21 (John Dyer) and 18 (Ted Smyth) from the 5th, with 86 (Sadler) and 82 (Rout, a New Zealander) from the 7th MGBs. None of these boats had worked together before.

This was another action for which Peter Dickens should be thanked for supplying an ultimate analysis many years after the event, written with complete humility and with the advantage of the enemy reports. These gave him the ability to correct those aspects of the original 'reports of proceedings' which were patently confused. Dickens demonstrates how, as many ships move around rapidly amid darkness, dazzling tracer and smoke, the acceptance of what is *believed* to be happening can often be totally wrong. In this case, he was told that aircraft had detected and attacked a sizeable *northbound* convoy off the Frisian Islands. The distance was so great that catching them would require a stern chase, rather than the preferred approach from ahead. So when the convoy was sighted – or rather when a flare burst overhead – the chase began, and the gunboats were sent on ahead to create their diversion.

Lt P.G.C. Dickens RN briefs the COs of the unit for an operation, 1942. (Courtesy IWM – D12517)

Almost at once it became apparent that the convoy was on the port bow and that Dickens' force was all inshore of them. They were also much closer than expected. It was some time before anybody realized that the convoy was *southbound*, not northbound as anticipated. The gunboats were confused when MGB 21 in the lead suddenly veered to starboard; Ted Smyth in 18, wanting to go on to attack (he was Irish and full of fight), was forced to cut across her stern. He drew much of the fire and in return his gunners wounded several of the escort's crew, but after suffering several hits on his own guns, and the coxswain being wounded in the face, 18 collided with MGB 82 and her bow crumpled. The escorts were firing heavily and all were armed with larger calibre guns than those of the attacking boats.

Suddenly MGB 18 found herself the centre of attention, being hammered from all directions despite making smoke. 86 was also being hit, and her CO Tom Sadler was killed almost at once. All these diversions did nothing to distract the leading escorts from the MTBs, who now sought to make their torpedo attacks, but were at a loss to decide on the correct approach and firing line because the reality seemed to bear no similarity to the expectation. Both made gallant attempts. Dickens soon got his two torpedoes off at the leading merchant ship. 230, which had been very heavily attacked and had two men severely wounded, chose to

A German seaman, Bernard Torzynski, of Vp 1313, who took part in the action on 1 October 1942 and later corresponded with John Perkins. (Courtesy J.P. Perkins)

approach from a different direction, and indeed penetrated the screen and fired one torpedo at each of two targets. There was a great column of smoke and Perkins thought he had struck with the first torpedo. Subsequent study of enemy reports reveals that this was MV *Thule* (a Swedish ship carrying iron ore – a valuable cargo); the second torpedo hit Vp 2003, an armed trawler, which also sank.

A fascinating 'reverse view' of this action is given by a German seaman aboard Vp 1313, Bernard Torzynski. He wrote to John Perkins in 1995, and his story does much to confirm many impressions of that night. (Appendix 1, Note 7)

Torzynski relates that he joined the ship in Hamburg straight from initial training, and that she sailed on her maiden voyage to Cuxhaven. There, she was allocated as an escort for a convoy which sailed towards Rotterdam on the morning of 30 September. They were positioned on the starboard side, just abaft the beam of the merchant ship *Thule*, towards the rear of the convoy. Torzynski manned the 88mm (he called it an 8.8cm) gun in the bows of 1313, which was not protected by any shield – the gun's crew stood in the open. He says:

> Just before midnight, the noise of aircraft resounded, then flares were dropped around the convoy and the fireworks started. Flare grenades [starshells] were shot into the air to enable us to see the enemy. On our port side we heard an explosion – I found out later it was a boat of our 20th Flak Ship Flotilla [Vp 2003]. To the left of us the merchantman *Thule* was sailing. Our combat helmsman evaded two torpedoes without receiving orders to do so, and if he had not, 1313 would have gone to the bottom of the North Sea on her very first trip – but he was later rebuked for acting without orders.
>
> The next few minutes are confused. Five of the upper deck crew – the gunners – were wounded, and the *Thule* blew up and sank, first breaking into two. Soon after, a British fast boat [MTB or MGB] was aiming to pass just in front of our bows, and one of the unwounded gun-aimers yelled 'load the gun, load it!' But four of my comrades were severely injured and I had been wounded in the left shoulder. I grabbed an 8.8cm grenade and pushed it into the barrel – and it hit the boat! [This must have been MGB 18 or MGB 86.]

Dickens managed to locate MGB 18, on fire and sinking; although delayed by Ted Smyth's attempts to speed up the sinking (once again petrol and a Very pistol featured – but this

Vp 1313, a heavily armed trawler of the 13th Vp Flotilla, which took part in several actions with the MTBs and MGBs, 1942. (Courtesy Bernard Torzynski via J.P Perkins)

time there was no explosion), he took off all the crew. 234 came under more heavy fire as she slowly moved away on two engines and with all her guns disabled; had it not been for PO Douglas Ross, a coxswain of another boat who had 'come for the ride' and brought his own gun with him, they may well have been lost. But Ross directed such accurate fire along the deck of Vp 2011 that her fire wavered as the gunners were hit, and eventually they switched aim to the abandoned MGB 18, already ablaze. Eventually – it seemed an age to those on board – 234 got clear and made her painful way back to Lowestoft.

The balance sheet showed one merchantship and its cargo of iron ore lost, and one escort sunk, against the precious life of a gallant young CO, and one gunboat. This success was due to the courage of many men, to the skill of 'Polly' Perkins and Petty Officer Ross, and to the leadership – however self-deprecated – of Peter Dickens. This action led to the strengthening of convoy escorts along the Dutch coast, and convoys began to sail during the day, preferring to chance aerial attacks by the RAF rather than challenge the MTBs. It was a clear result of the constant gamble of pitting small wooden boats against heavily armed escorts that within the next six days two more of the MGBs had been sunk in gallant attacks against superior forces.

Considering Perkins' success – two hits out of two – it seemed churlish of the Admiralty's torpedo expert to make the comment that he should have fired both torpedoes at the first target. Nevertheless, that was the lesson it was considered right to pass on to all COs.[1]

On 2/3 October Robert Hichens set out in MGB 77 with 78 (Duncan), 81 (Sykes) and 60 (Dixon), expecting to encounter the four armed trawlers so often found off Ymuiden. Nearly all his successes had relied on the

[1] MO 13348; ADM 199/782; Dickens, *Night Action*.

Sub Lt R.T. Sykes, CO of MGB 74, in Hichens' 8th MGB Flotilla, at HMS *Beehive*, November 1942. (Collection CFHT)

element of surprise but the moon was already up and visibility good, and so surprise would be difficult to achieve. However, he was supremely confident of the quality of his men and the lovely boats they now had, and he hoped that if three boats made a fast bold gun attack, the fourth could sneak in on the other side and make a depth charge attack that might sink one of these larger, more robust ships, which the gunboats' armament alone would have difficulty in achieving. Aware that George Duncan in 78 had been bitterly disappointed to be denied the chance a few nights earlier, he gave him the role this time.

Hichens' three boats gradually worked round ahead of the trawlers, and their diversionary attack on the port beam was not sighted until they were quite close. Immediately both sides began hammering away at each other, hopefully with the enemy's attention fully focused to port and ahead, leaving Duncan a clear approach from the starboard quarter, still down moon. Hichens saw 78's attack – a criss-cross of tracer – and then there was just silence and blackness. He crept in to take a closer look and saw the trawlers huddled together, with a pall of black smoke over them. It looked as though the attack had been delivered successfully. There was still no answer from 78 to his enquiry on the W/T, but that was not unusual after an engagement: aerials were often shot away.

MGB 77 went inshore, looking for the missing boat, but there were no signs of it. Eventually, believing that Duncan must have crept away and was already making his way back to Felixstowe, they too set out for base. But he wasn't there. It was possible that he was still struggling home, perhaps slowed by damage. They went out again to search in the early evening and were shot at from shore, but again they found no trace. It became clear that 78 must have sunk – but had her crew been picked up? Later came the news that some of them were prisoners-of-war. It was not until after the first lieutenant (Sub Lt Eggleston) had been repatriated that the disappearance was explained. 78 had been heavily hit and disabled while dropping her depth charge right under the target's stem, and she had eventually run aground. George Duncan was killed, but the enemy admitted that the trawler had been sunk.[2]

Another MGB from the 8th Flotilla was lost, together with MTB 29, three nights later, when four boats of 'Harpy' Lloyd's 4th MTB Flotilla went out on patrol accompanied by two MGBs. Robert Hichens was leading

[2] MO 3563; MO 3806; ADM 199/680; CFI 21; Hichens, *We Fought Them in Gun Boats*.

Two 'characters' from HMS *Beehive*: Lt Cdr J.S. ('Tubby') Cambridge DSC (left) and Lt L.C.R. ('Boffin') Campbell DSC, CO of MGB 76, one of Hichens' 'Band of Brothers'. (Collection CFHT)

aboard MGB 76, followed by 75 (Ladner). Details of the action in the records are vague, but the summary taken from CFI 21 says:

> The combined unit was surprised off Flushing by two Torpedo Boats accompanied by a group of E-boats, probably because recognition lights had been switched on briefly at the rendezvous of the MTBs with the MGBs, and had been sighted by the enemy. There was a short but fierce action, with damage to both sides, and it was during the crash start resulting from the surprise attack that MTB 29 was rammed by MTB 30 and eventually sank. MGB 76, which had clearly been hit by shells from the Torpedo Boats, was returning to Base when she blew up – probably from an incendiary shell in a petrol tank and a build-up of explosive mixture of air and vapour.

The crew was picked up by MGB 75. One of the survivors, L/MM (Leading Motor Mechanic) W. Donovan, provided the following account:

> L/MM Fred Phair and I were newly trained Motor Mechanics just arrived at Felixstowe, and had gone out in MGB 76 for experience. The Motor Mechanic of 76 was POMM Fred Innes, who was about to leave her for training for a commission. I recall a huge bang and a flash, and then being in the water. I believe Fred Innes was the only casualty: Hitch swam back past the blazing petrol, but could not save him.

The Petty Officer of the sick bay at HMS *Beehive*, much respected and known as 'The Old Doc'. (Collection CFHT)

Harpy Lloyd and the MTBs attacked an E-boat which became isolated, and sank it with gunfire from all three boats.[3]

Between these sad losses Dickens had an inconclusive brush with four M Class minesweepers, which kept the boats at bay with accurate fire. They made two attempts to attack but the alertness of the minesweepers crews made it impossible for them to get into a firing position, to their great frustration. Dickens reasoned that his boats urgently needed silencers on their main engines to enable a stealthy approach. He believed that an unobserved approach allowed a perfect attack, not only because the boat could get into the perfect position and fire her torpedoes with accuracy but also because she was more likely to be able to disengage safety. Securing the support of CCF and Cdr Barnard, the base CO at Lowestoft (HMS *Mantis*), he pressed the engineers to experiment and produce the necessary equipment.

Meanwhile the 9th Flotilla had been sent to Dartmouth because it was thought that MTBs would be of considerable value further west while activity in the Dover Strait was temporarily much reduced. While there, Lt Philpotts, SO of the 9th, was taken ill and Lt Christopher Dreyer, SO MTBs at Dover, was sent to take his place. The available (but comparatively slow) Thornycrofts of the 11th MTB Flotilla were also moved to Dartmouth in preparation for a special operation in the Western Channel. Intelligence had been aware for some time that a new enemy raider, the 4,000-ton *Komet*, had been commissioned and was now being moved from a German port down the Dutch coast in preparation for a dash down the Channel to break out into the Atlantic.

[3] MO 13807; CFI 21; Board of Enquiry report in ADM 199/180; W. Donovan.

On 12 October *Komet* reached Le Havre safely. Strong counter-measures were being rapidly prepared under the code-name Operation Bowery to intercept *Komet* and prevent her from getting through. It was known that she was fast and would be strongly escorted. Whether she would 'stage' at Cherbourg or Brest was uncertain.

By 13 October *Komet* had sailed, and a large force of Hunt Class destroyers, together with groups from the 9th and 11th MTBs, was dispatched to lie in wait west of the Cherbourg peninsula, with another group in reserve off the Channel Islands. There was great anxiety in the Admiralty that yet another important enemy major vessel might beat the blockade.

The most powerful force of destroyers, followed by the two groups of MTBs, moved southward from Dartmouth. After receiving an aircraft sighting report, the destroyers increased speed to be sure of being in place, and the slower Thornycrofts began to lose touch with the destroyers, and eventually lost them altogether, much to the frustration of the Vospers further astern. At the very rear of all the boats was MTB 236 of the 9th Flotilla, formerly the SO's boat but now commanded by its former first lieutenant, Sub Lt R.Q. Drayson. It was his first operation in command. Suddenly, to his horror, he realized (it was a very dark night) that the boat ahead had disappeared and he too was separated – and indeed he was on his own. His first reaction was to increase speed and carry on following the same course: it seemed likely that he had already overtaken his next ahead, whose signal to reduce speed – presumably for a conference – Drayson had seen and obeyed, but without then making contact.

Sub Lt Robert Drayson's report is worth quoting:

> I decided immediately to proceed direct to Cap de La Hague at 30 knots in order to intercept if possible, following C-in-C Plymouth's 2359A/13, giving enemy's anticipated position at 0045.
>
> At 0030 tracer and starshell in large quantities were seen in the direction of Cherbourg, approximately 7 miles distant. Course was set towards this position and speed increased to 35 knots.
>
> At 0047, speed was decreased and course altered to starboard; I was now 2–3 miles short of the tracer, and visibility was good due to starshell. I decided to proceed inshore and endeavour to intercept any ship which might pass through the destroyers' barrage.
>
> At 0055, a merchant ship was sighted at Red 50 [ship's head 160 degrees True]. It was firing astern at the area of tracer. She was considered to be of about 4,000 tons, and was making a speed of 15–18 knots.
>
> I closed this target unseen; she was clearly silhouetted by starshell at 1 mile. At 0105, main engines were cut and the target closed at 6 knots on auxiliaries. At 0110, when enemy was in torpedo sight, two torpedoes were fired, course altered to disengage to starboard with a 'crash start' on to main engines, and smoke was made. As soon as the torpedoes were fired, the gunfire from the target's stern guns (cannons) swung round and passed across my stern. An after life-line was severed but no casualties suffered. A few seconds later the torpedoes hit with two distinct explosions, and the target burst into flames from stem to stern and blew up, showering fragments of burning material past my ship. The flames spread rapidly and were capped by a thick pall of rolling smoke. The target was last seen lying on her side.
>
> My stern was lifted out of the water by the force of the explosion, and the centre engine broke down. The port engine overheated and had to be run on lower revs. Course was set for the Needles at 15 knots . . .

It was a highly creditable all-round performance by a young CO on his first operation in command. Generously, his report goes on to commend his first lieutenant, Sub Lt James Redgrove, and his motor mechanic, L/MM D. Mavor, who were also on their first operation in those roles.

Drayson, who went on to be a distinguished headmaster of Stowe School, was awarded the DSC. His sinking of *Komet* was one of the most significant of any by the MTBs in the whole of the war, bearing in mind the havoc this raider could have caused to Allied shipping had she broken out to the Atlantic.[4]

Patrols continued unabated in all areas, but with few enemy contacts. During one of these patrols, off the Dutch coast on 31 October, MTB 87 sank after an explosion which seemed – unusually for the 'short' boats – to have been caused by a mine.

In the North Sea it was impossible for destroyers to operate close to the Dutch coast, but in the Western Channel area there was deeper water along the coast, and at this time exercises were staged in the area to test the practicability of operating destroyers and MTBs together. The destroyers' radar was already of a very high standard and their fire-power was infinitely greater than that of the MTBs, but they had less chance of approaching unobserved or making close-range torpedo attacks. On 1/2 November a unit of the 9th MTBs from Dartmouth and led by Lt Hans Larive – a very experienced Dutch officer who was 'half leader' to the SO, Lt Christopher Philpotts – teamed up with HMS *Tynedale* and the Polish destroyer *Krakowiak* in an action off Brittany. Finding a convoy of two merchant vessels escorted by three M Class minesweepers and a trawler, the destroyers attacked immediately with accurate gunfire. Taking advantage of the confusion this caused, the MTBs then carried out a torpedo attack, and Larive in 203 was able to claim a hit on a 2,000-ton merchant ship. None of the others hit. The reports indicate that communications between the destroyers and the MTBs were faulty, leaving a good deal to be done in training if such joint operations were to continue.[5]

Dickens, still smarting from what he considered his failings in the action early in October, was still earnestly seeking to achieve an unobserved attack. The chance finally came on the night of 9 November. The 21st Flotilla boats were still dogged by reliability problems, however, and even his own 234 was unable to sail; despite leaving harbour with a unit of four, it was not long before two turned back. Dickens continued with just two boats to intercept and attack a reported convoy of eight merchant ships, likely to be well escorted, off Terschelling. He was embarked in MTB 233 (Jamie Fraser) and accompanied by 83 (David Felce) of the 22nd Flotilla.

They reached the convoy route before 2200 and almost immediately sighted the convoy steering serenely towards them. By a stroke of good fortune, a vast armada of Lancasters, probably en route for Hamburg, was flying overhead, making such a din that the enemy could not possibly hear the MTBs' approach. Moreover, the escorts' apparently poor lookout enabled Dickens to assess at his leisure the pattern of the path of the convoy. Once the heavily defended first group had passed, the fourth to sixth merchant ships in line seemed almost to overlap – with no escorts anywhere near.

The main difficulty Dickens faced was the long, anxious wait for them, all the time expecting starshell to burst overhead. At 2233 his chosen targets were in perfect position, still undisturbed, and the unit's four torpedoes were fired. As they disengaged, they saw one

[4] MO 14431; ADM 199/782; Robert Drayson.

[5] MO 14940; CFIs 21 and 22.

MTB 238 of the 22nd MTB Flotilla, off Felixstowe, November 1942. (Courtesy D.E.J. Hunt)

hit – a vast spout of black water blasted as high as the mast of a large tanker – and then tracer blinded them, although the crews were sure there was a second explosion.

With all the torpedoes gone, there was no point in hanging around. Peter Dickens had achieved his unobserved attack and quite properly was delighted. Better still, even before the two boats were out of sight, there were all the indications of a first-class battle going on – hopefully with the fire directed mistakenly at the more distant escorts.

A conservative type, Dickens claimed only one hit, but subsequent study of the German reports revealed that *three* of the four torpedoes had hit. Two struck the German ship *Rotersand* and the third the Swedish *Abisko* of 3,085 tons, carrying a cargo of coal. In the ensuing confusion two more of the convoy struck mines. The escort had in fact numbered eight: F 4 (an escort vessel), M8, M4 and M7 (all M Class minesweepers) and four Vps. Lastly Dickens discovered that those providential aircraft had been laying mines, not attacking Hamburg. Ultimately, the mines laid by Bomber Command sank more enemy ships than anyone else – a humbling thought.[6]

Only five nights later Dickens in MTB 83 (Felce), with 88 (Perkins, with the crew of his boat 230), of the 22nd Flotilla encountered two Torpedo Boats at very close range without any warning. One was the brand-new Elbing Class T 23, and the other was the Mowe Class *Kondor*. The MTBs were not spotted, and in fact were too close for an easy, accurate torpedo shot. To his eternal mortification Dickens missed with both, and Perkins never got a chance to fire, even though he tried again after the first encounter. It took Dickens a long time to forget that night.

[6] MO 15114; CFI 21; Dickens, *Night Action*.

At the end of the month the combined patrol by destroyers and four boats of the 9th MTB Flotilla at Dartmouth was repeated, with the same units as before. Once again Larive was able to claim a hit on a merchant vessel. But the SO Destroyers' lack of confidence in the communications – mainly in respect of protecting his own ships from inadvertent attack by the MTBs – led to a comprehensive series of papers proposing 'rules of attack' by the Admiralty's Operations Division.[7]

There were inconclusive brushes with the trawlers off the Dutch coast by the 8th and 7th MGB Flotillas in December but the weather was poor for much of the month and patrols were only possible on a limited number of days. However, on 18/19 December Dickens – who had just moved the 21st Flotilla back to *Beehive* at Felixstowe – took a unit to patrol off the Dutch coast. He was full of admiration for the base engineers, but knew that despite their best efforts the boats of his flotilla were still unreliable. They were especially prone to overheating of propeller shaft glands and time after time this had resulted in one or more boats not even completing the passage out to patrol. John Perkins, whose 230 was more often available for patrols than most at Lowestoft, tells how his motor mechanic once reported that one of the thrust blocks was red hot and sending off sparks: he was only able to keep it running by playing a hose on it. There had been no option but to return to harbour. On this occasion only MTB 241 was available for Dickens' patrol – this was the boat of the renowned young pair of Sub Lt Jim Macdonald and his even younger First Lieutenant Henry Franklin, who was larger in stature and one of the most extrovert of MTB officers. They made a formidable combination.

The patrol also included MTB 30 of the 4th MTB Flotilla. On passage to the Dutch coast, suddenly there was a flash and the roar and thump of an explosion – and there was 30 stopped in a minor maelstrom of seawater with her bow missing and wreckage all round. She must have hit a mine and it had certainly taken its toll. Tony Halstead, the CO, had been blown off his bridge and was clinging to flotsam some distance from the stricken boat. Four of the crew had been killed, and another died before he could be transferred to hospital. The rest of the crew were picked up. Henry Franklin and his motor mechanic tried to make 30 safe to tow, but she suddenly sank from under them and they only just got off in time.[8]

It was a sad end to 1942.

Sub Lt G.J. Macdonald DSC RNZNVR, CO of MTB 241 in Dickens' 21st MTB Flotilla, November 1942. (Collection CFHT)

[7] MO 14940; ADM 199/782.

[8] MO 1037; ADM 199/680.

CHAPTER 7

JANUARY TO MAY 1943

For over a year the men of Coastal Forces had been looking forward to 1943, anticipating the long-awaited delivery of new generations of more reliable boats. In January they looked back at the preliminary advances they had seen: the 71ft 6in British Power Boat MGBs of the 8th and 9th Flotillas; the newly arrived Vospers of the 22nd MTB Flotilla (still of the 1940/1941 classes, and less reliable than expected); and reports of a new 11th MTB Flotilla already working-up.

But for the most part, little real change had actually taken place. The Steam Gun Boats had brought a new dimension to the scene but had been beset with troubles, while the D Class Fairmiles, slowly churned out from the boat yards, were critically assessed. As yet there was not enough evidence to show how they would fit in to the offensive and defensive patterns of operations. In any case, four of their flotillas were gathering to go to the Mediterranean, and it looked as though only three of the four flotillas already completed would be available for east coast and Channel patrols, as the fourth was earmarked to be manned by Norwegian crews and to operate from Lerwick in the Shetland Islands. The one immediate benefit of these new 'long' boats was that the 'short' MGB flotillas would have to do fewer wearisome defensive patrols off the east coast convoy route – a duty for which they were, both in fact and even more in their own view, totally unsuited. The Fairmile C Class MGBs had proved throughout 1942 what valuable boats they were; they were now to find themselves constantly on convoy protection duties and acquitted themselves gallantly whenever they could get close enough to the E-boats.

In the Channel two more flotillas of 'short' boats also appeared. The Vospers of the 24th MTBs were initially under the command of Lt N. Poland RN and later Lt Basil Ward and Lt Christopher Dreyer RN, while the Free French 23rd MTBs were earmarked to operate from Dartmouth to cover the Western Channel and the waters around the Channel Islands. They were already at HMS *Bee* working-up and were expected to begin patrols in March.

There is no record of any contact with the enemy by the Dover flotillas during January 1943, although some patrols were mounted when weather permitted. This pattern was repeated in the North Sea, where the greater distances to patrol areas added another dimension to the hazards of operations in the shape of the weather, which was liable to worsen very quickly, even when apparently suitable as boats were preparing to set out. These 70ft craft were normally capable of getting home even in bad seas, but there was little point in despatching them when the conditions made accurate firing of guns or torpedoes impossible.

However, the weather improved on 18/19 January and Dickens, who had just moved to Felixstowe from Lowestoft with his 21st Flotilla, planned a new type of attack. A thoughtful strategist, he had until now accepted the conventional tactic of using diversionary attacks by MGBs to provide an opportunity for a 'blindside' attack by his MTBs. But suddenly he realized that diversions by another unit of MTBs could be just as successful – and might even give the chance of torpedo attacks from *both* sides.

Dickens decided to take a unit of five boats. Because only two of the 21st were available, he joined up with three from the 4th Flotilla, whose long-term SO, 'Harpy' Lloyd, had now been replaced by Lt John Weeden. He chose to lead Division 1 in 224, commanded by Lt Peter Magnus, with 241 (Macdonald) and 32 (Gardner) in support. Magnus had joined the 21st weeks before, but his boat had suffered constant defects and this was his first patrol with the flotilla. Weeden led Division 2 in 70 (Saunders) with 69 (Morgan) following.

They found two enemy trawlers off the Hook of Holland, and Dickens decided to attack, taking Division 1 round to the inshore side. He spent some time observing the trawlers, and suddenly saw a third, bigger and more worthy target for the new mark of torpedo he was carrying. He took 224 in alone to ensure an unobserved attack, and fired one torpedo. The torpedo hit, and the 'larger target' blew up in an enormous explosion. (Astonishingly, it was later identified as the 161-ton *Deli*, a harbour defence vessel!) The diversionary attack also worked perfectly, and 70 and 69 made an unobserved attack, hitting another trawler at the second attempt. After this, though, the third trawler engaged them fiercely, and Jack Saunders, the CO of 70, was wounded in the face.[1]

There was no other enemy contact in January, and February began with more action ashore than afloat. The control and organization of Coastal Forces had been under consideration for months, and major decisions were implemented at this stage. The general conclusions of the deliberations were that the role of Rear Admiral Coastal Forces (RACF), although carried out with energy and personal leadership by Rear Adm Piers Kekewick, had been formulated in such a way that it was impossible for him to coordinate all aspects of development, training, and technical matters. The task had been further hampered by the retention of all operational matters in the hands of the C-in-C of each Command, thus making centralized reporting and dissemination of best practice virtually impossible.

The office of RACF was abandoned, and a new structure established in the Admiralty, with departments dealing with Coastal Forces Materiel (DCFMD) and Operations, (DDOD-C). Coastal Forces Information Reports – known as CFIs – were replaced by Coastal Forces Periodical Reviews (CFPRs). These not only reported on operations involving all the Commands, but also promulgated information from all the technical departments – gunnery, torpedo, communications, tactical, etc., derived from detailed analysis of action reports. They were produced by Lt Cdr O.C.H. Giddy RN, another of the CMB commanders in the First World War who had been brought back to give first-class service to Coastal Forces at this time.

The process of improving efficiency was implemented most successfully by the appointment in February 1943 of a Captain Coastal Forces (Nore), with Headquarters at Chatham. This was a very necessary step in such a widely dispersed Command, whose units were more numerous than those in any other Command and whose bases were spread out along the east coast, particularly at Felixstowe, Lowestoft and Great Yarmouth. But the key to success lay in the man chosen for this post. Capt H.T. Armstrong DSO and Bar, DSC and Bar, threw himself into his duties with enormous energy, and concentrated on raising standards by intensive training throughout the Command

[1] CFPR 1 Feb 43; Summary from Actions List; Dickens, *Night Action*.

to supplement the basic training received at HMS *Bee*. His personality was such that this was taken up enthusiastically and, guided by talented Senior Officers, it brought about great improvements in standards generally.

In due course (but not immediately) Captains Coastal Forces were appointed to other Commands, and proved their value in advising C-in-Cs and in coordinating information and training. By this time the working-up base at Weymouth, HMS *Bee*, had developed a highly sophisticated training regime, tailored to the requirements and experience of COs and crews. Without doubt it provided a great service, particularly because such a high proportion of the crews now being formed came straight from initial training and had little or no experience of the sea, let alone of operations in small boats where each man had to play his part. There was no room for passengers. The lull in operations in the first six weeks of 1943 allowed all the flotillas an opportunity to train, and to store up reserves of energy for the more active times ahead.

There were changes of command at Dover. Christopher Dreyer had taken over from Lt B.C. Ward as SO of the 24th Flotilla, now based at Newhaven but preparing to leave for the Mediterranean. Basil Ward therefore became SO MTBs at Dover. The major German minefield in the Strait of Dover had restricted operations for the Dover boats for some months, and in any case the enemy were passing fewer ships through the Strait, realizing that they needed very strong escorts to counter the constant threat from the strong forces of MTBs and MGBs at Dover and Ramsgate respectively.

It was not until 17/18 February that Hichens' flotilla got a chance to take on the enemy. Two groups of E-boats had set out to attack an east coast convoy but were detected by the destroyer escort, whose signals resulted in the launching of the 8th MGB Flotilla, on short notice, to join the chase. Meanwhile HMS *Garth* made contact with the E-boats and engaged one group, sinking one E-boat and taking prisoners. Sadly, the MGBs had been alerted too late, and the retreating E-boats were able to avoid action.

Three nights later the 8th Flotilla was out again off Ymuiden, escorting A Class MLs laying a minefield near the harbour entrance. The MGBs were fired on by two M Class minesweepers but in order not to cause problems for the minelayers, Hichens ordered 'no reply', and the MLs were able to complete their lay and retire safely. At about the same time John Weeden's unit of the 4th MTBs detected small minesweepers off the Hook, but as they were under orders not to waste the precious Mark VIII torpedoes at this time they refrained from firing.[2]

On the night of 27/28 February several units were despatched from Lowestoft and Felixstowe. The 22nd MTB Flotilla was already gathering at Lowestoft, and three of the five boats available were sent to intercept a convoy reported off Egmond. 222 (Coombs), out for the first time, joined 83 (Felce) and 93 (Kennedy) but they never sighted the convoy, although they were fired on by heavy patrol vessels. Further south, the 8th MGBs, with Hichens leading in 77, supported by 79 (David James) and 111 (T.J. Mathias), had escorted another group of MLs minelaying; on their way back they found a convoy north of the Hook and attacked the escorts, hoping that a unit of the 4th MTB Flotilla would arrive in time to take on the larger ships of the convoy. Hichens became increasingly very frustrated as he shadowed the convoy, wishing he had torpedoes to use. As the convoy approached the harbour entrance, he decided to attack with guns.

[2] Summary List; Nore Signals 1436/18 and 1538/21.

The SO MGBs, Lt Cdr R.P. Hichens (left), and SO MTBs, Lt P.G.C. Dickens RN (right), at HMS *Beehive*, early 1943. Hichens was killed shortly after. (Collection G.M. Hudson)

In the ensuing battle, 79 was disabled and lay helpless in the water, surrounded by the enemy. Determined not to leave without at least trying to save David James and his crew, 77 and 111 both rushed in and began to pick up survivors during an unaccountable lull in the firing. Sadly, before they could rescue all the survivors, accurate firing began again and Hichens was forced to retire to save his remaining boats. James himself was picked up later by an enemy trawler and was taken prisoner. (Appendix 1, Note 8)

It was this incident that finally convinced Hichens that the idea he had been nursing for some time was indeed one he must pursue with the Admiralty. He reasoned that as the gunboats were now structurally strong enough, and his 71ft 6in boats had the room, they could be fitted with torpedo tubes so that opportunities to sink larger ships were not wasted. Although not everybody agreed, he put his case strongly through Cdr Kerr, the CO of HMS *Beehive*, and Capt Armstrong (CCF Nore), and it was arranged that when his own boat (77) went in for her next refit, two torpedo tubes would be fitted to her experimentally. In due course, this would lead to a major reorganization of the flotillas, with virtually all the MGBs in home waters redesignated MTBs. Many of the 'short' boats, however, continued to function as MGBs without tubes well into 1944.[3]

The 24th Flotilla, based at Newhaven, had very few opportunities to patrol successfully in the short period before it moved to the Mediterranean, but the boats were nevertheless vulnerable to the constant hazards of the Strait of Dover. During what should have been a routine passage from Newhaven to Dover on 5 March, off Dungeness, MTB 86 (Lt E. Young) was attacked suddenly by two FW190s. The bridge was hit, and two officers and four men were wounded. The boat returned fire, but the ferocity of the attack and the speed of the aircraft prevented them scoring any hits.

The 5th MGBs, based at Lowestoft, did not feature in many actions, but on 7/8 March they were on anti-E-boat patrol off the east coast when they got their chance. Lt J.S. Price in 20 was in the lead, followed by 21 (Lt G. Dale) and 17 (Lt C.A. Burk RCNVR), when HMS *Mackay* sighted E-boats approaching the convoy and drove them off. The MGBs intercepted them and sank the last in line. John Price, who served as a distinguished Senior Officer right through to the end of the war, earned his first DSC that night.[4]

[3] MO 3110; ADM 199/537; Scott, *Battle of the Narrow Seas*.

[4] MO 3621; ADM 199/536.

Left to right: Lt C.A. Burk RCNVR (MGB 17), Lt J.S. Price (20) and Lt G.A. Dale (21) of the 5th MGB Flotilla after their successful action on 7/8 March 1943. (Courtesy E. Keenan)

The 23rd MTB Flotilla consisted of 71ft Vospers built in six different boat yards around Britain, and was manned entirely by Free French officers and men (apart from the telegraphists who were all from the Royal Navy). Most of the men had already served in MLs at Portland, and were used to operating with the Royal Navy; a liaison officer helped to create a good rapport in Dartmouth, where they were based. All eight boats were completed by the end of 1942, and after trials at *Hornet* they worked-up at HMS *Bee* for four weeks before moving to Dartmouth in February 1943.

The depot ship at Dartmouth was HMS *Belfort*, originally a French sloop, and the base was housed in the Royal Dart Hotel. By March the 23rd Flotilla was ready and anxious to begin operations. Their first patrol on 6 March took them along the coast of Brittany, but brought no contact. They returned there on 10 March with just two boats, 94 and 96. The Senior Officer and CO of 94 was Capitaine de Corvette (Lt Cdr) E. Meurville, while 96 was commanded by LV (Senior Lt) L. Bourcy. The first lieutenant of 96 was EV2 (Sub-Lt) Philippe de Gaulle, the son of General de Gaulle, who not surprisingly took a very great interest in the flotilla and its activities.

The two boats spent the whole night close to the coast of Brittany, and were about to leave when two ships were sighted. One was identified as a 2,000-ton merchant ship, the

Loading a torpedo aboard MTB 94 of the 23rd Flotilla at the torpedo jetty, Weymouth, mid-1943. (Courtesy R.D. Fletcher)

General de Gaulle, whose son served in MTB 94 of the 23rd, at sea off Weymouth when visiting the flotilla, mid-1943. (Courtesy R.D. Fletcher)

other as an escort. Lt Cdr Meurville decided on a divided attack (in best Dickens' style). As 96 went in with guns blazing, which brought immediate return fire from both the enemy ships, he took 94 to the 'blindside' without being sighted and fired his torpedoes. Both hit, and he had the satisfaction of seeing the bows of the enemy ship rise high out of the water before she sank. It was a satisfying result for the exiled sailors, who were painfully aware that their homeland was enduring a harsh occupation.

The official summary of the action, written some years after the war, confirmed the sinking, but reported that enemy records claimed that only a minesweeping trawler had been sunk, rather than the 2,000-ton merchant vessel Meurville had thought. If the reports were true, it would by no means be the first time that an officer had over-estimated the size of a target.[5]

This action in the Western Channel area was followed almost at once by another successful sortie in the Strait of Dover – the first for many weeks. It was the first, too, for Lt Ward in his new role as SO MTBs at Dover, and for the newly formed 9th MGB

[5] MO 3621; ADM 199/1036.

MTB 94 at Dartmouth, 1943. (Collection G.M. Hudson)

Flotilla at Ramsgate. The 9th was led by Lt G.D.K. Richards RN, one of the great gunboat leaders, and was equipped with 71ft 6in BPBs built at Hythe. Its COs included a group of experienced officers, notably Lt R.M. Barge and Lt W.A. de Looze, one of the leading Dutch officers in Coastal Forces.

A unit of the 5th MTB Flotilla was at short notice in Dover harbour on the night of 11/12 March when an urgent message arrived. Intelligence had reported an enemy merchant ship just leaving Boulogne. Ward immediately went aboard MTB 38 (Mark Arnold-Forster) and set off to intercept, followed by 35 (R. Saunders) and 24 (Clarkson). The 9th MGBs had also been alerted and would soon catch them up. There was a brief pause when they met to discuss tactics, but not long after, as the heavy batteries at Dover and on the French coast joined in, a starshell burst over the scene and Ward sighted the enemy. The crews had been told that aircraft would make a simultaneous attack on the ship, but that was already in progress before they were within range. Both 38 and 35 fired their torpedoes at 700 yards, and Arnold-Forster's hit home with all the evidence required – a large explosion and column of water. Tracer erupted from the escorts and all three boats were hit, despite the intervention of Dicky Richards and Michael Bray in MGBs 110 and 113 on the other side, which drew the fire and enabled the MTBs to disengage. (Appendix 1, Note 9)

It was Bray's first action in command, although he had already experienced enemy fire when aboard Richards' boat as a spare CO. Like all who served with Dicky

Richards, Bray admired him as a wonderful and fearless – almost foolhardy – leader with an unquenchable desire to 'engage the enemy more closely'. In the attack, 113 suffered damage and casualties, with one of the gunners killed.

In 1945 a report by the Naval Intelligence Division (NID) revealed that the merchant ship sunk was SS *Dalila* of 3,176 tons – this was a pleasant surprise as Ward had estimated the target as a 300-ton coaster![6]

The activity continued on 15/16 March, and brought Lt D.G.H. (Jake) Wright his first action as a Senior Officer – he had recently taken over command of the 22nd MTB Flotilla from Lt Denis Long RN. The battle was fought off Terschelling, where only three nights earlier Lt K. Gemmell and a unit of Dog Boats had sunk two large merchant ships.

Wright embarked in MTB 88 (Eburah), with 93 (Kennedy) and 230 (Perkins) in company. They left Lowestoft at 1630 and their orders were to intercept and attack a northbound convoy off the Dutch coast. They set out at their cruising speed of 22 knots and after three hours were overflown three times by enemy aircraft. By 2245 the unit was close to its intercepting position, and it was here that their Type 286 radar began to prove itself an extremely valuable asset. At this time radar in the 'short' boats was not normally regarded as an effective aid, but Sub Lt P. Knowles, the radar officer from HMS *Mantis*

[6] MO 3571; ADM 199/1036; Michael Bray.

Dover COs after an action, March 1943. Left to right: Lt R. Saunders RANVR, Lt G.D.K. Richards RN, Lt B.C. Ward RN, Lt M. Arnold-Forster and Lt F.A.M. Bray. (Courtesy IWM – A14987)

Left to right: Lt D.G.H. Wright (SO), Lt J.P. Perkins, Lt N.G. Kennedy and Lt R.G. Eburah of the 22nd MTB Flotilla after the successful action on 16 March 1943. (Courtesy IWM – A15072)

(the Lowestoft Base), was aboard 88 and he proved to be a skilled operator able to get the best out of the apparatus. He picked up faint echoes ahead at 8,000 yards and they closed at a slower speed to avoid making a bow wave. At 6,500 yards a more detailed picture emerged, confirming that they had indeed intercepted their target convoy and that it consisted of three large merchant ships with at least three escorts, one of them possibly a Narvik Class destroyer. Wright demonstrated considerable skill in his choice of approach. Instead of continuing on his original bearing, which would have put him up-moon, he chose to move quietly round the stern of the convoy to the inshore side, carefully plotting the enemy's course and speed to make a more accurate attack possible when he reached the most advantageous bearing. All this took over an hour of painstaking stalking, but by 0005 the boats were in position 2,000 yards off the starboard beam of the convoy, which was up-moon and brightly silhouetted.

Wright now issued his orders: 88 would attack the leading ship, 93 the one in the middle, and 230 the rear one. The attack began at 0007. As soon as 88 and 93 turned in to close the range, the enemy opened heavy and well-directed fire, beginning with starshell. 88's torpedoes were fired, then 93's, but Perkins in 230 found himself dazzled by the starshell and tracer, and decided to wait.

93 observed a hit on the second ship, which by now was overlapping the first. John 'Polly' Perkins had already proved himself many times to be cool customer and an excellent marksman. He decided to move away for a time, and then to gain bearing before making his individual attack. His radar – and then visual sighting – showed two large targets, and he fired at 1,000 yards on a perfect approach angle. At once he turned away, and after only twenty seconds recorded the jarring of a large underwater explosion on his hull. He rejoined the others at 0530, and they re-entered Lowestoft harbour at 0850. In 1945 NID was able to confirm that they had indeed sunk two ships: SS *Agnete* of 1,458 tons, and SS *Mariatoft* of 2,302 tons.[7]

A week later, on 22/23 March, boats from Lowestoft were out again off Terschelling, and the new tactics that were emerging brought some results. In response to Intelligence reports that a westbound enemy convoy would pass along the Dutch coast, a unit of Dog Boats from the 31st Flotilla, led by Lt C.A. Law RCNVR (Appendix 1, Note 10), was joined by three of the 22nd MTB Vospers and each group was directed to take up position at either end of the convoy's probable line of progress. The 'short' boats to the south-west were initially delayed by hostile aircraft, and before they even sighted the convoy they were subjected to heavy fire, apparently from escorts, and driven off. The Dog Boats to the east sighted the convoy but they too encountered heavy fire from the escorts and a heated battle ensued. Two attempts were made to get through, but the only confirmed result was slight damage to an armed trawler.[8]

March had been a frustrating month for Peter Dickens' 21st MTBs; despite many patrols, his boats failed to find the enemy, although other units did. But April was to bring a flurry of activity. It began in the Channel on 4/5 April, when the 9th MGB Flotilla, led by Dicky Richards in MGB 110, followed by 117 (Outen) and 113 (Bray), was sent to patrol off Nieuport. At midnight they sighted a group of flak trawlers which seemed to have no inkling of the presence of the gunboats. Richards did not hesitate. Sweeping straight towards the nearest trawler, all three boats maintained very close station, firing their full broadsides with lethal effect. The trawler hardly had time to reply, but the others did – and all three MGBs were hit. But their selected target was stopped and burning fiercely, and when Richards led a second attack, it became apparent that the crew were already abandoning the ship and that the other trawlers had moved away, leaving the sinking ship to her fate. Richards ordered Michael Bray in 113 to rescue all the survivors he could, and to send a party on board to try to prevent the trawler from sinking. Bray's first lieutenant, Sub Lt Bill Fesq, an Australian, bravely boarded the trawler. He quickly returned with signal and code books, but reported that the fires had gained control. Richards then sent his motor mechanic aboard to open the sea cocks but she did not seem to be settling very fast, so he decided to sink her with a depth charge. His own effort to do so failed, so Bray was ordered to try. As the trawler was stopped, Bray reasoned that it could only be done effectively by taking the MGB very slowly alongside – a dangerous prospect. They lashed the charge to an empty oil-drum to slow down its descent, then bumped slowly along the side of the trawler; on a given signal they released the charge and then on full power roared away from the doomed trawler. The explosion came all too quickly, but the MGB was safe; the trawler's keel was broken and she sank.

[7] MO 3669; ADM 199/537; notes from J.P. Perkins.

[8] MO 3819; ADM 199/537.

The unit returned to Ramsgate with one killed and two others seriously wounded, and both 110 and 113 requiring repairs. It had been a typical Richards attack, and brought him a well-deserved DSO, reflecting his bravery in this and countless other operations. Bray and Outen also received DSCs.[9]

The 9th MGBs, in company with a unit of the 5th MTBs from Dover, again met the enemy off Berck on 9/10 April but were unable to press home their attack. Under orders not to waste torpedoes, they considered the targets not worthy of an attack.

On the night of 12/13 April 1943 came an event which shocked not only the men of Coastal Forces but the country as a whole. Lt Cdr Robert Hichens led a unit of his 8th MGB Flotilla from Felixstowe to give close escort to a group of MLs minelaying off the Dutch coast. Hitch and his crews did not expect this patrol to offer any great potential for action. However, when the minelayers had finished, Hitch and his boats set off to see what they could find. Recent reports had mentioned the appearance in this area of a new type of escort vessel known as gun-coasters.

Hichens was embarked in MGB 112, a newly commissioned boat commanded by Lt D.C. Sidebottom, who had won a great reputation for his gallant deeds in C Class MGBs. They found two enemy vessels which had clearly not sighted the four gunboats. Approaching from the port quarter, they sped along parallel to the enemy and hit them both very hard. As they drew ahead, the enemy fire increased but was generally inaccurate. Suddenly, however, a single burst of cannon shell struck the bridge of 112, with terrible results. Hichens was killed immediately – the only fatal casualty – and both the CO and the first lieutenant were wounded.

The atmosphere in Felixstowe when the boats returned demonstrated the enormous respect and affection with which Lt Cdr Robert Peverell Hichens was held. The BBC broadcast the news to a nationwide audience, who had read so frequently of his gallantry and brilliant leadership. But few of them knew the full story of his influence on strategic and tactical thinking in the operations of Coastal Forces.[10] Peter Dickens felt the loss of his friend particularly keenly. He believed that the loss of someone so outstanding was far-reaching and very significant: 'Remember Hichens? a perfect, gentle, indomitable knight in very truth.' He felt it was very important for the spirit of the crews and everyone else at *Beehive* that the 21st Flotilla should very soon find an enemy and get its teeth into him.

No one could have tried harder. All through March and early April he tried, but no targets could be found. It was particularly galling because at last it seemed that most of the problems of unreliability had been solved; a new rudder system made the boats more manoeuvrable, while persistent nagging had resulted in the fitting of Dumbflow silencers to eliminate the engine noise which had so appalled Dickens when he took over the flotilla.

On 17 April Dickens sailed in 234, with 241 (Macdonald) and 233 (Fraser) in company, and patrolled off Ymuiden all through a long night without finding any targets to attack. Hating the prospect of returning once again with a negative report, he decided to sweep fast southward towards the Hook. His crews knew what to do: if targets were sighted, they would have to come a sudden halt – dangerous after a

[9] MO 4435 and MO 4637; ADM 199/1036; Bray, *One Young Man's War*.

[10] MO 4763; ADM 199/537; Scott, *Battle of the Narrow Seas*.

Left to right: Sub Lt D.W. Moore, Sub Lt G.J. Macdonald RNZVR (241), Lt P.G.C. Dickens RN (SO 234), Lt A.C. Jensen, Sub Lt G.N. Fish of the 21st Flotilla after the action of 18/19 April 1943 when Sub Lt J. Fraser (233) was killed. (Collection CFHT)

35-knot romp – to prevent the enemy spotting him on this moonlit night.

This time they were lucky and an enemy convoy was spotted. Fraser in 233 moved off to seaward of the enemy, firing as he went, to draw the fire, while 234 and 241 sneaked up on the inshore side to make the attack. Fraser did so well – changes of speed, bursts of fire, rapid changes of course – that the enemy's report showed later they thought there were several boats attacking from that side. Both Dickens and Macdonald got their torpedoes away and one of the three armed trawlers (Vp 1409) definitely sank. As arranged, 234 disengaged northwards before returning to create a decoy attack in order to give 233 a chance to fire her torpedoes; 241 wove an intricate web to the southward with the same idea. But 233 was not attacking – and it was not until they found her on the way back that they discovered why. She had indeed gone in to fire her torpedoes, but had been seen and caught in devastating fire which raked the bridge. Jamie Fraser was killed and his redoubtable coxswain Bob Henry severely wounded, and the boat had suffered so much damage that the first lieutenant had no alternative but to withdraw.

For Dickens, the destruction of one enemy ship could never compensate for the loss of one of his most stalwart officers – but his task was to lead, and to work towards restoring morale, and this he did. His account of the action, written many years later after he had studied the trawlers' reports, revealed that the three Vps were armed with 88mm and 37mm guns, and that – most disturbing of all – their monitoring service had been able to receive and decode several of Dickens' W/T signals. Fortunately they had been using a short-term simple code and so this did not worry the Admiralty unduly. The enemy reports admitted that the loss of a Vp was a serious blow to their stretched resources, but claimed to have sunk at least one of the eight attacking MTBs, and damaged two others – a far cry from the truth.[11]

The run of successful actions from Felixstowe continued only two nights later, on 19/20 April, when a unit of the 4th MTB Flotilla found the enemy. This flotilla, which Lt 'Harpy' Lloyd had led for a very long time, was composed of early Vospers with the Isotta Fraschini engines that were much admired, but which had only been kept running by dedicated work from engineer officers, notably Lt (E) Herve Coatalen who took a particular pride in them. The 4th was being temporarily led by Lt Ian Trelawny DSC, who had been wounded in an action in 1942, and during his convalescence had been SOO – Staff Officer, Operations – at HMS *Beehive*. He was actually waiting to assume command of the 11th MTB Flotilla whose boats were gradually being completed and worked-up at this time.

The unit, 34 (Trelawny), 32 (Gardner) and 70 (Jack Saunders), was patrolling north of the Hook when Trelawny sighted a strongly escorted convoy moving southward. There was a bright moon to seaward, so the boats would be silhouetted up-moon, but he had no choice. He led the unit as quietly and slowly as he could while still gaining bearing, and could not understand why the boats were not sighted at 800 yards, although for a time cloud obscured the moon. When it cleared, they were starkly revealed and the enemy opened heavy fire.

There could be no more delay, and Trelawny took 34 in to make his attack. He hit, although he thought at first he had missed, as the torpedo seemed to take so long to strike, but his description of the effect is fascinating: 'a glow like a bonfire started on his water line – no enormous flash, no huge column of water, nothing dramatic at all. And then slowly he seemed to disintegrate, puffing out steam like a puff-ball puffs out dust when you tread on it . . . he seemed simply to deflate.'

The other two boats had not been able to attack, so he led them away to regroup and wait until cloud cover enabled them to approach again. It took two-and-a-half hours, but Jack Saunders in 70 was finally successful, and the explosion of his torpedo was far more obvious and dramatic. Trelawny, who had known Robert Hichens very well indeed, felt that this major success, just one week after his friend's death, was specially for him.[12]

Before the end of April Peter Dickens and his 21st Flotilla had two more actions. He describes them as 'the Bottom' and 'the Tops' because the first one, on the night of the 20th, was unsuccessful, while the second clearly had a considerable effect on enemy morale. Both actions took place off the Dutch coast, and involved attacks on Vp flotillas – these patrol boats were mainly armed trawlers, whose main task was escort duty for convoys, but at the time they seemed to be out trying to lure the MTBs into gun battles where their heavier armament gave them advantage. They also banked on the fact that they were not normally large enough targets for the MTBs to waste their torpedoes upon. But in fact the operational orders of the MTBs now gave commanders discretion to attack these escort trawlers towards the end of their patrols, as it was widely accepted that

[11] MO 5086; ADM 199/537; Dickens, *Night Action*.

[12] MO 5291; ADM 199/537; Trelawny; Scott, *Battle of the Narrow Seas*.

these vessels were irreplaceable assets whose loss considerably weakened the enemy's ability to defend his convoys.

Sadly, the first battle was thwarted by three adverse factors. Firstly, the moon was up and surprise was difficult to achieve. Second, the patrol was close in to the coast at the Hook, and thus in shallow water, so that although Dickens fired his two torpedoes with what he considered to be copybook accuracy, neither hit the target; it seems likely that they hit the seabed before reaching the targets. Lastly, it must be said that skilful manoeuvring by the enemy ships, which avoided torpedoes by 'combing the tracks', together with heavy and accurate gunfire which detracted from good aiming, also played a significant part. Dickens in 234 and Macdonald in 241 were disconsolate at missing their targets. The other two COs were the newly joined Tom Neill in 233 and Val Ohlenschlager in 232 who both attacked gallantly but suffered the same problems.[13]

The second action, on 28/29 April, involved the same group of the 14th Vp Flotilla that had escaped without loss a few nights earlier, although it was now further north, off Ymuiden. This time Dickens in 234 and Macdonald in 241 had with them another newcomer in 233, Peter Standley,

[13] MO 5266; ADM 199/537; Dickens, *Night Action*.

Left to right: Sub Lt J.H. Saunders (MTB 70), Lt I.C. Trelawny (MTB 34) and Lt N.S. Gardner (MTB 32) after the successful action on 19/20 April 1943. (Collection CFHT)

who had arrived to replace Jamie Fraser, sadly lost two weeks earlier.

It was a moonless night, with clear skies and good visibility, and Dickens took his unit inshore of the patrol and approached very quietly and slowly. Even so, they were sighted and came under heavy fire at 600 yards, making aiming very difficult, and Dickens missed. But Macdonald, given a clearer run in as the enemy was still firing mainly at 234, hit Vp 1408 – which by a strange coincidence was the same ship that had attacked 233 when Jamie Fraser was killed. Peter Standley, blinded by tracer at the first attack opportunity, then made several independent approaches and for his pains was beaten off by heavy fire which left his boat holed in a number of places and the starboard torpedo tube damaged.

Although Intelligence – and perusal of German reports – revealed that Vp 1408 was only a 107-ton tug, she was obviously a doughty fighter and one the enemy could ill afford to lose. Comments in the enemy reports indicated that the policy of enticement was not succeeding, and that the other strategic change – sending convoys by day – was also failing as the RAF was taking a heavy toll of them in the daylight hours. There was even a suggestion that E-boats armed with 37mm and 20mm guns but without their torpedoes – i.e. used as gunboats – could perhaps be allocated as 'MTB hunters'.[14]

It is perhaps obvious from the descriptions of these actions in March and April that with the onset of the better weather patrols were more numerous and the number of actions very much greater. In fact, the total number of actions in Coastal Forces as a whole showed a most encouraging increase over anything previously achieved. In this period, there were 34 actions, 13 of them by the 'short' boats and 9 by the 'long' boats in home waters, 9 in the Mediterranean and 3 off Norway.

A confused action took place in low visibility off the Brittany coast on 5/6 May when a unit of the Free French 23rd MTB Flotilla made a torpedo attack on enemy minesweepers and trawlers, but no hits were claimed. The first major success in May 1943 fell once again to Dickens, with four boats of the 21st Flotilla, on 13/14 May. Off the Hook of Holland they met the largest and most powerful force they had ever encountered: twelve fleet minesweepers escorted by nine R-boats. The former resembled small destroyers. The group had been minelaying further north and were returning to harbour where a trawler patrol was awaiting their arrival.

Dickens, as ever in his rejuvenated 234, detected a large force on his hydrophone from a listening position some distance to seaward of their track, and steered down the bearing to close them. He had 244 (Hartley) to port, with 241 (Macdonald) and 232 (Ohlenschlager) to starboard. They first sighted four large ships with several smaller escorts; poor visibility prevented them from seeing the others – perhaps if they had seen them, they would have been more wary. At least they were on the port bow of the advancing ships – a perfect position – without any conscious effort. Dickens quickly decided, as they had not yet been sighted, to make a double-pronged attack: 234 and 244 would go in immediately, fire their torpedoes and then disengage and draw the enemy fire while 241 and 232 followed in. After a quick shouted briefing in went the first pair. In no time they were at 400 yards, and as the first shells arrived, they fired four torpedoes. Very satisfactorily there were two distinct underwater concussions, and one of the large targets spurted flame. An enormous barrage of fire was now coming their way, so 234 and 244 made smoke and hared off at 40 knots

[14] MO 5553; ADM 199/537; NID in 005084/45; Dickens, *Night Action*.

MGB 108 (CO R.M. Barge) of the 9th MGB Flotilla at Ramsgate, May 1943. She became MTB 418 in September 1943. (Collection G.M. Hudson)

having made a very tight turn, 90 degrees to starboard.

Seeing that another of the large ships was going to help the survivors of the wreck, Dickens sent in 241 and then 232 one after the other: the R-boat escorts and the minesweepers (now identified) were firing furiously and both the MTBs were silhouetted up-moon. Macdonald fired at 600 yards, but the rescuing minesweeper saw the torpedo tracks and went full ahead, and avoided them successfully. Ohlenschlager (known as 'O') followed in; one of his torpedoes hit the wreck and finished it off completely. As the MTBs withdrew and turned for home, the minesweepers – now thoroughly alerted and trigger-happy – fired enthusiastically at the R-boats who were closing to render assistance. German reports revealed much later that the ship which was destroyed was M 8, an M Class fleet minesweeper, and that she was struck by no fewer than *three* torpedoes. Both M 4 and M 14 clearly had very lucky escapes, having been shielded by M 8.[15]

This chapter ends on another sad note. On 29/30 May Lt G.D.K. Richards RN in MGB 110 led a unit of his 9th MGB Flotilla to support a group of MTBs under the command of Lt Basil Ward RN (SO MTBs at Dover) who were to lay mines off Dunkirk. Richards was followed in 116 by Lt P.G. Lee (formerly his first lieutenant), 118 (O'Mahoney) and 108 (Barge). As ordered, they stopped some way to the west of the minelaying position, ready to act if Ward needed help. Dicky Richards thought this sort of operation too routine and dull to warrant any enthusiasm.

[15] MO 6155; ADM 199/537; Dickens, *Night Action*.

Messages began to come through from Ward that a patrol of enemy ships had stopped between his force and the minelaying position. He proposed to wait to see what they did. It was only 0115, and they were ordered to return to Base at 0300 if nothing further transpired. At 0230 Ward tried to slip past the enemy but was sighted and engaged. Richards did not even wait for the explanatory signal, but as soon as he saw the tracer he was off towards the targets. His boats closed very quickly. Ward had reported three trawlers, and in no time there they were. Richards, with the others abreast to starboard, roared straight at the leader and then turned sharply to port when only 100 yards off. Already one trawler was on fire. The unit then split up, and Barge peeled off to attack the third in line. 110 and 116 came in again to make a second attack on the first two, but the return fire seemed to redouble, and both boats were hit. Lee thought the first trawler was about to sink, but then realized that both he and his first lieutenant were wounded and his boat was damaged, so he withdrew. Barge was joined by Richards, and they were about to close in on and board the third trawler, already stopped, when suddenly six E-boats appeared at speed.

Richards immediately signalled 'Engage the enemy more closely', and a furious battle ensued. Boats charged at very close range down the line, exchanging broadsides, and all the boats suffered hits. Barge quickly realized 110 was on fire, and then he lost sight of her. The enemy – one of them burning – clustered around a burning wreck that must have been 110, and maintained withering fire that made it impossible to approach. Barge hung around till dawn, searching for any survivors, but found nothing, and returned to Ramsgate desperately anxious to learn the fate of Richards and his crew.[16]

[16] MO 6534; ADM 199/1036; Scott, *Battle of the Narrow Seas*.

The only news came in a German broadcast and was so obviously fabricated that it was totally unreliable. It claimed that 'a numerically inferior force of German ships' was attacked by seven MTBs, five of which were sunk and two others left blazing'. The only information about survivors was given in the statement that 'five British sailors were saved and taken back to port'. When the prisoners-of-war were eventually able to write to their families, it became apparent that Dicky Richards had died – as gallantly as he had lived – and with him his first lieutenant and all the upper deck crew.

The reports made by the COs of the three other boats were not able to tell the whole story, and only after the return of the prisoners could more details be pieced together. Leading Telegraphist William Lovel DSM, who had served with Lt Richards in every MGB he commanded, confirmed that only those below deck survived: two in the W/T cabin, and three in the engine room. All five were wounded but none seriously.

In the space of six weeks the three greatest leaders of the early MGB flotillas had all lost their lives in action. First, on 12 April, was Lt Cdr Robert Hichens, the first RNVR officer to command a flotilla. Next, on 28 April, was Lt Philip Francis Stewart Gould RN, who had served in the 1st MTB Flotilla from 1939 but had made his name as SO of the 3rd MGB Flotilla at Ramsgate. He had then taken a new flotilla of D Class Fairmile MTBs to the Mediterranean, where he was killed in a daylight operation off the Tunisian coast within a few weeks of arriving in his new theatre. And now Lt George Dick Kendall Richards RN had also gone. These men would be difficult to replace, but had surely set a tremendously high standard of dedication, aggression and fearlessness for others to emulate.

CHAPTER 8

JUNE TO DECEMBER 1943

After all the activity in the spring of 1943, it is difficult to find reasons for the almost complete absence of actions in June. Of course, there were many patrols from all the bases both on the east coast and in the Channel, but enemy convoys were difficult to find. Whether this resulted from improvements in the security of their signals, or from poorer than average detection by shore-based radar and aircraft is not known. Almost certainly the main factor was simply a reduction of the number of enemy ships sailing by night between their ports. It is now known that the strategy of passing their convoys by day to avoid attacks by night had failed because the RAF proved every bit as effective in sinking their ships during daylight hours as Coastal Forces were at night. Minefields, laid both by aircraft and by the A Class MLs from Dover and Felixstowe, had also taken a considerable toll. In addition, the policy of trying to lure MTBs towards groups of heavily armed trawlers off the Dutch coast, in the hope of sinking them with their 88mm guns, had proved so costly – a disproportionate number of trawlers and escorts were sunk – that it had been abandoned.

There was a constant flow of coastal convoys around the British coasts to be protected, but the incidence of E-boat attacks had also waned during June. Peter Dickens commented that his 21st MTB Flotilla was required to take a share of minelaying throughout the month; this was normally not a popular activity, but Dickens confesses to finding it comparatively relaxing. He had 40 knots to extricate himself from interference, and he knew that the minefields had become a major factor in the sinking of enemy coastal shipping (as indeed they were for our own ships). Despite the repugnance felt by all seafarers for this hidden menace, it was safer and more impersonal than dashing in to make close-range attacks, and led to fewer losses and casualties among those who normally took the war to the enemy.

It is perhaps not surprising that the only action recorded in June was an uncharacteristically confused and unsuccessful affair by a combined group of the 9th MGB and the 9th MTB Flotillas off Gravelines. It took place on the 7/8 June, only nine days after Dicky Richards had been killed. It involved a brief tangle with E-boats followed by an attack on convoy escorts, but neither the MGBs or the MTBs were really able to get to grips with the enemy. This was intended to be the first use of a new type of attack specific to the Dover Command; given the name 'Operation Dandy', it sought to help solve the problem of strong escorts keeping the attacking force at bay. The plan was to create a diversion with a coordinated strike by aircraft. Sadly on this first attempt the timing went wrong and it caused more confusion than assistance. Not only was Vice Adm Dover critical, but the SOs of both the MTB and the MGB flotillas were self-critical of the mistakes they made. One most unusual cause of confusion arose from the fact that both groups were challenged by the enemy with the same recognition signal as that allotted to them for this period, leading to hesitation and compromise.

The fact that there was much activity being reported from the Mediterranean was of scant reassurance to the frustrated crews in home waters. Out there, the Coastal Forces war had entered a new era with the arrival of many new flotillas, the end of the war in North Africa and the imminent launching of a long-anticipated invasion. In contrast, July – although not as full of constant activity as had been anticipated – at least saw a resumption of hostilities for several of the flotillas.

The first action came on 4/5 July and involved three boats of the 9th MTB Flotilla at Dover. The 9th Flotilla at this time was made up of four Dutch and four RN boats, but in August it was to be handed over completely to the Royal Netherlands Navy. The unit on this night was led by Lt Hans Larive, who was due to become the SO. He sailed in MTB 240 (Lt F. Visee), followed by 235 (Lt P. Tegelberg) and 202 (Lt J. May). This was meant to be another new tactical experiment, code-named 'Operation Dusty'. Taking advantage of the fact that Dover's coastal guns could reach the far shore, they were ordered to fire at the ships of a passing convoy, which would distract their crews, helping the MTBs to get in closer. Once again, the plan did not work in practice because the timing was wrong and also because the German batteries on Cap Gris-Nez were active.

On this occasion they met two Elbing Class Torpedo Boats heavily screened by assorted patrol craft. After first trailing the targets to ascertain their course and speed, and the precise positions of the escorts, 240 and 235 fired all four of their torpedoes in an unobserved zone attack on the rear-most target. Although the torpedoes ran true, no explosions followed; they assumed that the torpedoes had been set at too great a depth and had passed below the hull of the target. Bitterly disappointed at missing such a golden opportunity for a very important sinking, they returned to Dover.[1]

On 16/17 July it was the turn of the 22nd MTB Flotilla from Lowestoft, who set off for a patrol off Ymuiden. Four boats were led by 'Jake' Wright, the SO, in 238. He had with him 93 (Kennedy), 245 (Douglas Hunt, in his first action with the 22nd) and 83. They sighted a convoy of three small merchant ships escorted by two trawlers, and Wright decided to use all his torpedoes. Seven were fired, and although no hit was seen or felt, when they studied the convoy after the attack, only four ships could be seen, leading to a tentative claim that one had been sunk. Unfortunately this could not be confirmed by NID after post-war perusal of enemy records. The boats suffered a small amount of damage.

There was an interesting example in Wright's report of the flexibility and rapidity of response to suggestions from SOs by the staff of C-in-C. He commented that each of his boats now had a single Oerlikon for'd, and that on this occasion each of the four boats very quickly expended all eight of the magazines allocated. He suggested that this number should be increased. Not only did C-in-C agree and put this into orders, but he also made sure it was promulgated to other Commands.[2]

Several new COs had joined the 21st, and Peter Dickens, who had not seen action since mid-May, was increasingly frustrated. Patrols and training had continued, and he was sure that given an enemy to attack, his boats would acquit themselves well. At Felixstowe they had been cheered by the arrival of the first boats of the new 11th Flotilla, with Ian Trelawny, recovered from his injuries, as SO. One of the outstanding COs when Dickens had first been appointed to the 21st Flotilla, Trelawny was a valuable asset and volunteered to join a unit of four in his new

[1] MO 8359; ADM 199/1036.

[2] MO 8570; ADM 199/537.

Left to right: Lt J. Coombs, Lt N.G. Kennedy, Lt D.E.J. Hunt and Lt D.G.H. Wright (SO) of the 22nd MTB Flotilla, June 1943. (Courtesy D.E.J. Hunt)

boat MTB 356 – a Vosper with all the latest modifications.

On 17 July they set out for the Dutch coast, slightly disturbed by the moonlight which made visibility rather too good for MTB operations, as the possibility of an unobserved attack was virtually non-existent. Dickens led in 233, Tom Neill's boat, which was equipped with an efficient radar set, and had 244 (Hartley) in his division; Ian Trelawny in 356 was to lead the second group with 224 (Lee). The boats had a new camouflage, designed by Peter Scott, based on the well-observed fact that at night the background is lighter than the sea. It was to prove most effective.

Dickens chose to patrol several miles off shore, running south parallel to the main shipping lane between Ymuiden and the Hook; when they sighted a large convoy at about 4 miles, he decided to pause to plot its course and speed. He soon discovered that the ships were moving quite rapidly towards him, giving him less time to initiate the two-pronged attack he had intended. This manoeuvre, when begun, brought an immediate reaction from the enemy, who opened fire very aggressively on both units. Strangely, the enemy gunners lost both pairs, probably because of the confusion caused by the camouflage.

Each unit made its attack from a much closer range than they had expected. Trelawny was first, and got his torpedoes away at 700 yards, but close beside him 224 was hit. Left with only one engine in a very vulnerable position, Lee fought his way out very slowly. Trelawny could not understand how his torpedoes missed, but continued to charge in and out to divert attention away from the crippled 224. His diversion also helped Dickens' attack. He was able to get in to about 600 yards and both his boats fired unobserved on perfect angles. Frustratingly, not one of the six torpedoes had hit, although much later the German ships confirmed how lucky they had been, seeing the tracks pass close by bow and stern in every case. It also turned out that this was no strongly defended convoy – it was a force of ten large and well-armed minesweeping trawlers setting out to sweep the channel. To add to Dickens' misery, Ken Hartley was horribly wounded in the face by the only 20mm shell to burst on the bridge.[3]

Off Noordwijk on 22/23 July, a combined unit of MTBs from the 22nd Flotilla (SO Lt D.G.H. Wright) and the 71ft 6in MGBs of the 10th led by Lt A.N. Macpherson RN went into action against a formidable array of escort vessels, both MTBs and MGBs pressing home their attack repeatedly. The summary reads: 'Unit heavily engaged by convoy screen of M Class minesweepers and E- and R-boats, and from shore. Two R-boats thought to be severely damaged. Unit unable to close the convoy (to attack with torpedoes) before the area allocated to Dog Boats operating to the north was reached, so attack abandoned. MTB 222 (Coombs) disabled and towed home. Other boats damaged, 2 killed, 5 wounded. Confirmation (by NID in 1945) that one E-boat severely damaged.'

The CO of MGB 121 was Michael Bray, who remembers . . .

> the MGBs were suddenly illuminated by starshell which turned night into day. There, suddenly revealed, was an E/R-boat about 100 yards away going in the opposite direction. He was as surprised as we were, but we were quicker on the draw, and our guns raked him from stem to stern. I don't think he fired back at all – he may have been knocked out, but as the starshell went out, darkness returned and we lost him.[4]

Two nights later Peter Dickens led his boats for the last time. He had known for some time that he was to move on, eventually to command a destroyer, and his replacement as SO of the 21st MTBs had already arrived. Another RN officer with no previous experience in MTBs, Lt A.J. Hollings RN was given two weeks for an extended hand-over, and accompanied Dickens on the night of 24/25 July 1943. (Appendix 1, Note 11)

Naturally enough, Dickens hoped for a successful night. With his own boat now functioning more reliably, and accompanied by Ian Trelawny with two new boats of the 11th Flotilla, he had a large unit of seven boats to deploy.

They encountered the enemy off Ymuiden, and attacked what was later found to be a total of seven trawlers and Vps, the latter from the experienced 14th Vp Flotilla, who were becoming the MTBs' regular adversaries, now armed with 37mm and 88mm guns. Dickens organized his boats in three divisions, attacking in succession from opposite sides of the enemy force. The biggest drawback was the fact that on that night sea phosphorescence was particularly bright, and it seemed that however craftily they approached to close in for an attack the enemy saw them first, and sent out blankets of tracer, accompanied by the bigger 'crumps' of the heavier shells.

Dickens' seven boats made repeated attacks over three hours, but suffered more grievously than the enemy. Two men were killed and another wounded, and all the boats were hit, two of them by large shells. A German communiqué, while claiming to

[3] MO 8535; ADM 199/537; Dickens, *Night Action.*

[4] MO 9088; ADM 199/537; Bray, *One Young Man's War.*

have sunk two MTBs, admitted that one of their escorts had been sunk.[5]

On the same night in the Dover Strait two MGBs of the 9th Flotilla from Ramsgate, led now by Lt R.B. Rooper RN, were despatched to intercept E-boats from the Cherbourg flotilla, known to be on passage at speed en route for Germany. Rooper went out in MGB 116, accompanied by 118 (Lt M. Forsyth-Grant); having achieved the interception, they attacked immediately. There were only two E-boats and, to the MGBs' surprise, they separated as soon as the attack began, leaving the second E-boat at the mercy of the guns of both MGBs. Very quickly she blew up and sank. (It was later discovered from the survivors that one of the shells had hit a spare torpedo.) The MGBs were able to pick up four of the E-boat's crew, who confirmed that the boat was S 77, that the

[5] MO 9088; ADM 199/537; Dickens, *Night Action.*

Wrens loading a torpedo for MTB 234 of the 21st Flotilla, 1944. (Courtesy IWM – A25867)

Officers and men of the 21st MTB Flotilla at an investiture on 28 September 1943 at Buckingham Palace, following actions in April and May 1943. The group includes: J.H. Saunders, P.G.C. Dickens, I.C. Trelawny, V. Ohlenschlager, G.J. Macdonald RNZVR, with unindentified coxswains, motor mechanics and crew. (Collection CFHT)

captain had dived overboard after the explosion, and that the boat had a crew of 20.[6]

August 1943 was a very dead month for the 'short' MTBs, as an astonishingly long spell of very poor weather affected both the east coast and the Channel areas. On one of the few occasions that patrols were mounted, a unit of the old 6th MGB Flotilla's boats was forced to return to harbour, but MGB 64 broke her back in heavy seas and sank. Fortunately it was possible for the accompanying boats to take off all the crew and there were no casualties.

The only other patrol recorded in mid-August took place on the 16th by a combined unit of Dog Boats with two MTBs of the 14th Flotilla from Newhaven. This flotilla was equipped with boats built at the Samuel White yard at Cowes and powered by Sterling Admiral engines, and had only just begun to gather at Newhaven under their SO Lt F.E. McVie RN, who was also SO MTBs Portsmouth. Their arrival at Newhaven, a harbour mainly used by the SGBs and a Dog Boat flotilla, coincided with the establishment of new German radar stations linked to the shore batteries on the Normandy cliffs. This new development was to make 'lurking' patrols in this area far more hazardous, as was the case on this night. At a range of 4 miles one of the Dog Boats was hit by the first salvo from a shore battery, and although

[6] MO 8664; ADM 199/536.

MTB 252 (CO F.E. McVie RN, SO 14th Flotilla), a 71ft 6in Samuel White boat off Newhaven, late 1943. (Courtesy D. Rigg)

she struggled back to base the incident provided a salutary warning – especially as MGB 613, the victim, and the other three boats standing by were all subjected to shellfire as they returned across the Channel.

By August Ian Trelawny's 11th MTB Flotilla had almost all arrived at Felixstowe and were about to begin operations as a separate entity; previously they had made up mixed units. On 24/25 August the weather had begun to improve, and Trelawny in his own MTB 356 took 351 (Morrow), 348 (Bourne), 349 (Magnus) and 347 (Felce) on a patrol off Ymuiden. Trelawny was already renowned as a persistent battler, but on this occasion his unit unfortunately came up against two much larger enemy vessels, with escorts, which sighted the MTBs at long range and attacked them fiercely and accurately while keeping them out of effective range for a torpedo attack. 349 was badly hit, with one officer killed and another wounded, and 356 received a salvo of 20mm shells which caused considerable superficial damage.[7]

Behind the scenes in the Admiralty, decisions had been made which were to bring major organizational changes at flotilla and unit levels over the next two months. These decisions followed discussions that had stemmed particularly from reports by Robert Hichens much earlier in the year. After two actions in which the guns of his 8th MGB Flotilla had been unable to sink large, important targets, Hichens felt that the new boats – he had in mind the 71ft 6in British

[7] MO 10196; ADM 199/537.

Power Boats now being turned out in increasing numbers – had sufficient strength and space on the upper deck to be fitted with torpedoes and become 'combined MTB/MGBs'. The role of MGBs was changing. In addition to anti-E-boat patrols, creating diversions and attacking the smaller escorts of convoys, the same boats could now also act as Torpedo Boats. Peter Dickens had already begun to use his MTBs in a diversionary role, and thus implicitly supported Hichens' proposition.

After tests and trials on the boats, the 'short' MGBs were renumbered, labelled MTBs and formed into newly designated flotillas; the plan was also to be extended to D Class boats. There were, as ever, exceptions, and by no means all of the MGBs that had a new number stencilled on the hull actually received torpedo tubes. Some were allocated the alternative role of minelayers.

No doubt the men in the MGB flotillas with particularly proud records did not always take kindly to the changes. Just as army regiments have traditionally enhanced their *esprit de corps* by preserving traditions and emphasizing history, so the flotillas had followed suit. The 8th MGB Flotilla, which Hichens had led so effectively, suddenly became the 1st MTB Flotilla: again a break from tradition, as there had of course been a 1st Flotilla from 1936 to 1942. Gradually all the numbers changed, and newly-built boats joined the sturdiest of the older craft, to create new traditions and spirit. By October most of the changes were in place.

Although things had been comparatively quiet in the Channel for some time, the 14th MTB Flotilla with its new 'Sammy White' boats had a notable success on the night of 7/8 September. Operating from Newhaven, the unit was given very specific orders by the staff of C-in-C Portsmouth. These included precise limits of patrol, the nature of probable targets (which included TLC type IIIs – the armed F-Lighters), details of their return route and information about other units which would be either at sea or on immediate notice. The unit included one boat on loan from the 13th and consisted of MTBs 211 (Lt N.W.G. Taylor, with Lt Donal Rigg aboard as Senior Officer for the night), 255 (Sub Lt J.G. Hubbard) and 249 (Sub Lt L.P. Aspinall). The author possesses a copy of the complete report submitted by Donal Rigg, together with the subsequent comments of Base CO and C-in-C, and this provides the opportunity of indicating how closely such reports were monitored.

Rigg describes how he approached the coast until at 2243 he could see St-Valery ahead at about 3 miles range. He moved westward, aiming to close in to a position only half a mile off the coast and 3 miles to the west of the port. Eight minutes later a coastal searchlight came on; momentarily aimed in the direction of the patrol, it then shifted abruptly much closer to the St-Valery approaches, illuminating a ship that binoculars showed was clearly moving westward. Grateful for the enemy's help, Rigg decided to move closer, to be able to attack from inshore. Searchlight activity and even a vague challenge with the letter L and a single red tracer followed: it seemed that the enemy suspected their presence but could not see them. When starshell was fired towards the unit, Rigg decided to move quietly away further to the west, and then, when the moon came out of cloud, to wait until moonset at 2340.

His patience was rewarded. At 2344 he was able to close the coast again in darkness, still ahead of the enemy's course. Five targets were sighted at about 3,000 yards and all were tentatively identified as TLC IIIs. Rigg gave orders for the attack, indicating who was to take which section of the enemy patrol, and then moved in slowly and unseen to fire torpedoes. As 211 closed, the port torpedo depth setting was reduced to 2 ft, as Rigg was fearful of the torpedoes running under these shallow-draft ships. 211 and 255 fired in rapid succession as the last two ships of the line overlapped as they came into the sights, and after 38 seconds there was 'a great flash and all that remained to be seen was a large column of smoke'. After a further 7 seconds, a second distinct explosion was felt.

At this point the enemy opened fire, apparently sighting 255 as she disengaged. None of their shells was sufficiently accurate to hit 211, and the firing then ceased abruptly. Later it transpired that one 20mm shell had hit the bridge of 255, causing very slight injuries by wood splinters to the CO, first lieutenant and coxswain. 249 meanwhile had attacked the third ship in the line, a large trawler. Aspinall believed both his torpedoes had hit: certainly it sank within fifteen seconds. The three boats returned to Newhaven independently.

The reports of the SO and the COs of 255 and 249 were passed 'up the chain of command', first to the CO of HMS *Aggressive*, the base at Newhaven. He described the action as 'a brilliant example of the best possible use being made of torpedo-carrying Coastal Forces craft, resulting in a 100% successful attack with no loss to themselves'. He praised Rigg's deliberate, well-conceived and patient plan of attack, and commented that 'the previous training period that the boats had been able to have together had borne ample fruit'.

C-in-C Portsmouth (Adm Sir Charles Little) began his report in time-honoured fashion: 'Be pleased to lay before Their Lordships the attached report of the MTB action off Fécamp on the night of 7/8 September 1943.' The first three paragraphs (obviously drafted by his Command torpedo specialist) contained very detailed assessments of the torpedo attack. There were some criticisms, which, considering the levels of success implicit in the sinking of three ships (confirmed later by Intelligence) and the probability of four hits out of six torpedoes fired, seemed to give scant thought to the difficulties of decision-making in action at night. After all, on the bridge the CO had to contend with rapidly changing circumstances, often in poor visibility, making judgements based on very imprecise observation with no sophisticated aids. Analysis on paper in the comfort of an office is very different from the stress of close combat by very young, often inexperienced officers.

The report became much warmer in later paragraphs: 'I am very pleased with this attack following on some months of disappointing MTB work in this Command due to the general unreliability of the MTBs themselves and continual changes and lack of training as a consequence.' It went on:

> The favourable situation was well exploited by Lt D. Rigg RNVR. I have sent the following message:
>
> 'Please convey my congratulations and thanks to Lieutenant Rigg who led the successful operation last night . . . It was well conceived and executed and bears testimony to recent training . . . Please bring this message to the notice of the COs, officers and ships' companies of MTBs 211, 249 and 255.'

Two months later Donal Rigg was awarded the DSC, but he must have been very disappointed when his recommendations for honours and awards for the other officers and men involved were overlooked. (No wonder awards often led to dissatisfaction, as other far less obviously significant actions had been recognized by ten or more awards.)[8]

[8] MO 10298; ADM 199/1036; Donal Rigg; *Seedie's List of Coastal Forces Awards.*

MTB 349 (CO Lt P. Magnus) leaving harbour at HMS *Beehive*. (Courtesy R.D. Wickham)

Strangely, exactly the same unit met the enemy again off St-Valery three nights later, with the SO Lt F. McVie out in MTB 211. It says something about the lack of awareness of the lookouts in the enemy ships and the skill of the stalkers that once more the boats were able to make an unobserved attack from inshore, but sadly no hits were recorded.

Up on the east coast, it was the turn of Ian Trelawny's 11th Flotilla from *Beehive* to join battle with the enemy on 13/14 September. The flotilla was still smarting from its lack of success – accompanied by damage and casualties – off Ymuiden three weeks earlier.

Trelawny in his own MTB 356 took in his first division two boats which had just arrived at Felixstowe and were on their first operation. They were 355 (Sub Lt R.J. Dyke) and 360 (Sub Lt D.A. Hall). The second division was led by Lt Peter Magnus in 349, with 350 (Sub Lt H.G. Franklin). The five boats were about 13 miles off Ymuiden when in the excellent visibility of a nearly full moon they sighted a group of vessels about 4 miles ahead.

The two divisions were despatched to make their attacks, one from inshore and one from seaward of the seven targets (four escorts, with three larger vessels). As they got closer, Trelawny realized he would have to try to dispose of the largest escort vessel to allow 355 and 360 to fire at the principal targets. He had already been challenged and had bought time (successfully) by responding immediately with the same challenge. His torpedoes seemed to comb his target, and heavy fire was opened by the enemy. 356 made a diversion, drawing the fire, and in went the other two to make their attack. Their torpedoes did not hit, but they disengaged safely under fire.

Meanwhile, 349 and 350 were now in position to attack from inshore, and Trelawny once again drew the enemy fire to give them a chance to attack. This time one of the four torpedoes hit – it was probably one of 350's – and the strike was observed from both sides of the convoy. The boats then shadowed the convoy as far as the Hook, where another patrol was operating, and then returned to base. In these early days of the 11th, this could almost be regarded as a 'training exercise in earnest', but Trelawny was disappointed with just a single hit from ten torpedoes. It was confirmed later that the 372-ton trawler *Walrus* was sunk.[9]

It is an indication of the constant pressure upon these Dutch coast convoys, forcing the deployment of more and more of the small reserve of escorts at the enemy's disposal, that on the next night they were attacked again – this time off Noordwijk by four boats of the 21st Flotilla from Felixstowe under Lt Tony Hollings RN who had now succeeded Peter Dickens as SO. This time the enemy used a patrol of six R-boats, so no torpedoes were fired, but there was a short fierce exchange of gunfire. The MTBs were unharmed and the crews believed some damage may have been inflicted.

In the course of these three books covering the operations of the MTBs and MGBs, there have been several mentions of the Fairmile A and B Class MLs, even though their activities lie outside the strict terms of the text. They were magnificent sea-boats and performed many functions, including minesweeping, minelaying, anti-submarine patrols, air-sea rescue and clandestine operations. But their main role was as convoy escort, and they were essential elements in the meagre defensive resources which strove to protect the constant flow of merchant ships supplying all parts of the British Isles. It was not often they hit the headlines, but on 24/25 September, off Harwich, they 'joined the ranks of the MGBs' by sinking an E-boat, and this feat certainly deserves a mention here. Few craft other than the 40-knot MTBs and MGBs were fast enough to catch an E-boat in flight, but there were occasions when circumstances conspired to allow other boats to attack them. When MLs 150 (Lt J.O. Thomas) and 145 (Lt R. Seddon) suddenly sighted two or three E-boats at close range, without hesitation both set out to ram one of them. They succeeded, and sank S 596, at considerable cost to the bows of the two MLs. Sixteen survivors were picked up. The work of the MLs was greatly respected by the men of the MTBs and deserves far more recognition than it has generally received.

In both the other books of this trilogy,[10] reference has been made to a special issue of the *London Gazette* dated 18 October 1948, which contains full details of four Coastal Forces actions, selected to illustrate a variety of theatres of war, types of boat and circumstances. The second of these covers an action in the Channel by the 9th MTB Flotilla, with a unit composed entirely of boats manned by officers and crews of the Royal Netherlands Navy, together with a unit of the 9th MGB Flotilla, all under the Dover Command. Both units were under the command of Lt E.H. Larive, RNethN, who was embarked in MTB 202 (Lt J.L. Bommezyn RNethN), with MTBs 204 (Lt H.C. Jorissen RNethN) and 231 (Lt C.H. Vaneeghen RNethN), in company with MGBs 108 (Lt L.E. Thompson), 118 (Lt M.O. Forsyth-Grant) and 117 (Sub Lt D.W.B. Woolven).

Aerial reconnaissance had reported the presence in Le Havre of two enemy merchant ships, which were expected to attempt the passage of the Dover Strait. Vice Admiral Dover therefore sailed the force to arrive off the Berck Buoy (7 miles offshore, about

[9] MO 10831; ADM 199/537.

[10] Reynolds, *Dog Boats at War*, 1998; Reynolds and Cooper, *Mediterranean MTBs at War*, 1999.

HRH Prince Bernhard of the Netherlands (left) visiting the 9th MTB Flotilla of Dutch-manned boats. He is on the bridge with the SO, Lt Cdr E.H. Larive DSC RNethN (centre). (Courtesy H. van Rossem)

25 miles south of Boulogne) at about 0200 on the 27th. When they reached their patrol area, they lay stopped about 5 miles off the coast, but when Larive saw that the horizon to westward was far brighter than towards the coast, he decided to move much closer inshore. The weather was squally and the wind 4–5 and gusting – on the limits of normal MTB operations for launching torpedoes accurately. The enemy was first sighted at 0308, and Larive moved his force even closer inshore, reaching a point about 2 miles from the cliffs.

Suddenly at 0320 starshell burst overhead, making an attack impossible from their position, so Larive moved at speed (it was very rough) to get out of the illuminated area. But they could already see the bow waves of the nine E/R-boats protecting the convoy, and although it seemed that they must have sighted the MTBs, they did not open fire. As soon as the combined unit got ahead of the convoy, the MGBs peeled off to make their diversionary attack, and the three MTBs moved inshore again, but this time well ahead and unobserved. Gradually the convoy approached and as the main escort screen passed the main target – a large three-island merchant ship – came in to a perfect position for an attack. Five torpedoes were fired (one misfired) and a hit was clearly obtained by 204 on the main target. Further approaches were made in order to fire the remaining torpedo despite heavy enemy fire, and eventually they disengaged at about 0500. The MGBs reported that they had made two gun attacks on the escorts, met heavy retaliatory fire, and suffered very slight damage with one man wounded.

Intelligence was later able to confirm that the major target, SS *Madali*, 3,014 tons, was sunk. Despite minor critical comments from SO MTBs Dover, Vice-Admiral Dover (Sir Henry Pridham-Whippell) praised the planning and skill which both MTBs and MGBs employed in achieving surprise despite the presence of an escort totalling about fifteen vessels.[11]

Jubilation in Dover and Ramsgate at this success was tempered three nights later, on 29/30 September, when Larive went out with a very similar unit in much the same area. After a long fruitless patrol, they were retiring when they were attacked by a strong force of R-boats. Two boats – 433 and 436 – were very considerably damaged, suffering one killed and seven wounded, but first they had silenced one of the R-boats.

The report on this operation indicates the date at which the renumbering of the 9th MGB Flotilla took place. The boat that three nights earlier had been MGB 117 was now MTB 436, while MGB 118 was now MTB 437.[12]

No actions were reported in the first half of October, even though operations obviously continued whenever weather permitted. The hazards from radar-controlled shore batteries on the Normandy cliffs were emphasized when boats of the 14th Flotilla, together with some Dog Boats, were shelled at a range of 6 miles. They were not hit, but the splashes were close enough to demonstrate what an effective force these batteries could be. Similarly, further to the west, two boats of the Free French 23rd Flotilla met two Torpedo Boats off Brittany, which were able to keep them well out of range with their higher calibre guns.

However, the outcome of another clash with superior forces on 15/16 October was not so fortunate. Ian Trelawny took five boats of his 11th Flotilla on patrol between the Hook and Ymuiden, and at 2338 sighted a force of two large trawlers and two gun coasters – all expected to be armed with 88mm guns. Trelawny could see that direct confrontation was not the answer, and turned away to gain time to decide on his approach. They were spotted and challenged, and then illuminated by starshell. Almost at once the enemy opened fire with their main and secondary armament, and MTB 356, the SO's boat in the lead, received a number of hits. Trelawny decided to increase speed, drop smoke floats and make smoke in order to attack from the starboard side.

Unfortunately almost at once 356 was hit in the engine room by an 88mm shell. It blew a large hole in the boat's side, destroyed the starboard engine, blew out the petrol compartment bulkhead and burst at least one petrol tank. Throttles and telegraphs jammed, the boat lost way and began to settle rapidly by the stern. MTB 349 (Peter Magnus) quickly appeared alongside and took off the crew, three of whom were wounded. Demolition charges were set, which exploded later when enemy trawlers were investigating the wreck.

German reports indicate that the enemy force actually consisted of three well-armed Vps, one gun coaster (AF42) and an armed trawler, and that beyond that screen were the eight fleet minesweepers of the 34th Flotilla – indeed a formidable array. But Trelawny was saved: yet another SO whose ship – always the most vulnerable as they led the way towards the enemy – was sunk beneath him.[13]

11 MO 11204; ADM 199/536; *London Gazette*, 15 Oct. 1942; NID in OD 5084.
12 MO 11477; ADM 199/1036.

13 MO 11831; ADM 199/536; NHB Search Document.

VENTURE
ARY 2006

ky Star 1	Lucky Star 2
5	6
1	8
4	7
3	8
5	8
3	7
3	5
3	7
1	3
2	9
1	6
6	8
3	7
1	9

The Dutch boats of the 9th MTB Flotilla were active in the Dover Strait at this time, and had two actions within two days on 25/26 and 27/28 October, in both of which Lt F. 'Happy' Visee RNethN was involved. In the first, a two-boat unit found a merchant ship, and unobserved fired torpedoes at long range. They believed they had missed but NID later revealed that a trawler had been hit – but whether the size of the target had been over-estimated or the trawler was unseen and extremely unlucky was never discovered. In the second action, two boats were suddenly confronted by two E-boats. Only a brief exchange of fire was possible before the two units separated; our boats had four wounded and believed one E-boat was damaged.

Mark Arnold-Forster has already cropped up in connection with actions in the Channel, and he will continue to do so. He was a youthful – some say boyish – figure who by November 1943 was SO of the 13th Flotilla and was highly regarded as a first-class MTB CO and leader. The 13th MTB Flotilla boats (205–212) were built by Whites using Vosper drawings supplied directly by the Admiralty, without the knowledge of Peter Du Cane of Vosper, who had designed them. Due to the shortage of Packard engines, these and all subsequent White-built MTBs received the heavier Sterling Admiral engines which added 2 tons' extra weight; these boats initially suffered countless teething troubles since the engines were incompatible with the hulls.

On 3/4 November Arnold-Forster in 211 (Lt N.G.G. Taylor) with 207 and 212 were sent to lie off Cap d'Antifer in wait for two German destroyers which Intelligence reported were likely to pass during the night. It transpired that three other boats had failed to intercept them as they passed Fécamp. Neil Taylor describes how an engine failure had reduced 211's available speed to 18 knots, so it was essential that their first torpedo attack should be successful – as they would certainly not be able to get away if it was not.

It was a disaster. As the destroyers approached, 211 and 207 were in perfect position to fire as their torpedo sights came on – but they were spotted and to their horror the two destroyers altered course directly towards them and fired starshell. They were cornered and trapped. With all the resourcefulness at their command, they used guile, smoke, and what speed and agility they could muster, with their superior turning circle, and they did escape – but it was a very close-run thing.[14]

Back in the North Sea the weather was interrupting operations as winter began to bite, but on 10/11 November four boats of the 22nd Flotilla on patrol off Zanddyck had a nightmare experience while shadowing an enemy force under the cover of thick fog banks. Having stopped to listen in nil visibility, they suddenly realized that the enemy was bearing down on them. Making a crash start, they tried to escape but almost immediately there was a horrendous collision. In accelerating away 222 rammed 230 amidships, leaving her with a huge hole in the engine room, filling fast and sinking. The crew were taken off and she was scuttled. 222 herself had a gaping hole in the bow. Leading Stoker A. Rowberry described her efforts to get back to base:

> 222 could only go astern, but after a short while, because we were so close to the enemy coast, the SO [Jake Wright] ordered the CO [Lt J.Whife] to fire her scuttling charges to avoid capture. The charges failed. We were then towed stern first to westward; the weather turned really foul and it was decided to sink her – gunnery

[14] MO 12755; Summary of Actions; Neil Taylor's notes.

An original painting by David Cobb presented to D.E.J. Hunt, organizer since 1947 of the reunions of the MTB/MGB Officers' Association. It depicts three of the 22nd Flotilla with MTB 245 (D.E.J. Hunt) in the foreground. (Courtesy D.E.J. Hunt)

practice for the two remaining boats of the unit – but in the sea that was running they couldn't achieve that. The SO called up some Ds on patrol to sink her with their 6-pounders. By the time she sank, forty hours had passed since the unit left Lowestoft.[15]

[15] MO 13142 and MO 14028; ADM 199/536; notes from L/Sto A. Rowberry.

The only other reported contact with the enemy in home waters in November occurred on the night of the 26th when the 14th MTB Flotilla was patrolling off Cap d'Antifer. Mark Arnold-Forster in 205 was SO, and had three boats in Division 1. At midnight he sent Division 2, led by Donal Rigg in 254 with 256 in company, to patrol from the south-western limit of the patrol area. In this way, the search for targets could cover a greater area.

It was not until 0445 that Rigg sighted a ship, and then two more, to the east, some 5 miles distant and apparently moving northward. Blessed with the newly acquired TCS voice radio, he was able to report his sighting to the SO further north. Rigg attempted to close in order to maintain contact, but found his unit illuminated by accurate starshell at 3 miles. At 0525 shelling began – again it was far too close for comfort and was obviously from enemy vessels of destroyer size. It was decided to withdraw temporarily, but even at 35 knots, the shelling kept pace with them for ten long minutes, through the smoke they had laid.

In view of the impossibility of shadowing at such long range, and the lack of time before dawn, it was reluctantly agreed to abandon the patrol. It was frustrating, as on a darker night they might have been able to get close enough to attack, and in their reports the view was expressed that there was scope for patrols to be reinforced by destroyers. This led – once again – to prolonged discussion in the Command and in the Admiralty, but destroyer captains were still reluctant at this time to work with Coastal Forces until far more training together and more efficient communications had reduced the risks![16]

On 9/10 December it was the turn of Ian Trelawny's 11th Flotilla to mount an important and successful patrol. The 11th had been very busy for weeks but had not been rewarded with the targets they hoped for. Trelawny had a reputation for efficiency and thoughtfulness, and in this he was continuing Dickens' work from Felixstowe. His flotilla was well worked up and had reliable boats.

On this occasion he took to sea a large unit of six boats: 355 (his own), 352 (J.H. Moore), 360 (D.A. Hall) as Division 1, with Peter Magnus as Division 2 leader in 350 (K. Harris), 348 (F.W. Bourne) and 351 (N.C. Morrow). It was to be a very long night: they were off Egmond by 2041 and beginning their patrol. They had specific orders to attack a convoy with two large ships further north, so they avoided contact with two trawlers and a TLC picked up on radar. At 2330 they were stopped 11 miles off Ymuiden when their radar showed the convoy they were after – at least ten ships, with two larger 'blips' on the screen. They closed until they had visual contact and could see a merchant ship of about 2,500 tons and a tanker of 2,000 tons, surrounded by large trawlers and R-boats, well disposed ahead, astern and on both flanks.

Their orders were to make a 'zone' attack – that is, a spread of torpedoes. This was considered to give the greatest chance of a hit even when they were forced to make the longer-range attacks required of them in most circumstances. In fact, it had been a suggestion of Trelawny's some months earlier, so he was committed to the concept. He told Division 2 to hold back while he attacked the merchant ship, and moved in to get as close as possible. Almost at once starshell burst overhead, followed by well-directed 40mm and 20mm fire. He gave the order to fire the spread, and was disappointed to see that only four torpedoes were fired: 360 had not received the signal. But what mattered most was that two explosions were seen and felt on the target, and she was clearly doomed. Trelawny disengaged and rejoined his boats, and immediately sent in 348 and 360 to make a second attack, this time on the tanker. They got off their torpedoes, but saw no hits. By this time the fire from the escorts was very heavy and the weather was worsening. They spent two more hours stalking and probing the convoy's defences, but in the end had to conclude that they could not get through.

[16] MO 13631; ADM 199/782.

They left the trigger-happy escorts engaged in a blistering cross-fire – which they hoped would do the job for them.

Despite Trelawny's admission in his report that he thought he had made some wrong decisions, C-in-C was very complimentary and gave credit to the SO for having initiated the idea of zone firing. He was delighted that it had brought at least one success to justify the concept. Among several awards, Trelawny received a Bar to his DSC.[17]

The last action of 1943 took place on 23/24 December but did not, alas, bring any reward. Intelligence reported the imminent passage of a large 400ft merchant vessel from Boulogne through the Strait of Dover to Dunkirk, and emphasized that it would be very heavily escorted. The Dover Command still had bad memories of the failure to stop the *Scharnhorst*, *Gneisenau* and *Prinz Eugen* nearly two years earlier. Now they had far more powerful and reliable boats, and a force of eleven short boats and two Ds, organized in four groups, was despatched to attack this plum target.

In the event, with visibility very poor indeed, the first group sought the enemy in vain (they had probably already passed), but the Dog Boats attacked escorts and damaged two R-boats further north. The convoy then crossed the minefield which had been laid for such an eventuality; one escort was sunk but the main target seemed to bear a charmed life. Off Dunkirk a truly gallant attack was launched by two new MTBs of the 5th flotilla, followed by three recently renumbered MGBs (still without tubes) of the 9th, now the 2nd MTB Flotilla. The attack faced the combined fire of seven large M Class minesweepers: all three MTBs suffered damage (357 so badly that although she got back to Dover she was deemed 'uneconomic to repair') and could not penetrate the screen. The gunboats followed in, got even closer and began to register hits. Then 437 (ex-MGB 118, CO Lt M. Forsyth-Grant) suffered several hits which set her on fire, killed the first lieutenant (Ian Galbraith) and disabled the for'd gun (the Pom-Pom), wounding one of its crew. 436 (ex-117) astern was also damaged, her CO (Lt Woolven), the coxswain and signalman being wounded. Both vessels returned to Ramsgate independently.

They simply could not get in close enough to attack the merchant ship, which was later discovered to be the 6,000-ton *Aalen*, which reached the safety of Dunkirk harbour. 437 was paid off for repairs which lasted three months.[18]

[17] MO 14240; ADM 199/536; *Seedie's List of Coastal Forces Awards.*

[18] MO 1687/44; Search document at NHB; Forsyth-Grant, *Courage in Adversity*; notes from Charles Burford, gunner in MTB 437.

CHAPTER 9

JANUARY TO MAY 1944

Throughout 1943 there had been constant development of boats, equipment and training in Coastal Forces, but not at the pace that many had expected or thought necessary. The new principle of combined torpedo and gun armament was looked upon with optimism, although some of the old 'gunboat brigade' were not convinced. In fact very few of the older gunboats were fitted with tubes. The new boats which received them did lose some speed but gained in return additional attack potential. In general 1944 was to provide the big step forward in quantity and quality of craft.

The newly numbered 1st, 2nd and 3rd MTB Flotillas of 71ft 6in British Power Boats were, as the new year began, all immediately available; the newly formed 35th Flotilla led by Lt J.D. Dixon was soon ready, followed by the 4th Flotilla. This was manned mainly by the personnel of the Elco boats of the 7th MGB Flotilla which had gained a great reputation over the previous two years operating from Lowestoft. Their new 71ft 6in boats arrived between December and April, and their first action took place in February 1944.

The existing flotillas – the 5th, 9th (Dutch), 11th, 13th, 14th, 21st, 22nd and 23rd (Free French) – all had boats which were at least the most recent available from Vosper yards, or Samuel Whites of Vosper design. Several more flotillas were well advanced in building, particularly the 29th, with all-Canadian crews under Lt C.A. Law RCNVR, the new 22nd (Lt R.G. Eburah) and the 30th (Lt P. Magnus) – all of which were destined to play a significant part later in the year.

The overall war situation was naturally the subject of much discussion and speculation among the men of Coastal Forces, in common with the whole nation and the media. Since the successful occupation of Sicily in August 1943, and the subsequent assaults on mainland Italy (now meeting stiff opposition), everyone was expecting the launch of the long-awaited Second Front by the Allies, to begin a drive towards Germany itself, and relieve the pressure on the Russian Front.

Whenever and wherever the assault was made, it would clearly involve a large proportion of the available Coastal Forces craft. Rumours abounded, and the amateur strategists – the dogmatic and the balanced, the cautious and the bold – put forward their theories. It was certain that to be truly effective it would have to be targeted at one of the stretches of coast between the Netherlands and Brittany – the very areas in which all the home waters MTB flotillas plied their trade. The most thoughtful of the strategists realized that when decisions were made about time and place, pointers would be available in advance to indicate the start of preparations. Certainly several months of planning would be required, however much effort had already been expended in the creation of provisional plans. After all, this was surely destined to be the greatest enterprise ever yet undertaken in war: the number of men and the enormous quantities of arms and supplies which would need to be put ashore on the territory of a prepared enemy, and then sustained for months, would require a vast naval commitment quite separate from the land and air battles which would ensue.

Through January and much of February 1944 there were very few signs of an increase in the pace of war – indeed for the MTBs it seemed to be the reverse. The fact that the 'short' MTBs in particular needed a relatively calm sea state to provide a stable enough platform to use their guns and torpedoes effectively was bound to restrict activity in the winter months, however anxious they were to get to sea. The 'long' boats could operate in worse weather, but with some risk to their hulls: patience was required to make best use of them.

There was another factor, too, in the small number of effective interceptions of enemy shipping made at this time. Intelligence sources established that far fewer convoys were being routed on the inshore shipping lanes. Without doubt, the tenacious attacks on them by MTBs, aircraft and mines, had made their passages extremely hazardous in the last few months of 1943, and the force of available escorts had suffered considerably. The enemy had certainly strengthened and improved his coastal defences, too. The shore batteries had better radar-controlled directors and heavier calibre guns than in the past. It was galling to learn that the E-boats still seemed able to make a number of raids on our convoys – especially along the south coast – but the destroyer shield was generally successful in beating them off.

On the few occasions in the Channel, both in the west and in the Dover Strait, that the MTBs were sent out in January they met poor visibility and failed to intercept. The first recorded action of the month was on 29/30 January, when a significant target – the 360ft *Sperrbrecher* 32, a large heavily armed minesweeper used as a flak ship – sailed westward from Dunkirk. This was deemed so important that a force of nine boats from four different flotillas, together with two Dog Boats, was despatched from Dover. The long-range guns at Dover attacked first, followed by six individual and zone attacks, but none was successful. The main reason was the heavy fire from the escorts (and the *Sperrbrecher*), which forced the boats to fire their torpedoes from longer range. However, despite the heavy retaliation which left MTBs 418, 203 and 240 with some damage but no casualties, two boats made gun attacks on an M Class minesweeper which they considered they had damaged, and scored some hits on two E-boats.[1]

Two nights later, on 31 January/ 1 February, a similar group of boats from the 9th and 13th Flotillas, again in company with two D Boats, had much the same experience off Wissant when attempting to attack a merchant ship which had left Boulogne to sail towards the Dover Strait. The weather was bad and totally unsuitable for the 'short' boats, and once again no hits were obtained. At least mines were laid off Dunkirk.[2]

After a completely blank month for the whole of January, the east coast flotillas had just two nights in mid-February when there were opportunities to engage the enemy. The first, on the night of the 12th, brought only frustration. Two E-boat groups from Ymuiden tracked a group of minesweeping trawlers off the Humber beyond the range of shore radar, and sank the *Cap d'Antifer*. Boats from the 11th and 21st Flotillas tried to intercept the E-boats on their return to Ymuiden, but narrowly missed them. As the 21st Flotilla boats were returning to base, 223 was attacked by a Beaufighter, and suffered casualties: Sub Lt Derek Smith, the first lieutenant, and POMM John Evans both died in this unfortunate incident.[3]

The new 3rd MTB Flotilla, composed of 71ft 6in boats previously in the 10th MGB

[1] MO 2083; ADM 199/261.
[2] MO 2056; ADM 199/261.
[3] MO 2518; ADM 199/265.

'The bulkhead held'. Four of the Dutch crew of MTB 240 (9th MTB Flotilla) display the missing bow after a collision off Dover. It was repaired in time for Operation Neptune, by May 1944. (Courtesy H. van Rossem)

Flotilla, had not yet received torpedoes. When their SO, Lt E.D.W. Leaf DSC, was given orders on 14/15 February to carry out an anti-E-boat patrol, he took along a similar boat of the 4th Flotilla (455) which did have torpedoes 'in case they might be useful'. This apparently innocuous assignment was to lead to a series of fierce engagements that were ultimately well detailed in the ROPs and in a War Intelligence Report.

The unit had reached its patrol position well to seaward of the east coast convoy route by 19.00, when Leaf was instructed by the shore plot to move fast (at 38 knots) to a position much closer to the Dutch coast. A large group of E-boats had been repelled by two corvettes and they were now returning to base.

The E-boats were almost certainly ahead of them, so Leaf pressed on towards Ymuiden and closed the harbour entrance, hoping he might be in time to catch them as they slowed to enter. No sooner had Leaf arrived than he sighted not E-boats but two trawlers and a low-lying flak ship. He ordered 455 (Lt M.V. Rout RNZNVR) to make a torpedo attack, and then, leading in his own 444, he followed in to draw fire away from her, with 439 (Lt C.A. Burk RCNVR), 443 (Lt G.R. Dale) and 441 (Lt J.S. Price) in close company. 455 hit her target with both torpedoes (the detonations were clearly felt and the mast was seen to collapse as a flash spread around the upper deck). The four gunboats silenced the leading trawler, and then sped away to disengage and prepare for a second attack. It was at this moment that a previously unseen flak ship opened fire directly at 444, inflicting immediate damage and casualties. The Oerlikon gunner was killed, and the SO,

Derek Leaf, mortally wounded, along with two others on the bridge. Somehow the first lieutenant – Sub Lt Peter Davis – managed to extricate 444 and with great difficulty coaxed her back to base. The other three boats, led by the Canadian 'Bones' Burk in 439, attacked the flak ship at short range, inflicting further damage with Pom-Pom and 20mm fire, and then disengaged to look for 444 and 455 which had lost contact. Both had been seen to get clear, and as no distress signals were received it was assumed that they had returned to Lowestoft.

Burk had not finished yet. As they sped away, they found six E-boats to starboard and once more closed to attack, savaging the first and second in line so that the leader stopped dead and was on fire. 441 (John Price) lost touch briefly, and then found and attacked several more E-boats to port before losing touch altogether. Burk persisted even longer and twice more went in with 439 and 443 to engage two more groups of E-boats before discovering that it was 0440 and time to leave the far coast. Although his two boats had, miraculously, suffered only minimal damage and few casualties, they had W/T problems and the whole unit returned to base independently.

There they discovered that their highly respected leader, Derek Leaf, had been killed. They pieced together the events and results of a very long night, beginning with the anti-E-boat patrol off the Humber and concluding with the series of attacks in which they had certainly damaged several of the seventeen returning E-boats, after two successful torpedo hits on one of the larger targets. They mourned the loss of a fine officer and the three crewmen killed, and knew that Derek Leaf would have been proud of the results achieved by the aggressive spirit of his flotilla in attacking such a numerically superior enemy.

C-in-C (Adm Sir Jack Tovey) described Lt Leaf's death as a great loss to Coastal Forces. He had led this operation with a high standard of dash and efficiency. Radar was efficiently used, and weapons well maintained. He also commended Lt Burk for the way he had taken over when the SO was killed. He noted that this was the first MTB operation in which the newly fitted 18in torpedoes had sunk a target, and expressed profound disagreement with those who had suggested that they should be removed from the 71ft 6in boats.[4]

This stirring action, coming as it did after seven weeks of comparative (and very unusual) sterility in the operations from the east coast bases, was like a beacon in the dark. In the Channel, too, the few brief spasms of activity in January and February had been frustrating, but the pattern was shortly to be relieved by the onset of a period of high activity in March. Before that, there were two brushes with the enemy for the Dartmouth and Newhaven boats, further west. The new 1st Flotilla cut its teeth on 26/27 February when 415 and 431 (both without tubes), led by Lt T.J. Mathias, maintained the traditions of Hichens' 8th MGB Flotilla when they attacked a convoy entering harbour in Jersey, and claimed to have severely damaged a trawler. On the same night the 14th Flotilla was patrolling off Cap d'Antifer when 249 lost contact with the other four boats, and then found herself under heavy fire from an enemy convoy. Despite being alone, 249 attacked, firing one torpedo (the other misfired), sadly with no result.[5]

It must have been as obvious to the German High Command as to the rank and file of all the British Services that in these early months decisions would be made to launch the Second Front. It is not surprising

[4] MO 2476 and MO 2527; ADM 199/265.

[5] MO 3072, Summary; MO 2774; ADM 199/261.

MTB 434 (Lts E. Archer and Patrick McNee) and 415 (Lts P. Beck and F.S. Large) of the 1st MTB Flotilla alongside HMS *Aberdonian* at Dartmouth, spring 1944. (Courtesy F.S. Large)

that E-boat activity in the Channel was at an extremely high level in these first few weeks of March 1944, and it was matched by equally watchful defensive plans involving destroyers, Coastal Forces and aircraft. The high-speed forays by the E-boats towards the south coast of Britain were clearly intended both to attack the increasingly numerous coastal convoys and to lay mines. As the enemy had no command of the air by this time, aerial reconnaissance was difficult for them, and it was presumed that some E-boats were simply probing for evidence of changes in convoy patterns, concentrations of shipping and positions of shore batteries.

The congregation areas for the eastward convoys had been in Mevagissy Bay and Lyme Bay, and particular care was taken over the defence of these areas, with Coastal Force patrols waiting off the Lizard, ready to be vectored to attack E-boats from Cherbourg. The Coastal Forces Control Officer, Lt Guy Fison, was based at the Start Point radar station, to marshal the defensive patrols. On both the 1 and 2/3 March E-boats were plotted off Falmouth and Lyme Bay, but they retired at speed after shore battery fire, and evaded interception by MTBs. There was no evidence of minelaying. Such sallies became commonplace over the next few months, but were generally repelled. The E-boats were under orders to avoid action with both 'long' and 'short' MTBs but they had in the recent past occasionally shown their teeth; clearly they were being saved for future missions if no targets were found.

Although MTB actions came thick and fast in the Dover and Channel areas in the second half of March, the boats from the east coast bases were denied contact with the enemy except on 5/6 March and again at the very end of the month.

When Peter Dickens left the 21st Flotilla of 1941 Vospers in July 1943, he handed over to Lt Hollings RN. When he in turn moved on, CCF Nore took note of recommendations from HMS *Beehive* and appointed the New Zealander Lt G.J. Macdonald as SO at the age of twenty-one. It was an unprecedented move but, after all, Macdonald had proved himself with Dickens and already wore the ribbons of a DSC and Bar.

The new SO was leading (in his own boat, 241) a unit of six MTBs of the 21st Flotilla (241, 224, 225, 234, 244, 232) – all with experienced COs – off Ymuiden, when at 0430 on 6 March, after sighting and stalking a patrol of two trawlers, he formed the unit into two divisions and went in to make a zone attack at the long range of 1,100 yards, but at a perfect angle of approach. It seemed that the targets were not keeping a good lookout as there was no enemy fire. No fewer than three explosions were seen as one trawler was hit, with the tell-tale concussions felt on the hulls of his boats. He sent in the second division, but they were beaten off by heavy enemy fire in bright moonlight. C-in-C,

Officers of the 21st MTB Flotilla at Lowestoft, 1944. COs standing in front row, first four, left to right: D. Gill (225), A.J. Lee (224), G.J. Macdonald (SO and 234) and J. Wolfe (232). (Courtesy J.S. Hawkins)

MTB 224 (A.J. Lee) of the 21st Flotilla. (Courtesy J.S. Hawkins)

noting that this was Macdonald's first action as SO, also took the opportunity of driving home his conviction that zone attacks were essential to success at long range.[6]

On 8 March 1944 the first formal (though secret and not at once generally known) step was taken towards the preparation of the plan which would detail the part Coastal Forces would play in the 'Invasion'. (Appendix 1, Note 12) The appointment a year earlier of Captain Coastal Forces (CCF) Nore was followed when Captain P.V. McLaughlin RN was named as CCF (Channel). His roles were to coordinate the use of Coastal Forces craft throughout the Channel, to operate them in the Portsmouth Command and to plan their use in Operation Neptune. He was to be a member of the staff of C-in-C Portsmouth, and would exercise command over all CF bases in the Command.

This was all revealed gradually, as security was of necessity extremely tight. Operation Neptune was the code-name for all the naval aspects of Operation Overlord – the plan for the landing and subsequent development of the assault forces on the coast of north-west Europe.

Capt McLaughlin very quickly appointed the first member of his staff, which eventually comprised four 'Operating Staff Officers', a Signal Officer, a Torpedo Officer, an Engineer

[6] MO 3550; ADM 199/265.

Officer and a Secretary, and established his offices in the Portsmouth Combined Headquarters in a chalk tunnel safe from bombing. Some of his staff were already well known to the men of Coastal Forces. Lt C.W.S. Dreyer DSO DSC RN and Lt Cdr P.M. Scott MBE DSC RNVR both had proven pedigrees in Coastal Forces warfare. (Appendix 1, Note 13)

CCF did not waste time. Within a few days he had visited almost all the HQs of other relevant Commands, including the Nore, and the major Coastal Forces bases on the east and south coasts. His Operating Staff Officers were in place and took over their duties on 15 March. As these included the overseeing of all operations in the Channel, this was a far more overt expression to all the men of Coastal Forces that major changes were afoot.

The task for Coastal Forces in the period running up to the invasion was clearly the continuing harassment of enemy shipping in all areas: anything else would surely have indicated to the enemy a change of emphasis in operations. For months the pattern in the Dover Strait had been difficult and frustrating for the MTB/MGB crews, as the enemy was passing fewer and fewer ships through the Strait, and those that did venture out were very heavily escorted and protected by shore batteries. But units were sent out most nights, and both 'short' and 'long' boats hammered away, trying to find a way through the enemy defences.

On 15/16 March three D boats from Dover were sent out to attack a target, thought to be a small merchant vessel. It was escorted by a force more notable for quantity than for the size of individual ships: two auxiliary trawlers and ten R-boats. With the Dog Boats was one 'short' MTB of the 5th Flotilla, 353 (Lt J.D. Dempster), and the combination worked well. While the withering broadsides from the Dogs distracted the escorts, 353 crept in unseen and torpedoed the main target.[7]

The next night four boats were vectored to attack a patrol of six armed trawlers off Cap Gris-Nez. Lt R.B. Rooper RN, SO MGBs at Dover, was embarked in 417 (Sub Lt T.G. Wilson), supported by three other ex-gunboats of the 2nd Flotilla, two of which became detached, leaving only 417 and 418 (Lt L. Thompson) to make the attack. Their approach was detected and they were met by a curtain of gunfire, much of it from 88mm and 37mm guns, from Vps 1802, 1803, 1804, 1810, 1811 and 1815. Several 88mm shells from 1810 and 1811 hit 417 which immediately burst into flames and sank with all hands. 418 very gallantly attempted to approach to see if anyone could be saved, but was beaten off by the continuing barrage. Lt Rooper, who had been awarded a DSC for an action in September 1943, had suffered the same fate as Dicky Richards, the SO he had succeeded. Vice Admiral Dover commended Lt L.E. Thompson and his crew for their spirited single-handed attack and believed one R-boat was sunk.[8]

Twice more in the next three days attempts were made to attack enemy craft off Wissant, but they were beaten off by heavy fire from both patrols and shore batteries. Another effort was made on 20/21 March, when Mark Arnold-Forster in 212, with 206, attacked a large tanker (T 38), which had left Boulogne at 20.30 moving eastward. They were beaten off, 212 with slight damage. A second attack by 359, 354 and 362 met with similar response, but their accurate reporting enabled the Dover batteries to gain a hit on the tanker, and she was reported to have sunk off Calais.[9]

[7] MO 4504; Dover 15/1226, Summary.

[8] MO 4299; ADM 199/261; Search Document NHB.

[9] Dover 21/1211, Summary.

The for'd Oerlikon on a 71ft Vosper of the 21st Flotilla, with its gun's crew. (Courtesy J.E.H. Davies)

This astonishing week – quite out of keeping with past experience – was followed by a further eight occasions between 21 and 31 March when interceptions were attempted, some from Dover and others from Newhaven. Many variations were tried, including greater involvement of the Dover shore batteries, and operations code-named Dandy which were coordinated with aircraft attacks. The 'short' boats frequently worked with a unit of Dog Boats of the 59th Flotilla, based at Dover. Most of the earlier contacts were in the Dover Strait area, but later they occurred further west in the Baie de la Seine, reached more readily by David Shaw's 14th Flotilla from Newhaven. Here there was evidence that the enemy was very aware that the MTBs were equipped with radar, and enemy aircraft were seen dropping 'window' to jam effective use of the sets.

Off the Dutch coast the Dog Boats had enjoyed most of the contacts throughout March since Macdonald's spirited action on the 5th. But at the end of the month, both Wright's 4th and Price's 3rd Flotillas, which had a confused brush with a large enemy force on a very black night, and then Macdonald on the 30th, were back in action. With the benefit of information obtained from German records, it is possible to piece together a clearer understanding of the unequal odds facing the five boats of the 21st which were sent to intercept a convoy off Ymuiden. Macdonald was leading in 241 with 224 and 244 in the first division, while the second division consisted of 223 and 350

(Henry Franklin in his new command, from the 11th Flotilla). The convoy was a far larger one than usual, with six 'steamers' (all named) and an escort numbering eighteen vessels. Sweeping ahead were eight R-boats of the 9th Flotilla. Astern of them came the minefield escort of four large M Class minesweepers of the 27th Flotilla, while close escort was provided by six Vps of the 8th and 11th Flotillas. Macdonald devised an approach that he hoped would allow him to penetrate the screen and make a zone torpedo attack on the rich harvest of shipping, by deploying the first division on the inshore bow of the northbound convoy, and the second on the seaward bow. Unfortunately they were sighted as they began the attack, and were met by very heavy fire from the R-boats and M Class ships. Macdonald disengaged to the north-west across the bow of the convoy, but 241 was hit underwater in the engine room by a very large shell – probably a 105mm from the Ms – and completely disabled. Macdonald transferred to 224 (Lee), leaving 244 (Saunders) attempting to tow 241 home stern-first.

Two more attacks were made – one a zone firing of six torpedoes – but the boats were kept at too great a range to be successful. Meanwhile, after 244 had towed 241 laboriously towards base for six hours, the tow parted. By this time, 241 was awash aft and had a heavy list to starboard. The tow was replaced but again parted, and at 0800, eight hours after the attack began, 241 rolled over and sank. Macdonald had commanded her since March 1942 – over two years – and felt her loss deeply. But the crew were all saved, to his relief.[10]

Operations in April 1944 were very greatly affected by the preparations for Operation Neptune. There were a few offensive patrols, usually vectored towards known shipping movements. Success was unlikely owing to the enemy's greater defensive power and numbers compared with the small offensive units pitted against them, just as in March. But this type of patrol was at this time assuming a lower priority than several other activities, all described in CCF Channel's report on Neptune several months later, but difficult to piece together chronologically.

The highest priority for every flotilla with boats to spare was the protection of the convoys plying east–west and west–east along the south coast, increasing by the day in both frequency and size as the material requirements for the great invasion were redistributed to their required destinations. The whole of southern Britain was becoming a seething mass of humanity on shore, and training in new skills required vast resources of every conceivable kind. The MTB flotillas were used to bolster the defensive screen against E-boat attack, joining destroyers and frigates to prevent any possibility of the successful torpedoing of precious ships and cargoes. Despite the acknowledged superiority of the E-boats' speed and sea-going qualities, the quality of the radar scanning and the skill of those marshalling the defensive forces managed to keep them at bay, but few were actually destroyed at this time. In the conclusion of his report much later in the year, CCF (Channel) bemoaned this difference in speed with as much vehemence as was felt by every MTB CO attempting unsuccessfully to intercept a fleeing E-boat.

Perhaps the most significant of all the new Coastal Forces' operating techniques proposed for Operation Neptune was the introduction of frigate control. MTB flotillas were to be allocated to specific groups of frigates, the leaders of which would carry Coastal Force Control Officers specially

[10] MO 4430; ADM 199/265; Search Document NHB.

Gun barrels being taken ashore for overhaul after an action by the 22nd Flotilla. (Courtesy IWM – A17973)

trained to interpret plots and convey orders to the MTBs. Very tight discipline was required to delineate the areas in which each group could operate to prevent confusion when the defence of the invasion's supply route, and ultimately the anchorage, would mean a very large number of vessels in close proximity. All this was going to need training for the officers and telegraphists, and exercises to make that training come alive. That process also began in April.

Yet another requirement was to build up the level of boat availability to a hitherto unknown level of readiness. This required the completion of repairs, the speedy execution of routine refits and engine overhauls, and the acceleration of the programme for the fitting of new equipment. Slotting in all these elements to the overall plan was no mean task for the planners, and throughout April and May 1944 it kept everyone on their toes. To cap it all, came the first directly operational tasks of the grand plan to be carried out by the MTBs – the laying of minefields. Some of this minelaying was carried out off the Dutch coast by the 21st and 22nd MTB Flotillas, although no detail is given in CCF (Channel)'s Report.

The vital tasks of routine minelaying and the establishment of new minefields in the Channel were shared between the Dog Boats of the 64th Flotilla and two flotillas of 'short' boats, Mark Arnold-Forster's 13th and David Shaw's 14th. The 13th had been operating from Dover, but were now ready to move as required; the 14th was moved on 14 April from Newhaven to *Hornet*. The whole minelaying operation was code-named

'Maple'. The 'short' boats laid ground mines, while the 64th laid moored mines. The two types of mines were designed to create a zone of danger and to deter not only E-boats and destroyers but also Torpedo Boats and larger ships.

Maple began on 18/19 April and the first lay was described as 'routine'. MTBs 246, 250 and 249 of the 14th Flotilla laid four mines each – presumably to reinforce an existing minefield rather than create a new field. Thereafter, between them the three flotillas were involved in laying fields off Le Havre (Scallops area), Cherbourg (Greengage area) and east of Cap d'Antifer (Peach area). None of the lays was free of hazard: simply having the mines on deck was risky if the lay was detected either by shore batteries or surface craft. It took time to make each lay with precision – which was essential if our own craft were not to be endangered. And, of course, the fields were always in positions where detection was probable rather than unlikely. The weather took a hand on several occasions, but in general lays were completed as ordered and to the great satisfaction of the planners. Between mid-April and 13 June Coastal Forces laid in the Channel a total of 334 moored mines and 228 ground mines; of the latter, the 13th laid 56 and the 14th 172. It was a very significant contribution to the success of Operation Overlord.[11]

Another facet of the preparations for Neptune concerned the imminent arrival of two new flotillas, which were to play very important parts during the next three months. They were in the final stages of their completion, working-up and absorbing special training for their tasks. They were briefly mentioned earlier, but a more detailed introduction is now justified.

[11] Report on Operation Overlord by CCF (Channel).

The 29th Flotilla had 71ft 6in British Power Boats and was manned entirely by Canadian officers and crews. The first eight boats (MTBs 459–466) were all completed during March and April 1944 and had every modification and improvement available at that time. The Senior Officer, Lt Cdr C.A. (Tony) Law had enjoyed a very long and varied career in MTBs, and had been Mentioned in Despatches when in command of MTB 48 in the action against the *Scharnhorst* and *Gneisenau* in February 1942. Later he had served for a year as CO of a Dog Boat. His divisional leader was Lt C.A. (Bones) Burk, an equally experienced and very aggressive CO. Early in April the first boats of the flotilla gathered for working-up at HMS *Bee*, which had transferred from Weymouth to Holyhead, away from the crowded south coast. By May they were established at Ramsgate, awaiting the final instructions on their role in Neptune.

The 35th Flotilla was also equipped with British Power Boats. The first eight boats had been completed between August and December 1943, but their working-up had been delayed by very bad weather. The flotilla gathered at Felixstowe, and had carried out only a few patrols – without actions – before being transferred to Newhaven, whence they patrolled off Cherbourg. Nearer to D-Day they were moved to Portsmouth, which was so crowded that *Hornet* used berthing facilities at both HMS *Dolphin* (the submarine base) and HMS *Vernon*, where the 35th was based.

The biggest advantage of most of these new boats was the great increase in their fire-power. Never before had fast 'short' MTBs been armed with torpedoes, a 6-pounder forward and two Oerlikons. The comparison with the boats which had begun the war was staggering to veterans like Tony Law.

These general considerations could not obscure the importance of offensive operations which, despite the demands on boats and personnel, were still continued throughout April and into May. The introduction of frigate control, and the rigours of being vectored to intercept known enemy movements, had increased the number of contacts in the eastern Channel but the strength of the escorts was still preventing conclusive results.

When May began it seemed that the pattern would continue, but on 7/8 May the Free French 23rd Flotilla at last seized an opportunity for close action and turned it into a successful attack. MTBs 91, 92, 227 and 239 were patrolling in pairs on a bright moonlit night off the coast of Jersey. At midnight a convoy was sighted, consisting of two cargo vessels, thought to be of 3,000 and 1,500 tons, escorted by a screen of eight patrol boats. The SO decided to move round the stern of the convoy in order to attack from the down-moon side, but suddenly the convoy altered course to enter St Peter Port.

It was now a case of making an immediate attack before it was too late, so the SO sent two boats to the up-moon side on full, noisy, power, drawing the attention of the escorts. The other boats were then able to fire four torpedoes. The main target, later identified as SS *Bizon*, was hit, blew up and sank. The shore batteries on Guernsey joined in, and 227 was damaged but got away. The other three boats attacked again, and four more torpedoes were fired at a group of escorts entering harbour. One hit was claimed.[12]

[12] MO 5778; Higgins, *The Free French at Kingswear.*

MTB 449 of the 35th Flotilla (note no torpedo tubes fitted) working up at HMS *Bee*, early 1944. (Courtesy IWM – A25314)

The semi-automatic feed on the Mark VII 6-pounder in MTB 467 of the 4th Flotilla, mid-1944. (Collection G.M. Hudson)

It is recorded that General de Gaulle was so delighted with the success of this operation that he visited the flotilla and presented each of the four boats with the Ordre de l'Armée, a decoration unique to the French Navy in that it is bestowed on a ship, not an individual. (Appendix 1, Note 14)

There were very few notable actions by the short boats in May, but on the 10th, units from the 3rd Flotilla (not fitted with torpedoes, and still acting as gunboats) and the 4th Flotilla were patrolling in company in the Schelde estuary area, near the island of Schouwen, when four trawlers were sighted in the path of the moon. The gunboats, led by John Price in 445, followed by 441, 443 and 438, attacked first and in a fierce engagement set one trawler on fire. As they disengaged, 438 was badly hit and disabled. It seemed that she would have to be abandoned, but the fire was brought under control and she was towed back to Lowestoft.

The 4th MTBs followed in to make their torpedo attack, led by Lt M.V. Rout RNZNVR in 458, followed by 467, 468 and 455. In the approach, 458 was hit in the engine room and dropped astern, but 467's torpedoes ran true and hit one of the trawlers, which broke in two and sank. No further hits were recorded. All the boats suffered damage, and sustained casualties, with one killed and three wounded.[13]

Even more significant to the preparations for the invasion, however, was the successful action

[13] MO 5933; ADM 199/265; WIR 19.5.44.

fought off Cherbourg on 11/12 May by the new 35th Flotilla led by Lt John Dudley Dixon, very soon after they had moved to Newhaven from Felixstowe. Dixon had served with Hichens in the 6th MGB Flotilla and proved to be a very similar type of commander. His unit on this first Channel patrol was 450, 453 (Lt Neil Watson RNZNVR) and 454 (Lt Eoin Glennie). Signals from the Portsmouth plot directed them to intercept unidentified vessels moving west from Cherbourg. They stopped to keep hydrophone watch and detected ships now moving east, so they took up a position closer to the entrance of Cherbourg harbour. After stalking for two hours, they finally sighted a line of four ships – two large trawlers, a large merchantman, and a fourth vessel, possibly another trawler.

Despite being in an up-moon position, Dixon decided he could not delay his attack any further, as the ships could so easily enter Cherbourg. 450 and 453 moved in to deliver a zone attack, and were able to close to 1,200 yards before heavy fire was met. They went on regardless, and fired four torpedoes at the largest target from 700 yards. A large tongue of flame erupted from her forecastle, and shortly after there was a further explosion and she keeled over to starboard.

At once Dixon split his force and disengaged, taking 450 to port to attack the trawlers and sending 454 and 453 to starboard to fire at the fourth in line. 450, with a 2-pounder Pom-Pom for'd, set the second trawler on fire, while the others, with their even more potent 6-pounders, savaged the last in line. All boats suffered damage and casualties: in 450 Dixon himself was wounded in both thighs, one of the crew was killed and five more (including two officers on the bridge) were injured. The CO of 453 and two of 454's crew were also wounded, one later dying of his wounds.

Both the CO of HMS *Aggressive* at Newhaven (who particularly praised Dixon's courage in bringing 450 back and steering her alongside even though painfully wounded) and Adm Charles Little, C-in-C Portsmouth, commended Dixon and the crews of his boats for the way in which the attack had been pressed home so gallantly.[14]

Although only one example of the clandestine operations which preceded the invasion is mentioned here, there is no doubt that a very large number of such operations were carried out on the coast of France in this period. Small parties of specially trained personnel were landed to check beaches, examine defences and generally reconnoitre any area where decisions had to be made about their suitability for action. A typical operation was carried out on 15/16 May by a unit of the 5th MTB Flotilla, recently re-formed with new boats under Lt Roland Plugge RN.

His orders were to take two boats, 354 and 359 (Lt A.W.A. Rickards), to a point just north of the Somme estuary between Dieppe and Boulogne, land a small military party of two officers and four other ranks, and then three hours later to pick them up again and return to Dover. Code-named Operation Tarbrush 8, it required not only iron nerves to remain close inshore for so long, but also extremely precise navigation. The new device known as QH made accurate navigation much simpler than had hitherto been possible. Every aspect of the operation went perfectly, despite worries about the weather. The party landed by dory and rubber dinghy from a predetermined anchored position, the signalling routine ensured safe homing back to the MTB, and her hydrophone picked up the dory engine five minutes before the tiny craft returned. By 0550 the landing party was back in Dover, making the report on its findings.[15]

[14] MO 6493; ADM 199/261; WIR 19.5.44.

[15] ROP held by the author.

The crew of a Flying Fortress of the USAAF with the officers of MTB 245, who picked them up in the North Sea, June 1944. (Courtesy D.E.J. Hunt)

The Free French 23rd Flotilla based at Dartmouth had another success on 19/20 May when after lying in wait west of Jersey, MTB 90 torpedoed a stationary trawler and damaged its partner with gunfire. In the next few days there were contacts and brushes with the enemy further east on several occasions, including a first clash for the Canadian 29th, but none was significant until 23/24 May when the 13th and 14th Flotillas took time off from their vital minelaying tasks to score a notable success against a formidable group of ships.

Mark Arnold-Forster had with him 209 (Lt J.Y. Ferguson) and 208 (Lt P. Liddell), while David Shaw had 246 (Sub Lt C.D. Cobb) and 247 (Sub Lt I. Brett). They had been escorting minelaying MLs when they were vectored to attack a patrol of five Torpedo Boats and three minesweepers, all heavily armed. Aircraft were to make a coordinated attack. Fortune was with 208 and 209 who found themselves in a position to make an unobserved approach and fire a spread of torpedoes, whereas 246 and 247 received such a barrage that they had to withdraw rapidly. 208 hit and sank one Torpedo Boat, but 209's torpedoes did not run true.[16]

The stirring story of the next three months in the Channel, during which a vast army of Allied soldiers was carried across to Normandy, landed, supplied and defended from attack is best told in a new chapter. The *Dramatis Personae* have now been introduced, but the twists and turns of the plot have still to be revealed.

[16] MO 6783; ADM 199/264.

CHAPTER 10

JUNE TO AUGUST 1944 – OPERATION NEPTUNE

The Portsmouth Operational Orders for this operation were issued on 30 May under a Top Secret heading, and went first to every naval authority involved, including the Senior Officers of five MTB flotillas. The flotillas that fell under the operational command of Vice Admiral Dover and C-in-C Plymouth received their orders separately from their own authorities, but all came under the coordinating umbrella of CCF (Channel).

Quite apart from the C Class MGBs, the SGBs, the MLs and the HDMLs, which all had their parts to play – many of them very significant – there were eventually fifteen MTB flotillas involved, and they were later joined by two squadrons of USN Patrol Torpedo Boats. This made a total of 158 boats, 71 of them 'short' MTBs, 57 D Boats, and 30 PTs – the largest group of MTBs ever deployed in one operation.

Naturally, in the interests of security, no date was promulgated for D-Day or H-Hour, but the orders covered every aspect of the rigorous planning for the assault and its support for as many weeks or months as necessary. Boundaries were clearly laid down for the responsibilities of each Command. Perhaps the most significant special information was the carefully delineated cross-Channel convoy route from a position south-east of the Isle of Wight to the mouth of the Baie de la Seine, fed by routes from the east and west, and from the eastern and western entrances to the Solent. This channel was known as the 'Spout', and the major task for the MTBs was clearly going to be the prevention of attacks on it by any enemy forces, but most particularly by E-boats and whatever larger ships (Torpedo Boats and destroyers) the enemy could throw against this vital artery. This was not to be a purely defensive role: wherever possible, E-boats would be intercepted as they left their home ports or made their way towards their targets. Le Havre in the east and Cherbourg in the west were well-established bases with concrete E-boat pens, and they were already well known to the flotillas.

In general, boats based in Portsmouth were at first assigned to the protection of the western flank of the 'Spout'. HMS *Hornet*, despite being a major (and essential) administrative and repair base since the earliest days of Coastal Forces, had rarely hosted more than one flotilla, but now it was having to accommodate as many as nine. Arrangements were made for HMS *Dolphin*, the submarine base, to provide berthing and maintenance facilities for Dog Boats, while HMS *Vernon* housed its share of 'short' boats. Dover and Newhaven boats were responsible for the eastern flank, while Plymouth Command, which operated the flotillas from Dartmouth and Brixham, would cover the approaches from the west, assisted by Portsmouth as required.

The implication of these arrangements for the MTBs in their offensive rather than defensive mode was that the E-boat flotillas in their two main Channel bases at Le Havre

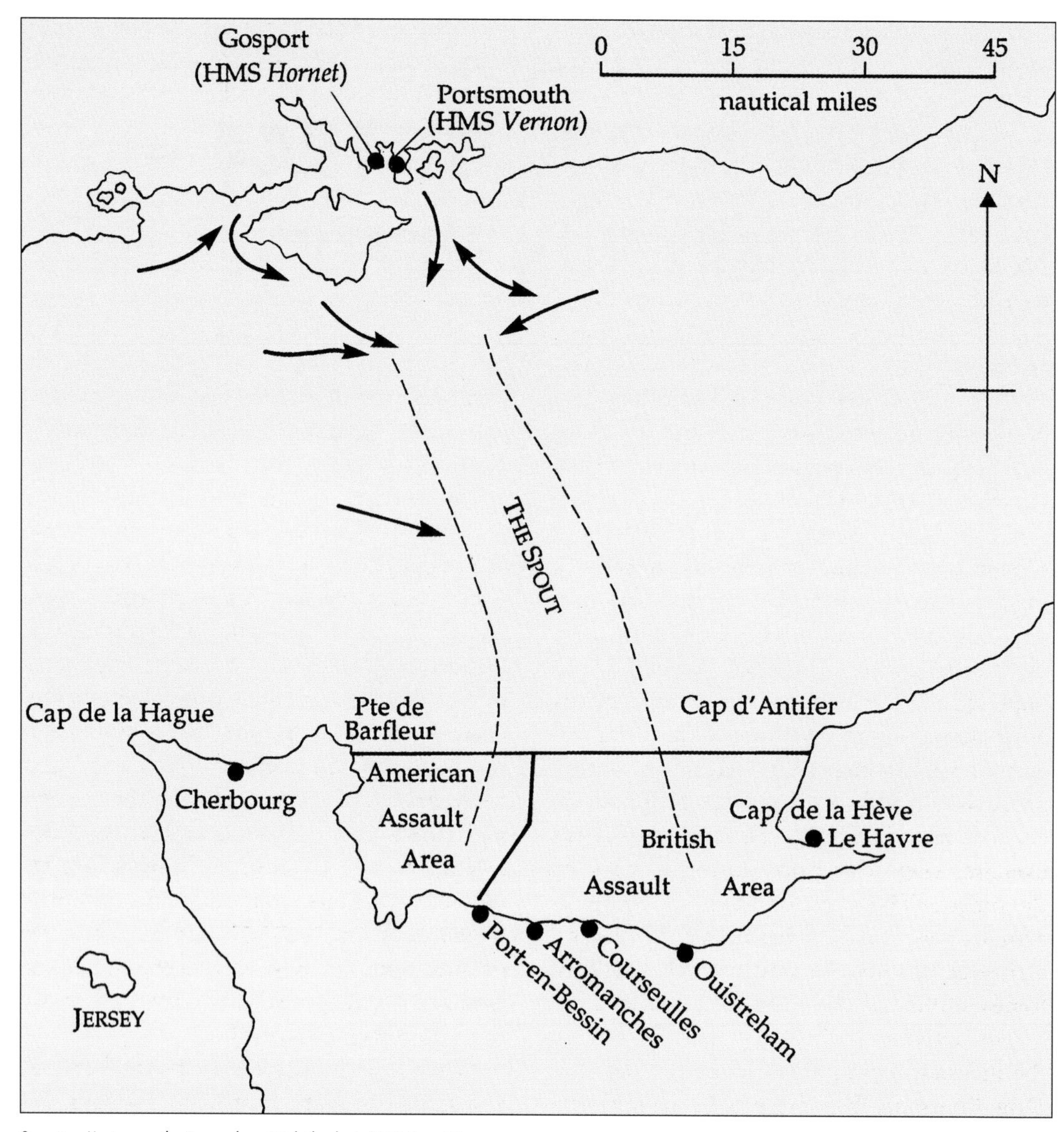

Operation Neptune – the Approaches. (With thanks to CCF's Report.)

and Cherbourg would be their main concern. They would not be hovering as a last line of defence, but actively intercepting the E-boats in the most favourable positions for attack, as directed by the control frigates. Training in frigate control had proceeded during May, and was to prove very valuable, providing constantly updated information from the expertly run plot in each of the frigates. In the event it was also essential in avoiding clashes with our own forces.

On each side of the 'Spout', frigates would patrol along a defensive line (the 'frigate line') as ordered, with MTBs attached. The Senior Officers' frigates acted as the control ships for each area, receiving reports from the other frigates, collating them on the plot and passing orders to the MTBs by either R/T or

W/T. Major exercises were held on both sides of the 'Spout', and the team of Coastal Forces COs trained as Control Officers was expanded, with Lt R.G.O. (Guy) Hudson and Lt C.J. (Cedric) Wright DSC attached to the frigates of the eastern line, and Lt P.G. (Philip) Lee DSC* and Lt H.A.J. (Tony) Hollings DSC RN to those on the western flank. All were well known in the close-knit circle of MTB and MGB officers, and this fact contributed greatly to the successful introduction of a new and complex system that could so easily have brought as much confusion as help.[1]

One of the last exercises to be held by the Naval Commander Eastern Task Force (NCETF) was designed to test the defence organization planned for the far shore once the expeditionary force had been established. The exercise involved the Canadian 29th Flotilla, together with the C and D Class boats, some of which were designated enemy craft attempting to penetrate. CCF (Channel) later remarked that an interesting situation arose when real E-boats were found to be active some 20 miles to the south during the exercise. They were held and turned back by the outer MTB screen, and the mock E-boats actually penetrated further than the real ones, although it must be said that the defence forces refrained from opening fire on them.

The activities of the Dog Boat flotillas in the invasion period are described in detail in *Dog Boats at War*, with a brief acknowledgement of the work of the 'short' MTBs and of the MLs and HDMLs. In this book, the emphasis is reversed. In the initial stages the 55th Flotilla of Ds, led by Lt Cdr D.G. Bradford RNR, worked closely in the east with Tony Law's Canadian 29th Flotilla, while Lt Cdr David Wilkie's 64th Flotilla of D Boats joined with David Shaw's 14th Flotilla in the minelaying role.

[1] Report of CCF (Channel).

These four flotillas featured strongly on the night before D-Day (5/6 June), although other flotillas were patrolling to the east and west. The two groups had very different roles, but in the 'Spout' itself the minesweeping MLs and the HDMLs (acting as navigational leaders) were in the van of the whole enterprise, and should be accorded their proper place in history. There was even a group of HDMLs in a very vulnerable position close inshore in the Pas de Calais, playing a vital part in the deception plan with their 'radar-spoofing' operation. (Appendix 1, Note 15)

On the eastern flank, close in, the 29th was required to provide a unit to protect the minesweepers. Law describes how on the previous day he and his divisional leader, Lt C.A. Burk (nicknamed 'Bones' at Lowestoft because of his strange cries when rolling dice, though after becoming a father, he was known as 'Daddy' Burk throughout the flotilla), had travelled to Fort Southwick to be briefed. They learned that the weather had already delayed the operation, and that D-Day was now to be 6 June, when the whole enormous and complex timetable would click into action. Their part in it was detailed and they now carried the ponderous weight of responsibility for the most significant secret of their lives.

When 5 June arrived, it dawned as dull and miserable as the previous two days. But the die was cast – whatever the weather, there could now be no pulling back. The order to go had been given and the Armada would sail at various times during the day, ready to land the next day. Law had divided his flotilla into two divisions to enable some form of rotation for patrols. On the first night the boats on duty were Burk in 461 and 464 (Lt Craig Bishop). They set off in the late afternoon into a Channel which looked less inviting than ever before – it was extremely rough, and even for hardened small boat sailors it was really grim. They thought of all the soldiers who would also be making this voyage, and wondered how they would ever be able to fight if their landing was strongly opposed.

Burk was back the next morning, showing all the signs of strain about the outcome of the landing operation and of weariness after a night of being soaked and battered by sea and wind. His story was almost unbelievable. He told of hundreds of aircraft droning inexorably overhead to bomb every coastal defence target and military installation over a tremendously broad front during a quiet night with no interference whatsoever from the enemy's surface ships or aircraft, and he described the safe delivery of the shock troops to the beaches. It seemed that total surprise had been achieved. The poor weather had led the German High Command to believe that no landing could possibly take place while the deception strategies had been so successful that the main defence forces were concentrated further east. The Allies had achieved the apparently impossible.

The task facing David Shaw's 14th Flotilla was totally different. Written into the master plan as Operation Monastic, it involved the laying of the last protective minefield, which had been left to the last minute. The lay was off Cap d'Antifer to the north of Le Havre, and Shaw was more concerned about the weather than about the enemy. His unit consisted of his own 250, with 251, 248 and 249. He confessed that the sea was far too rough for his boats, but knowing that this

Rough passage! The sea state on D-Day. (Source unknown)

task was the most important of all they had carried out over the preceding months, they simply could not turn back. The lay was, in fact, carried out successfully, but tragedy struck as they reformed to return to base. In the heavy seas 248 (Lt Brian McGinty) collided first with 249 and then with 251, and sank. All the crew were safely taken off and shortly after they took over another boat.[2]

On the morning of D-Day, 6 June, as the British landings proceeded at pace on the most easterly beaches, the first surface intervention took place. The Mowe Class Torpedo Boats from Le Havre sailed towards the 'Spout' but were intercepted and held by destroyers; they did not affect the progress of the landings at all. (Appendix 1, Note 16)

The 29th, this time with Law's division of 459, 460 (Killam), 465 (Chaffey) and 466 (Marshall), set out at 1400 on 6 June, and saw the whole vast invasion force as they raced past on their way to the Assault Area. There were ships of every size and shape, the merchant ships with barrage balloons overhead and the landing craft wallowing in great discomfort. Then the traffic began to be two-way, as the first wave returned empty. They eventually found their Control Ship, HMS *Scylla* – the flagship of the Eastern Task Force – and snatched some sleep before being briefed by Lt Pat Edge, the Admiral's Coastal Forces staff officer. They were to patrol close to Lt Bradford's 55th off Le Havre. For several hours they saw nothing, but suddenly the situation changed: the 55th sent an enemy sighting report and began an attack. As Law closed him, he sighted a group of six vessels and speedily reduced the range until he could identify them as R-boats. A furious battle ensued, with the four Pom-Poms and every other gun that could be brought to bear pouring shells into each R-boat in turn. One certainly exploded and others were set on fire, but 459 and 466 both suffered serious casualties among the gun crews, and all four received damage in the close-range encounter. (MO 11301)

Another hazard became apparent as they disengaged. Mines began to detonate around them and they realized that in the heat of battle they had strayed into the British Scallops minefield. They carefully extricated themselves and set off to find *Scylla* and get medical attention for the wounded. The first two hospital ships were already overcrowded with casualties, but eventually they were sent to an LST with hospital facilities, and with great difficulty passed over their wounded.

At last they could snatch some sleep, berthed alongside a merchant ship, but soon they were directed to go alongside *Scylla*, where Adm Vian, the Naval Commander of the Eastern Task Force, wished to see the COs. He congratulated them on their action and wished them well. Pat Edge then told them they were free until 1700, so once again they found a resting place and got what sleep they could against the constant roar of gunfire from the battleships and cruisers bombarding targets ashore.

Over on the western flank, the only engagement on the night of 6/7 June involved a two-boat unit of the 35th Flotilla. Lt R.T. Sykes as SO in 448 had 478 (Ashby) in company and was patrolling off Barfleur in much the same unpleasant weather as the 29th encountered further east. The unit was vectored by its control frigate HMS *Stayner* to a point closer to shore, where they found two boats lying stopped. When challenged, both boats replied with the correct letter and both switched on the correct mast display before moving off westward. Unconvinced, Rodney Sykes decided to close and take a clearer visual sighting. At about 50 yards, he recognized them as E-boats and opened fire,

[2] Report of CCF (Channel); MO 7417.

MTB 447 (Lt E.C. Glennie) of the 35th Flotilla. (Courtesy R. Wrayton)

securing numerous hits. The enemy made smoke and set off to the west and then south, being pursued and driven into the Greengage Plus minefield.

448 had some superficial damage. Sykes concluded that the apparent knowledge of recognition signals must either mean the Germans were in possession of those signals for the relevant period or that they had means of decoding such information. He also reported that pounding into heavy seas had rendered his Type 291 radar unserviceable, which had made it impossible to hold contact with an enemy unwilling to join action. (MO 13001)

The night of 7/8 June was much busier, as might have been expected, given that the enemy had had time to assess his options and tactics. Sent back to the same area as on the previous night, the 29th encountered the Mowe Class Torpedo Boats: as their torpedo tubes had been replaced by depth charges they could only do their best in a valiant gun attack, but their armament was unlikely to cause more than superficial damage. (MO 3001)

Meanwhile several two-boat units of the 35th were off Barfleur, two of which met E-boat patrols seeking a path through to attack the convoy route. The first pair, 453 (Watson) leading, with 447 (Glennie), sighted a total of seventeen and found that in the calm conditions the 71ft 6in boats could match the speed of the E-boats. In four separate actions they engaged ten of them – four were claimed as severely damaged, their speed being reduced and guns silenced. One was set on fire aft. The 6-pounder and 2-pounder guns gave them far greater fire-power than MTBs had ever had before. Neil Watson was ordered to break off ···ack by the control frigate *Stayner*, but ··· ·ggrieved as he felt that ···uld have been ···aged, but not

···John Collins in ··· company, was ··· to five E-boats ···, made smoke and ···tempting to avoid ··· to illuminate them, ··· weapon, and two of ···aged before getting ···O 7417)

··· together with the ···Boats, frigates and ···that despite numerous ··· no effect on the build- ··· far shore.

···inued at much the same ···nd the wisdom of rotating ···y proved itself for both the ···Antifer and the 35th off Barfleur. Burk was back out with his three boats (461, 462 and 463), and although they lost track of a group of E-boats in worsening weather, the rough seas forced them to return to Le Havre. Burk was then able, like Law the night before, to mount an attack on two Mowes. He inflicted some hits, but faced withering return fire; casualties mounting (464 had one killed), they were forced to disengage under smoke. (MO 13001)

Over at Barfleur the SO of the 35th, John Dudley Dixon, was leading a fresh unit – 450 and 478 (Warren) – and was vectored to intercept five E-boats. Despite the heavy seas they sighted them and closed to less than 300 yards, engaging the leading three before they turned south and escaped under smoke. There they were intercepted by Ds of the 53rd, and forced to return to Cherbourg. (MO 7417)

After this period of feverish activity in the Channel, the flotillas, had a brief respite on 9/10 June when the only contact for the patrols was an inconclusive brush with the enemy. However, on the 10th a unit of the 35th was involved in a fierce battle with several E-boats. Although the night's SO Lt Rodney Sykes (448) later made an amplifying report, the main narrative was supplied by Lt Neil Watson RNZNVR (453). As soon as the E-boats were sighted, Sykes attacked at full speed with the intention of making a depth charge attack as he cut through their line, to complete the first gun attack. He wanted to ensure that the E-boats had no chance of making their escape and to force them into a decisive action. 448 passed only a few yards astern of the first E-boat, and a similar distance ahead of the second, and Sykes let his depth charge go, seeing it explode very close abeam of the second target. Both E-boats had taken considerable damage, particularly from the Pom-Pom fire, but 448 was then hit by several 40mm shells below the waterline and she began to settle and lose way. 453 continued to fire at the second and third E-boats, expending 70 6-pounder shells and 400 Oerlikon rounds, many of which hit. All three E-boats appeared to be in distress.

453 took off 448's crew, two of whom were wounded, and a war correspondent who had been killed, before sinking 448 by gunfire as her scuttling charge had failed. She then transferred 448's survivors to HMS *Stayner* before joining a unit of Ds – the 53rd Flotilla led by Lt Cdr McCowen DSO – which attacked a further four E-boats. One of them was stopped, disabled and on fire, and 453 was sent in to pick up survivors. Five were found and the unwounded prisoners handed over to HMS *Duff* before 453 returned to Portsmouth at best speed to land the wounded at Haslar. It was by now 0745, the end of an exhausting and eventful night during which at least one E-boat had been

The devastating effects of the RAF's massive raid on Le Havre on 14/15 June 1944 in which fourteen E-boats were destroyed. This attack altered the balance of the Coastal Forces campaign in the Channel. (Collection G.M. Hudson)

sunk and three more severely damaged. (MO 7417)

On the same night three boats of the Free French 23rd Flotilla attacked an enemy patrol off Sark. MTB 98 fired her torpedoes at 300 yards but did not claim a hit. Her two officers were both wounded.

The records show that over the next three nights the flotillas were active but had no positive encounters, and on the night of 14/15 June the RAF mounted a devastating raid on Le Havre, especially targeting the E-boat pens. It was so successful that not only were the pens rendered unusable, but 14 E-boats, 3 Möwe Class Torpedo Boats and 17 other minesweepers and escort vessels were destroyed or sunk. It was a crippling blow and for the next seven days and nights there was no enemy activity in the Assault Area.[3]

This was a crucial time for the E-boats in the Channel. Not only had they lost a large proportion of their battle-hardened boats at Le Havre, but at the same time, one of their most experienced Senior Officers was killed and another wounded. To cap that disaster, the US Army was closing in on Cherbourg and it would not be long before it fell. The German Naval Command wasted no time: the remaining E-boats in Cherbourg were sailed to reinforce Le Havre, but were turned back by destroyers. The 2nd S-boat Flotilla was

[3] Rohwer & Hummelchen, *Chronology of the War at Sea*.

moved to Le Havre from Boulogne, and E-boats from Ostend began to operate through the Dover Strait into the invasion area. The Germans were desperate not to have any E-boats caught in Cherbourg, so they were sailed first to St-Malo and then to Alderney.[4]

The setbacks were not all on the enemy side. A fierce storm raged from 19 to 22 June, and conditions in the Assault Area became untenable. Even within the Mulberry harbours, which had been constructed from robust pontoons to provide sheltered water for anchorages, many smaller ships dragged anchor and were driven ashore.

On the night of 23/24 June the enemy evacuated Cherbourg, but lurking outside was the 14th Flotilla, whose two divisions made short work of attacking some comparatively innocuous targets. Lt G.H. Baker in 250, leading the second division of 249 (Oldfield) and 251 (Morrish), scored torpedo hits on two coasters, a trawler and a tug, while the first division, led by the SO with 254 (Rigg), 255 (Aspinall) and 257 (Hawkes), followed up with more hits. Only one coaster attempted to get away, and that was sunk by McCowen's Ds.[5]

Within a very short space of time, the whole naval situation in the Channel had changed. The threat from the west was now confined to the possibility of U-boat attacks, which were not regarded as a Coastal Forces' responsibility, or from the destroyers at present hemmed in to their Atlantic ports – Brest and Lorient – by blockading British destroyers. It was now possible for more boats to be deployed to reinforce the eastern flank and to assist in nullifying the main threat, the E-boat base at Le Havre, now reinforced by fresh flotillas, despite the destruction of pens and loss of personnel.

[4] Rohwer & Hummelchen, *Chronology of the War at Sea.*

[5] MO 8082; ADM 199/262.

Throughout the whole of June this feverish activity was concentrated in the Channel, but the east coast flotillas had not been idle. They continued to patrol relentlessly whenever the strangely fickle weather of this momentous month allowed, but until 24/25 June there had not been any action of note by the short boats. On that night, 444, 440 and 441 of the 3rd MTBs – built as 71ft 6in MGBs – found four heavily armed trawlers off the West Schelde. Concentrating on the rearmost two of the group, they made a series of six gun attacks despite heavy fire, and even tried, unsuccessfully, to make a depth charge attack. They left both trawlers severely mauled and one on fire, at the unexpectedly small expense of superficial damage and one man wounded.

There were several brushes with the enemy in both the eastern and western areas of the Channel as June turned into July. The 1st Flotilla repelled an E-boat raid, and the 9th from Dover were also involved. The Canadian 29th had been maintaining a constant presence in the Assault Area, and had sustained a number of casualties. All the boats were suffering from hull and propeller damage from floating debris, but somehow relief craft were always found when boats had to return to Portsmouth for repairs. On successive days, 459 (Law's own boat) damaged two propellers, and then came the tragic news that 460 (Lt David Killam DSC) had been sunk by a mine, and only six survivors had been picked up. Both officers (Killam and Howard Hunt) were killed. This was a great shock to the newly formed flotilla which had already developed very strong close relationships. It seemed that the enemy's new pressure mines were already taking their toll, and it took some time for all the crews to quell their apprehension as they crossed the sea areas in which they were most vulnerable. Within a week of the loss of 460, 463 (Creba) was also mined, although all the crew were taken off before she sank. The 29th were certainly suffering.

By now most of the 29th had had their torpedo tubes replaced, and felt much more comfortable. They resumed the patrols off Le Havre, and soon found themselves facing constant bombardment from the coastal batteries. On 4/5 July Law's division was operating with two Dog Boats of the 55th Flotilla when they met nine E/R-boats and several M Class minesweepers. The 'shorts' damaged three of the E/R-boats, the Ds finishing off two with torpedoes, and their heavy armament left two Ms and another R-boat crippled. It was a profitable encounter.

News came through of a particularly fine action off Terschelling involving the 21st Flotilla, now led by Lt G.J. Macdonald, at twenty-one the youngest flotilla SO ever appointed. He had been tireless in his patrolling but targets since the invasion had dried up. On the night of 4/5 July he took out a five-boat unit, with 234 now back in the lead, followed by 224, 225, 232 and 244. They found a convoy by radar, tracked it and then attacked. The strong escort fought them off, and the convoy was led into the safe harbour in West Gat. Macdonald split his force into two divisions and continued to search, and his group met a second convoy upon which they made a zone attack with a spread of six torpedoes at 1,000 yards. One coaster was hit and left in flames. The second division then attacked individually from inshore and claimed a hit on one of the escorts at 1,800 yards.

Briefly at ease in the Assault Area, June 1944. Left to right: Lt Cam Gough (416), Lt F. Head (414) and Sub Lt G. Baptie (1st Lt 416) on the bridge of 416 of the 1st Flotilla. (Courtesy F.S. Large)

Macdonald thought that these two could be regarded as sunk, and this was confirmed by air reconnaissance. Surprisingly, enemy radio admitted that in fact vessels had been sunk. Macdonald was awarded a DSO to add to the DSC and two Bars already won during the previous two years of constant patrolling and action.

One of the flotillas to be transferred from the western flank to operate off Cap d'Antifer in the blockade of Le Havre was John Dudley Dixon's 35th, which had been in the thick of the action off Cherbourg as the main strike force in that area. The second division, led by John Collins (like all Collinses in the Navy, he was always called 'Jumper'), was out on the night of 7/8 July with the 55th, accompanied by 463 (Creba) of the 29th on the night she was sunk. It was about this time that the enemy began to use human torpedoes of several designs. On the first night they appeared, a wave of these new weapons achieved some success by virtue of surprise, but thereafter the destroyers and Coastal Force boats had their measure and large numbers were sunk.

The most unusual feature of the complex pattern of patrolling on the 7th was that Collins' unit of the 35th had two completely separate actions, each as the result of vectoring by frigate control. The first, at 0127, was against a group of three E-boats 8 miles off Cap d'Antifer. Collins' boats (451 and 447) were at first able to close them and engage, but the E-boats increased to maximum speed and began to draw ahead, and the action turned into a chase. The rearmost E-boat was hit, but not decisively, and the boats were recalled to the frigate.

At about 0230 they were sent off again to a position further out from Cap d'Antifer, and almost at once met four more E-boats. This time the range was much closer – down to 150 yards when fire was exchanged. The E-boats repeatedly altered course but Collins kept them in range, and two of the E-boats were heavily damaged. Return fire of 37mm and 20mm calibre was heavy and accurate, and suddenly disaster struck. At almost the same moment, Eoin Glennie in 447 was wounded in the face and blinded by blood, while 451 in the lead sustained a hit on the bridge which killed the SO John Collins and wounded everyone on the bridge except the coxswain. As he fell, Collins must have caught the throttle. The combination of the two incidents led to a collision in which 447 sustained such damage that she had to be towed back to base with the help of Dog Boats.[6]

Lt Cdr G.J. Macdonald DSO DSC** RNZNVR, CO MTB 234 and SO 21st Flotilla. (Courtesy J.S. Hawkins)

That casualties and boat losses were mounting is hardly surprising in retrospect, as

[6] MO 8082; ADM 199/262.

Lt D.E.J. Hunt DSC*, of MTB 245 in the 22nd Flotilla and later SO of the 31st Flotilla. (Collection L.C. Reynolds)

the intensity of operations caused by the concentration of enemy forces and their relentless detection and interception far exceeded any previous period. In the first month of Operation Neptune there had been fifty-six actions in the Channel, despite the bad weather in mid-June and the reduction in enemy activity in the week after the bombing of Le Havre.

This inevitability was not readily accepted by the comrades of those who were lost, and of course the steady reduction in numbers of boats available caused concern to Senior Officers. But the speed of repairs exceeded anything previously known, and already a new flotilla (Peter Magnus's 30th MTBs) was ready to join the fray and replacement boats were coming from the boat yards. The British Power Boats yard at Hythe was completing boats at an unprecedented rate, although the Admiralty, with an eye to economy, was keeping new orders under constant review, ready to reduce them as soon as the operational need began to wane.

The activity in the North Sea, although much quieter than that in the Channel in terms of contacts with the enemy, continued, with a special eye on the prevention of reinforcements sailing southward towards the Strait of Dover. On 8/9 July a unit of the 22nd Flotilla, led by Lt D.E.J. Hunt in 245 with 93, 88 and 238, met and attacked a superior force of armed trawlers off Scheveningen. The return fire was very heavy, but 238 and 88 fired their torpedoes independently, and hit and sank one of the targets. In a second attack 245 and 93 made a zone attack under fire, and secured two more hits with the newly available CCR pistols fitted to their torpedoes. (Appendix 1, Note 17)

245 suffered a hit by a shell on the waterline at the bow and began to settle. Determined to save her if it was possible, Douglas Hunt got under way stern first; when it became possible, 93 towed her that way over the wide expanse of the North Sea at 5 knots. As the weather worsened, the water crept over the deck for'd. An ML took over the tow, and later the base at Felixstowe sent out a tug to bring her in. She arrived at 1900, totally awash after twenty hours of towing, but she lived to fight another day. She was finally paid off in December.[7]

On the same night it was business as usual in the Assault Area. Law in 459, with 461 and 464, were lying about 3 miles off shore between Le Havre and Cap d'Antifer. John

[7] MO 8152; ADM 199/266.

MTBs 415 and 431 at (comparative) rest on a line from a battleship off the Mulberry harbour, June 1944. (Courtesy F.S. Large)

Mathias with 430 and 434 (Archer) of the 1st Flotilla – originally members of Hichens' renowned 8th MGB Flotilla and still operating as gunboats – lay 7 miles to the north. It soon became apparent that the gunboats were in action, and Law moved northward to help. As they approached, they could see that one of them (434) was on fire and surrounded by R-boats. 430 had also been damaged and could not get near enough to do more than pick up one group of survivors, including the CO, Eric Archer.

The 29th came roaring in, using 461 ('Daddy' Burk) to lay a smokescreen, and attacked the R-boats furiously. 459 was hit by a 37mm shell in the coxswain's cabin, but the R-boats backed off far enough to permit those survivors clinging to two Carley floats to be picked up. Several were wounded. The Canadian boats then made a hasty departure and set off to find help for the wounded. This took far longer than expected. Eventually, after being sent on by the designated hospital ship which had no room to take them, they appealed for help from the battleship HMS *Rodney*, which took them all and looked after them royally. At last the Canadian boats, escorting the damaged 430, were able to make their way back to HMS *Vernon*.

Eric Archer, the CO of 434, later supplied more detail of her loss. In the first run in to attack he found himself engaged heavily by each R-boat as he passed along the line, and it was not long before the Oerlikon magazine was hit, causing a fire directly over the fuel tanks:

> To disengage I increased speed but although it took 434 away from the

> R-boats, the airstream made the ship into a blowtorch: but this was, I thought, preferable to being shot to pieces. As soon as I thought we were out of range I stopped and evacuated the engine room, operating the remote control methyl bromide extinguishers in both that area and the tank space, but to no avail. There was no choice but to abandon ship. John [Mathias] came back and picked up four or five of us. The remainder of the crew were nowhere to be seen. Stoker Haywood had been killed and several others wounded. I did not discover until long afterwards that it was Tony Law who saved the rest of the crew.[8]

Although the number of actions in the Nore Command could not compare with the feverish activity in the Channel, whenever the patrols met the enemy they were becoming more and more successful, even against larger and more heavily armed ships. The 4th MTB Flotilla, successors of the 7th MGBs, and led at this time by 'Jake' Wright, proved this on 13/14 July in an action off Ymuiden. In heavy seas and low visibility, he took out a very large group, seven of the eight boats under his command at Lowestoft. Finding a patrol of three armed trawlers he made his approach from astern, but was detected in dazzling phosphorescence. Six of his boats were able to make independent attacks. 458 (Wright) and 467 (R.R. Crosley) fired at the leading trawler and sank it, watching as it blew up, and 469 (A.A. Podd) also secured a hit. The calm manner in which Wright carried out the attack in difficult conditions brought him a second Bar to his DSC. Several of the boats were damaged, and the unit had two killed and two wounded.[9]

[8] MO 10117; Law, *White Plumes Astern*; notes from Eric Archer.

[9] MO 8159; ADM 199/266; N.W. Gerhard; *Seedie's List of Coastal Forces Awards.*

As predicted, the 30th Flotilla had arrived at Portsmouth to reinforce the hard-pressed boats on the nightly blockade of Le Havre and to protect the Allied anchorage from attacks from the east. One feature of Peter Magnus' flotilla was that four of his COs were vastly experienced, having served with distinction for two years in the Mediterranean. Lt The Hon F.M.A. Shore in 474, Lt D.D. Owen-Pawson in 472, Lt J.J. Aimers in 473 and Lt R. Campbell RCNVR in 480 all featured in *Mediterranean MTBs at War* in the campaigns along the North African coast off Tunisia, then in the invasion of Sicily and in the Italian campaign. It said a great deal for their dedication that they were once again in the thick of the fray.

Freddie Shore led the first unit of the flotilla to meet the enemy, off Cap d'Antifer on 14/15 July, with Ross Campbell and Jeff Aimers. They were vectored to a group of E-boats which fled as soon as the attack began, and it never developed beyond a brief long-range skirmish. Their turn would come again. (MO 8082)

On the same night the second division of the 29th, led by Burk, was off Le Havre. They found two M Class minesweepers escorted by eight E/R-boats, fired four torpedoes and engaged in a brisk gun action. Having sustained some serious casualties, they returned to their control frigate, where they were told that one of the 'M's had disappeared from the radar screen after their torpedo attack. (MO 10117)

A different challenge faced Law and his division on 16/17 July, when after an active night enemy aircraft dropped flares over the unit about 3 miles off Cap de La Heve, and the shore batteries began a relentless barrage, culminating in a direct hit on the engine room of 459 (Law's own boat), leaving a hole 14ft long the full height of the ship's side. She began to settle, but 466 was able to tow her back to HMS *Duff*, which held her alongside

An MTB passes the 'Pens' at Dover approaching the berths in the Submarine Basin. (Courtesy D. Ridgeon)

secured with a steel hawser, until a salvage vessel could take her away in the morning. Two of the engine room crew had died.

More and more flotillas were now entering the fray, and on 16/17 there were no fewer than five actions, including two by the 2nd and 5th Flotillas from Dover, and the 35th led by Dixon off Cap d'Antifer, in addition to or in conjunction with D Boats of three different flotillas. And so it went on, night after night, and despite damage to boats and casualties, the pressure was kept up and there were no major successes by the enemy in getting through to the Anchorage.

A CFMU (Coastal Forces Mobile Unit) was established at Arromanches under the watchful eye of Cdr M.A. Brind RN, previously the base CO at Yarmouth, and this enabled some boats to avoid having to return to Portsmouth for repairs. A lull during eight nights of bad weather provided a breather from 19–26 July, except for another battle with E-boats for Shore's unit of the 30th Flotilla on 22/23 July.

On the night of the 26th John Mathias was leading a unit of the 1st Flotilla in 430, with 412 and 431 in support, off Cap d'Antifer, and intercepted six E-boats. Mathias led his boats at speed through the E-boats' line; in the process, 430 was rammed by S 182 and blew up. 412 (Salmon) following in close order astern, could not avoid colliding with the wreckage of 430 and suffered so much damage to her hull that she too had to be sunk later. However, S 182 also sank, and in the gun attack one other E-boat was severely damaged. Ten of 430's crew were missing and the total casualties other than these were one killed (Sub Lt D. Okey), and eight wounded.[10]

On the same night, the second division – or rather the five remaining boats – of the Canadian 29th had their last action in the Assault Area before being withdrawn after seven weeks of continuous fighting. With 'Daddy' Burk leading, they found the usual group of M Class ships with their numerous R-boat escorts, and made a visual zone firing followed by a gun attack. They believed that one M was hit by a torpedo, and that one of the R-boats was severely damaged. (MO 10117)

The latest reinforcements to be transferred from the western flank to Portsmouth for operations in the east were six USN PT boats. They had the considerable advantage over their British counterparts of far more advanced radar sets, although this was less significant than in the Mediterranean, because in the Channel, operations were controlled by frigates with even more powerful sets. The PTs arrived on 4 August, and were soon into action when on 5/6 August three Elco boats led by Lt McSwan USNR in PT 510, with 512 and 514, intercepted three E-boats well out from Cap d'Antifer and engaged them vigorously at 500 yards, turning them back to the coast.

A different unit of three Higgins boats (PT 460, SO Lt L.F. Jones USNR, with 459 and 457), shadowed and attacked four R-boats rather closer in to the Cape on 7/8 August, and with their superior speed were able to close rapidly and inflict some damage, driving them off westward. These two brushes were valuable in giving the PTs experience of frigate control and opportunities of close cooperation which they seized wholeheartedly, gaining the approval of the C-in-C, Adm Sir Charles Little.[11]

Activity in the Le Havre area between 8 and 23 August was continuous and on almost every night units of the 1st, 13th, 29th, 30th and 35th Flotillas, together with Dog Boats and C Class MGBs and PTs, were successfully vectored by the controlling frigates to meet the enemy. The E-boats, R-boats and occasionally larger vessels could neither approach Le Havre to reinforce it from the north nor leave it to attack the Anchorage without being intercepted and mauled or turned back.

The shore batteries were always a threat to the MTBs, and frequent near-misses by heavy shells after starshell illumination made their task very difficult. The Germans also brought into the battle two new weapons: the human torpedo and the explosive motor boat (EMB). Both were fairly unsophisticated and their crews were extremely unlikely to survive in the event of being sighted. They proved very easy to sink and had virtually no success, being met by MTBs, MLs and other craft. On 8 August reports indicate that no fewer than thirty-four EMBs were sunk.

Not every brush with the enemy led to positive results, but on 8/9 August a unit of the 30th led by Freddie Shore had a rare encounter with a merchant vessel, sank her and damaged her R-boat escort. Two nights later he led a different unit and had a tough battle with an unpleasant *Sperrbrecher* and its escort.

Records show that on 17/18 August eight human torpedoes attempting to attack the Anchorage were sunk. On the 18th two boats

[10] MO 9084; ADM 199/264; report of CCF (Channel).

[11] Report of CCF (Channel).

of Arnold-Forster's 13th Flotilla tackled an M Class minesweeper escorted by R-boats, and MTB 208 torpedoed an R-boat (R218) at 600 yards. Eighteen survivors were taken prisoner. (MO 9829)

On the following night Shore's unit of the 30th made an unsuccessful torpedo attack on six R-boats, and without pause followed this up with a gun attack, cutting through the enemy line and savagely raking the boats with gunfire on either side. Enemy radio admitted that one R-boat was sunk, and two others were known to have been damaged.

And so it went on. On 20/21 August another three boats of the 30th Flotilla, this time led by Lt Peter Standley in 471, had a very similar close-range gun battle with R-boats off Cap d'Antifer. Both sides suffered damage and casualties: 476 and 477 were badly hit (477 had to be towed home) and both 471 and 476 lost men, with others severely wounded. Three of the R-boats were seen to be in difficulties, one of them in a sinking condition.

At this stage, with Le Havre threatened by the Allied armies that were closing in on the port, it was decided to increase the patrols at night to counteract the efforts that the enemy were certain to make to extract the vessels based there before they were trapped in harbour. It was expected that renewed efforts might be made to pass through reinforcements of supplies and men, and more escorts to help any evacuation. With so many boats (and destroyers) involved, careful planning was essential and the frigates with their Coastal Forces Control Officers played an important part in this. Daily briefings were held at HMS *Dolphin* – now temporarily a major Coastal Forces base – usually conducted by Lt Christopher Dreyer, who prepared the plot each day after assessing all the results and movements of the night before.

That first night gave some indication of the fierceness of the battle ahead. The shore batteries along the whole coast from Cap d'Antifer to Cap de La Heve made things very difficult with accurate illumination and shelling. The Hunt Class destroyer HMS *Talybont*, escorting a unit of Dog Boats of the 53rd Flotilla, was beaten off, but another Hunt, HMS *Melbreak*, gave covering fire to Arnold-Forster's 13th MTBs attacking from inshore; almost certainly they sank a merchant vessel at 700 yards. The third group, further south, could not get in an effective attack owing to the continuous shelling, but *Melbreak* sank a gun coaster and a trawler, making it a successful night.[12]

The pressure was kept up on the following night (24/25 August) with no fewer than four flotillas supplying units. The activity is briefly described in the *Coastal Forces Periodical Review* (*CFPR*) of August 1944:

> The control frigate vectored a unit of US PTs to a group of R-boats. They badly damaged two. The frigate then detected a convoy leaving Le Havre and vectored a unit of the 14th (254, 256 and 257) to attack. They fired a zone of six torpedoes at 1,000 yards, hitting and sinking one trawler. HMS *Retalick* later sank one E-boat. A second MTB attack on the convoy by 452 (Yock), 447 and 453 of the 35th Flotilla was beaten off but returned and fought the R-boats, severely damaging two more. Yet another attack was launched by the 13th Flotilla, led by Mark Arnold-Forster in 205 (Irvine), 209 and 210 under cover of a destroyer with diversion, but was at first beaten off by a group of five TLCs [landing craft adapted for convoy defence mounting three 88mm guns] but

[12] *Coastal Forces Periodical Review*, August 1944.

MTB 358 (CO Lt P. Allen) of the 5th MTB Flotilla enters Dover. (Courtesy D. Ridgeon)

returned to fire a zone of six torpedoes, and 210 (Percy Everett) sank one TLC.

A note is appended to this report indicating that the success in sinking this target with its very shallow draft was due to the torpedo having a CCR pistol, enabling it to explode within the magnetic field of the ship without actually striking its hull.

The blockade continued for three more nights, with increasing intensity and even more success. On 25/26 August it was the turn of Dudley Dixon, leading a different unit of the 35th in 450. They were the first to meet yet another convoy attempting to reinforce the garrison. The heavy escort kept them at bay, although a coaster was set on fire and one E-boat was seen to be severely damaged. Even more significantly the convoy was halted and this enabled the French-manned Hunt *La Combattante* to get in and sink three merchant ships and one E/R-boat with direct hits. The unit from the 14th, led by their SO David Shaw, fired a zone spread of six torpedoes, sinking a TLC and an R-boat. Other attacks were made by Dog Boats and PTs.

Astonishingly, the enemy made a last effort to reinforce Le Havre on the night of the 26th but the convoy was intercepted off St-Valery, well short of their objective and the units of the 13th and 14th, and the PTs with HMS *Middleton* sank no fewer than six of the eight ships which made the attempt.

The last night of this unremitting battle was fought on 27/28 August when those ships which could sail left Le Havre, which had been for so long the enemy's lynch-pin of resistance in the Channel. They sailed northward towards the uncertain safety of the Dover Strait and the North Sea. Before they passed out of the blockade area, Dixon's 35th sank two more merchant ships, and *La Combattante* one more. The remnants struggled on to Fécamp and over the next two nights attempted to run the gauntlet of the Dover Strait, with two of the Dover flotillas (the 5th under Lt Roland Plugge and the 9th led by Hans Larive) sinking three more.

At last the Channel was virtually free of enemy shipping and Operation Neptune was successfully completed. For the MTB flotillas it had been a period of intense and increasingly successful operations which left many boats battered and their crews worn out from the strain of their ceaseless efforts. They deserved not only great credit, but a pause before regrouping for the last stages of this unprecedented activity. They were not alone in deserving the plaudits of Their Lordships of the Admiralty, as those who had planned the complex pattern of operations, together with the control frigates and their Coastal Forces Control Officers, had all played a vital part. And in all the bases the maintenance staff had worked night and day to ensure there were always boats ready to take their place in the units required for patrol. The reliability of the MTBs had increased dramatically from the early years of the war when breakdowns had been frustratingly all too common.

All this was recognized handsomely by an Admiralty signal sent early in September. (Appendix 1, Note 18)

> Their Lordships are particularly impressed with the recent fine work carried out by Coastal Forces craft off the coasts of France and the Low Countries, and congratulate not only the crews themselves but also those concerned with the direction and administration of the craft. Their efforts have contributed largely to the success of operations in France.

CHAPTER 11

AUGUST 1944 TO MAY 1945

The dramatic sea battles off Le Havre for the five weeks to the end of August have led to attention being concentrated in this area to the detriment of the continuing war in the North Sea. Yet there had been a very important role for the east coast flotillas to play. After the bombing of Le Havre in mid-June, and the destruction of large numbers of E-boats and other enemy escort vessels, it was vital to prevent or impede reinforcements from reaching the Channel from the ports of the Low Countries.

The German E-boat Command was clearly aware that several MTB flotillas of both 'short' and 'long' boats had been switched to the Channel for the invasion, and that this gave them the opportunity to use sea transport with less risk of interference. Strangely, though, there was no great increase in activity. There had been few convoys moving along the coasts of Belgium and Holland, and the east coast flotillas had carried out dozens of fruitless patrols, meeting the enemy only on comparatively few occasions. The men of those flotillas, conscious of the intensity of the operations in the Channel, had been very frustrated when night after night they went out on patrol, tired, cold and wet, with no reward.

There had, of course, been a few notable victories for both the 'short' boats and the Dog Boat flotillas (which by virtue of their much heavier armament were better equipped to attack the well-armed trawlers, gun coasters and minesweepers that made up the bulk of the targets in the area).

Successes for the 3rd Flotilla on the 24/25 June, the 21st under Jim Macdonald on 4/5 July, the 22nd led by Douglas Hunt on 8/9 July and the 4th Flotilla under Jake Wright on 13/14 July have been mentioned briefly in Chapter 10, but for the sake of completeness, it is necessary to return to the night of 20/21 July, when yet again the 21st, with its proud record of operations, fought a successful battle off Scheveningen.

Macdonald in 234, with 224 (A.J. Lee), formed Division 1 and 225 (Gill) and 232 (Wolfe) were Division 2. A patrol of trawlers was detected and attacked, using the classic method of approaching from opposite sides with coordinated timing of zone attacks. The second division was first to record a hit, while the first group had to make a second approach but they believed they too had secured a hit, judging by the concussion felt by all the boats. CCR pistols were once again a boon: throughout Coastal Forces there was an air of disbelief that a weapon which brought such an immediate increase in the success rate of torpedo firing should have been so long in arriving because of development problems.[1]

On 26/27 August it was the turn of the 4th Flotilla, now led by Lt J.S. Price. He was in 468 (Bazeley), with 457, 470 and 467. They detected two M Class minesweepers off Noordwyk. 468 and 457 made the first attack, and 468 hit and sank the leading M at 700 yards. Both 468 and 457 suffered damage under heavy fire, and withdrew. They later met a TLC patrol and had a brief brush before returning to base.[2]

1 MO 8737; ADM 100/266.

2 MO 9953; Summary of Actions.

The crew of MTB 358 at 'Exercise Action Stations' in Dover Harbour, September 1944. (Courtesy D. Ridgeon)

It was at this stage, after the fall of Le Havre, that the concentration of flotillas in the Channel was no longer required, and a period of reassessment of priorities began. It was also a time when Coastal Forces could be said to have reached at last the high level of overall quality which had been the aim right from the start of the war. Quite apart from the injection of power which the Dog Boats had brought, many of the short boat flotillas were now equipped either with 71ft 6in British Power Boats or the latest 73ft Vospers, all purpose-built boats with enhanced armament and much greater reliability than the earlier boats. Another important factor was that the boats were now manned by a far higher proportion of experienced officers and men. As new boats came from the yards, the older craft were paid off and the crews, their skills honed in countless patrols, wherever possible were kept together in the new boats, maintaining the sense of mutual reliance and team-work already developed in action.

Gradually flotillas were transferred from Portsmouth to Lowestoft and Felixstowe, to reinforce the long-serving east coast boats. Even though they had not had the same opportunities for constant action, the 3rd, 4th, 11th, 21st and 22nd Flotillas had provided the constant patrols which had for months been sent across the North Sea. Their task had been to ensure that the enemy could never venture to sea unhindered. Each of these patrols covered a far greater distance than those in the Channel, and in view of the time they were at sea there was a greater chance that fierce weather might blow up before their return.

Most of these flotillas had either received or were awaiting their new boats, but the 21st, which had been the main strike force since Peter Dickens' energetic leadership had begun in early 1942, was still operating in its original 1941 type Vospers which had given so much trouble in the early days of the flotilla's formation. Under Lt G.J. Macdonald RNZNVR they had proudly maintained the reputation of their flotilla. Macdonald had an amazing record: appointed to command at nineteen, he had become SO of the 21st Flotilla at the age of twenty-one, and had already earned a DSO and DSC and Bar. The replacement boats for his flotilla did not begin to come through until November, but in September and October Macdonald saw three more actions in the original boats; they proved to be the last actions of any significance that the 21st would have.

In the first, on 14/15 September, Macdonald in 234 led seven boats to patrol off Terschelling: five of his own flotilla (234, 233, 232, 223 and 244) and two of the 22nd (83 and 88). As meticulous as ever in his observation and judgement, he embarked on a lengthy stalk of a convoy to establish its size, course and speed, and then decided to take the first division to the inshore side to make the opening attack. This led to early detection and a fierce response from the heavy escort, causing him to move away temporarily. But as he had hoped, the second

The crew of MTB 234 at Felixstowe, October 1944. The CO was G.J. Macdonald RNZNVR and the First Lt D. Moore. (Collection CFHT)

division, led by John Wolfe in 232, had not been sighted and were able to make a zone attack from seaward, securing two hits on a 2,000-ton merchant vessel at 1,500 yards. As ever, Macdonald was not content to leave it at that, and he made a second attack from inshore. The spread of torpedoes from his boats was skilfully avoided by the trawlers of the escort, and no hits were obtained. It had been a copybook action involving careful plotting, a two-sided attack and zone firing – all regarded as 'best practice' at the time,[3] and it deserved more success.

Without any direct record of the enemy's strategic intentions, it is very difficult to see any pattern to their attempts to sail convoys, which seemed to be few and far between. Certainly the Allied armies were probing forward fast, and were urgently in need of supplies, which made the importance of clearing Ostend and particularly Antwerp a very high priority. Montgomery's 21st Army Group had swept into Belgium, and in a brilliant stroke had moved so fast that the enemy troops in Antwerp were taken by surprise, and this vital port was occupied on 4 September. However, because of the situation further to the west of the advance, he was not permitted to move on to clear the north flank of the vital Schelde estuary and thus enable the port there – 50 miles from the open sea, and guarded by the well-garrisoned island of Walcheren at the entrance – to be cleared.

All these considerations must have drastically affected enemy troop dispositions and movements of supplies, but it was not until the night of 30 September/1 October that convoys were sighted and attacked. The 30th Flotilla led by Peter Magnus met the enemy for the first time in this new sphere of operations off Texel, but were not able to reach a successful conclusion. Further south, however, the 11th Flotilla, led on this occasion by Lt F.W. Bourne, was engaged in a battle off Ymuiden, which for gallantry and determination was rarely surpassed in the history of Coastal Forces.

Freddie Bourne had long experience in normal MTB operations, and in MTB 344 had carried out more clandestine activities than any other 'short' boat. His report of this operation is long and detailed, and remarkably clear considering that he was wounded and that the movements of both divisions were complex. He was embarked in 351 (N.C. Morrow), which along with 360 (D.A. Hall) and 349 (K.E. Harris) made up the first division; the second was formed by 347 (Alec Foster) and 350 (H.G. Franklin)

When they reached the Dutch coast at 2043, visibility was exceptional, and they turned southward about 7 miles from the land. Three hours later, with cloud and rain having reduced visibility, they sighted a convoy of at least twelve ships. After nearly an hour's stalking, Bourne began the first attack; 347 and 350 were to follow them in, but some distance astern. By this time he had fired illuminating rockets and it was possible to make out details on the ships of the convoy, whose size and number made them an impressive group of targets. There were two or three good-sized merchant vessels escorted by a TLC and trawlers both ahead and astern, and more ships were further astern, obscured by cloud. The first division boats closed at 12 knots and soon realized they had penetrated the screen unobserved. As the enemy began to open fire, 349 fired first and her torpedoes ran true, along two lanes of tracer from the main target; 360 followed a few seconds later. Sadly her torpedoes exploded prematurely, and 351 was unable to fire. They were now under heavy fire from guns of all calibres, and they disengaged to starboard. As they did so, there

[3] MO 10649; Summary of Actions.

was a heavy explosion as 349's torpedoes hit and a large cloud of black smoke obscured the target. The nearest trawler was now engaged by 351's twin Oerlikons and was set on fire aft, and was clearly hit on the bridge.

360 had made smoke, but was being repeatedly hit by heavy calibre shells. Her bridge was on fire and she was veering off to port with her steering jammed. Her twin Oerlikons continued to fire at the enemy, but finally all her main engines were hit and she stopped, sinking and burning; the crew had no choice but to abandon ship.

Meanwhile, the second division had begun its attack, firing rockets to provide light, and securing hits on a trawler as they closed their target, the second merchant ship. 347 came under very heavy fire, and both torpedo tubes were damaged and unable to fire. Henry Franklin in 350, realizing 347's condition, carried on alone and fired both torpedoes at the second merchant ship. He was rewarded by two large explosions on her hull. Fire from the escorts increased and as 350 disengaged she found herself passing between the lanes of enemy ships on a reciprocal course, and her gunners were able to engage and set on fire yet another trawler. Running on, Franklin passed a tug and, further aft, a large ship with destroyer lines, which was not firing.

As he ran clear of the convoy, he saw a burning MTB to the northward, and closed to render assistance, despite the gunfire from two trawlers nearby. He managed to pick up five survivors and discovered they were from 360.

While all this was happening, Alec Foster in 347 was disengaging, but the boat was still under fire. One shell hit the centre engine and blew a hole in the bottom of the boat, and another hit the starboard engine. The engine room crew somehow managed to get the boat under way by running the port engine on the inboard bank of cylinders, and as she slowly moved away the Oerlikons continued to fire at the trawlers, the tug and finally the destroyer. As the wreck of 347 began to sink, Foster carried out all the procedures for security of codebooks, and ensuring nothing of use to the enemy could be left. Finally the crew was gathered into and around a Carley float, and they were eventually rescued by 351 which took the thirteen men aboard. It was noon before the three boats were back at their base.

In all such battles decisive close action carried the risk of boats being sunk, but it was the loss of lives and the number of seriously wounded which really hurt the flotilla. On this occasion nine of 360's crew did not return and two were gravely injured. Considering the damage 347 had suffered, the toll of five slightly wounded was amazingly low. Freddie Bourne was himself wounded. The enemy had lost two merchant ships, and two of their trawlers had been set on fire.

Perhaps the outstanding feature of the action was the way in which both the doomed MTBs had continued to attack the enemy while making huge efforts to prevent the loss of their boats to the enemy. It was this aspect among others that received particular praise from Capt Robson, CCF (Nore), in passing on the report to C-in-C.

> This was a most gallant and spirited action in which the conduct of all officers and men seems to have been exemplary . . . both divisions succeeded in penetrating the enemy's screen unobserved and in making an attack from close range. . . . The manner in which Lt A.D. Foster in 347 pressed in to 800 yards after being heavily hit was admirable . . . as was the way in which 350 closed to 500 yards to score her two hits on the target. . . . The efforts to save 347 while under fire are beyond praise.[4]

[4] MO 11253; ADM 199/265.

MTB 458 of the 4th MTB Flotilla, SO's boat with Type 970 radar, 1945. (Courtesy W.J.R. Howard)

In the following ten days there were three more actions off the Dutch coast for the 'short' boats. Two of them took place on 8/9 October. In the first, Lt E. Whife led a unit of the 4th Flotilla in 458, with 468, 457 and 467, off the Hook where they met a patrol of armed trawlers. In the first attack the return fire was so intense that they were forced to withdraw, with 467 so damaged that she was sent home. A second attack was then made, and this time each boat fired independently and 458 secured a hit on one of the trawlers. Enemy radio later confirmed it had been sunk.[5]

On the same night further north, off Texel, Macdonald took a patrol from the 21st and 22nd Flotillas, very similar in composition to the group which had sunk a merchant ship in September off Terschelling. They were equally successful, with an M Class minesweeper being sunk in a zone attack by the second division, consisting of 83 and 88 of the 22nd Flotilla. Jack Coombs of 83 and his coxswain PO L.W. Pratt were both decorated for their roles in these two operations, as were John Wolfe and the coxswain of 232. Although the 21st had one more brush with the enemy, this was their last taste of success, and very soon afterwards the flotilla received new boats. Sadly they never had the opportunity to record a victory with them. The 21st Flotilla had a long and proud record of harassing the enemy, and Jim Macdonald, the young and intrepid New Zealander, had been involved throughout the whole of its existence.[6]

The last of these three actions took place on 10/11 October, when Peter Magnus in 475, leading five boats from his recently transferred 30th Flotilla, had the satisfaction

[5] MO 11739; ADM 199/265.

[6] MO 11454; Summary of Actions; *Seedie's List of Coastal Forces Awards*.

of firing the torpedoes which sank a trawler. (MO 11884)

The comparative dearth of convoys in the area continued through October, although patrols by enemy trawlers and M Class minesweepers were maintained, thought to be associated with minelaying activity. The vitally important Allied supply route to Antwerp could not be secure until the Schelde estuary was in Allied hands. This at last became a probability when on 1 November, a seaborne assault was launched on the heavily defended island of Walcheren; Canadian divisions simultaneously attacked the mainland areas to take Zeebrugge and its hinterland to the south, and the northern flank of the West Schelde. The battle for Walcheren was hard fought, and many landing craft were sunk, but on 8 November the island fell; minesweeping began, and the first Allied convoy of eighteen supply ships sailed into Antwerp by 28 November. (Appendix 1, Note 19) This was the signal for a new phase of operations at sea, in which the E-boats (mainly from Ymuiden and Texel) repeatedly set out to attack shipping in the approaches to the Schelde and in the estuary itself. This resulted in turn in a new pattern of operations for the boats of the Nore Command, involving three types of patrol. A group of MLs and D Boats manned the Z line, 5 miles to seaward and parallel to the east coast convoy route, between the

MTB 393, a 73ft Vosper with Type 970 radar for the SO, one of the long-awaited new boats for the 21st Flotilla, with Jim Macdonald (left) on the bridge, late 1944. (Courtesy J.E.H. Davies)

'I see it!' Dennis Neale, CO of MTB 381 of the 31st Flotilla. (Courtesy T.H. Stewart)

Thames estuary and Great Yarmouth and beyond. A second patrol line, protecting the convoy route to Antwerp, ran eastward across the North Sea to the mouth of the Schelde, 25 miles north of Ostend. This was manned by control frigates, each able to deploy a destroyer and two units of MTBs. The third type, code-named 'Bangor' was the more usual offensive form of patrol for MTBs, sweeping the enemy coast northward from the Hook to Texel searching for enemy patrols or convoys.

In all these operations the cooperation and assistance of the RAF had been stepped up in a most useful way. Aircraft of Coastal Command fitted with air-sea radar were now able to find and track E-boats. Unfortunately, there was a hitch in communications as their VHF (voice) radio signals could be received by the frigates but not directly by the MTBs.

Coastal Forces had also gained one new asset. The Belgian port of Ostend had fallen in September during Montgomery's initial push into Belgium, although the German defence line breached in the early stages of the Walcheren operation on 1 November had reached the coast at Zeebrugge only 12 miles to the east. Cdr Brind's CFMU had moved up from Arromanches to Ostend at the end of September, and it became an important advanced base from which the flotillas could launch patrols without the long slog across the North Sea. They still returned to Felixstowe, Lowestoft and Great Yarmouth for more serious maintenance and repairs.

Even so, apart from a flurry of activity on 1/2 November when units of the 4th, 29th and 30th Flotillas met enemy patrols off the Hook and Ymuiden, the 'short' boats were not involved in any significant action until

22/23 December – a very long delay, especially in the light of their experiences in the summer and early autumn. Clearly the enemy was extremely cautious about sailing convoys now that they only held the Dutch coast from Ymuiden northward towards the north German ports.

It seemed that the battle was now to be fought largely against the E-boats, which soon proved to be operating very gallantly in ever greater numbers around the Schelde and against the North Sea coastal convoys which had been their major targets since 1941. The Allied supply line across the North Sea to Antwerp had a main feeder from the Thames, joined by branches from north and south. This route was known as the Thames–Schelde Channel, a phrase which recurs constantly in the official descriptions for the rest of the war.

The action of 22/23 December was a complex battle involving initially seven boats of Peter Magnus's 30th Flotilla, and later a force of destroyers, frigates and the 53rd Flotilla of Dog Boats.

Magnus' report reveals that the 30th was ordered to make an anti-E-boat patrol off the Hook, 'with freedom of action to attack any enemy shipping south of 52 degrees north'. His seven boats were organized in two divisions, with 475 (SO), 473, 472 and 471 (Bradley) in the first, and 474 (Shore), 476 and 477 in the second. They were approaching their patrol position at 17 knots when Magnus's radar detected vessels at 2,800 yards and closing, on either bow. A few seconds later six E-boats were sighted, moving across the unit's line of advance at 30 knots. Knowing that his boats had a maximum continuous speed of only 30 knots, he deemed it essential to attack at once, and he closed to just 100 yards before opening fire and running along the enemy line. There was no reply for fifteen seconds, and when the response came it was wild and high, which seemed to indicate that the E-boats were shaken by the ferocity of the attack. The third, fourth and fifth E-boats in the line were particularly hard hit, and the fourth, which had taken many 6-pounder and Oerlikon shells, blew up with a large red explosion and clouds of black smoke. In a very short time the MTBs had run the full extent of the E-boats' line, and Magnus sent the second division in pursuit but to no avail.

The unit resumed its patrol position and half an hour later obtained echoes at 5,000 yards. Almost immediately the MTBs were illuminated by well-aimed starshells and began to be shelled by high-calibre shells from an enemy they could not even see. After several near-misses, Magnus decided to move away, intending to return later, but he lost radar contact. 471 had been hit in the engine room and had to return to base. Intelligence later revealed that it was the E-boat S 185 which had been sunk.

Further phases of the action involved two more groups of E-boats which fell foul of the Dog Boats, *Walpole*, *Curzon* and several other frigates and destroyers. Three more E-boats were sunk, two of which were identified as S 192 and S 182. It had been a bad night for the E-boat flotillas. Peter Magnus received a Bar to his DSC.[7]

As the war entered 1945 there was a continuous succession of E-boat raids against Allied convoys. The flotillas were constantly deployed, but it was the destroyers and frigates, with their high-quality radar and heavier armament, which bore the brunt of detection and attack. The E-boats coped with bad weather far better than was possible for the 'short' boats, and it was not until 22/23 January 1945 that boats of the 35th Flotilla met the enemy.

[7] MO 910; ROP held by the author; Rohwer & Hummelchen, *Chronology of the War at Sea*; *Seedie's List of Coastal Forces Awards*.

On that night three groups of E-boats set out to attack the convoys; they were cleverly dispersed to different areas in order to stretch the thinly spread resources of available escorts. The first group evaded all patrols and were able to attack a convoy entering the Schelde estuary, damaging one of the merchant ships. They were then intercepted by two units of the 35th, vectored by HMS *Stayner*; the second unit engaged in 'a fierce chase' during which one E-boat was hit by a 6-pounder shell, and 495 was hit in the engine room.

The second group of E-boats headed towards Walcheren but were driven off. The third group of five E-boats was shadowed by aircraft but managed to shake them off; they then appeared near Tongue Sand off the Thames estuary, where they were briefly engaged by 451 (McGinty), 452 and 450, and then by the Tongue Fort. In a confused action one E-boat (S 199) was sunk, and several survivors were picked up.[8]

In a fascinating exchange of correspondence many years later, the CO of S 199 vehemently asserted that his boat was sunk not by the Fort or the MTBs, but as a result of a collision with one of his own boats in the course of the action. To confuse the issue still further, the CO of the anti-aircraft battery on the Tongue Fort describes his own pattern of fire as the E-boats came very close, and submits 'that it may be considered whether this E-boat was in fact sunk as a result of my fire'. The E-boat commander (who was taken prisoner) gave evidence for the collision: 'I was convinced that I had rammed an enemy boat, but in fact we had collided with S 701, also fighting the MGBs. Later on they found, on the deck of S 701, a magazine from our foc's'le gun marked S 199'! He seems to have proved his point. (Appendix 1, Note 20)

[8] MO 424; ROP held by the author.

On 14 February 1945 Coastal Forces suffered its greatest disaster of the war. On that day there were thirty-two boats crammed along the cramped berthing quays in Ostend Harbour, in front of the offices of CFMU. This number was made up of eleven 'short' boats, sixteen D Class, two Camper & Nicolsons and three MLs. Almost all these boats were in trots of four. At 1602 fire broke out on the surface of the water very near the closed end of the 'Creek', a narrow extension to the main berthing area just inside the lock gates. Within five minutes there was a tremendous explosion as MTB 462, the inboard boat of Trot 'B', blew up; and a short while after there was a second explosion when 465 disintegrated. From then on the fire spread like lightning and there were several further explosions. All the boats in the Creek, except for those in Trot 'A' which were ahead of the outbreak of fire, and the outboard Dogboat in Trot 'D' (the 'knuckle' berth), a total of twelve boats, were involved.

There was frantic activity in all the boats, but as in all such situations there was much confusion. The personnel necessary for fire-fighting, or for releasing lines and starting engines, were either overtaken by events or missing or were simply overwhelmed by the enormity of all that was happening. Some distinguished themselves and were commended, while others were held responsible both for starting the fire and for a lack of preventative regulations. The casualties were horrifying. In all, 5 officers and 59 ratings were killed or missing, and 5 officers and 60 ratings were listed as wounded. Nine civilians were also killed.

The Board of Enquiry established that the fire was caused by the igniting of petrol which had been inadvertently pumped out of a fuel tank when trying to clear it of water contamination. There had been some urgency as the boat concerned was required for patrol that night, but the motor mechanic had

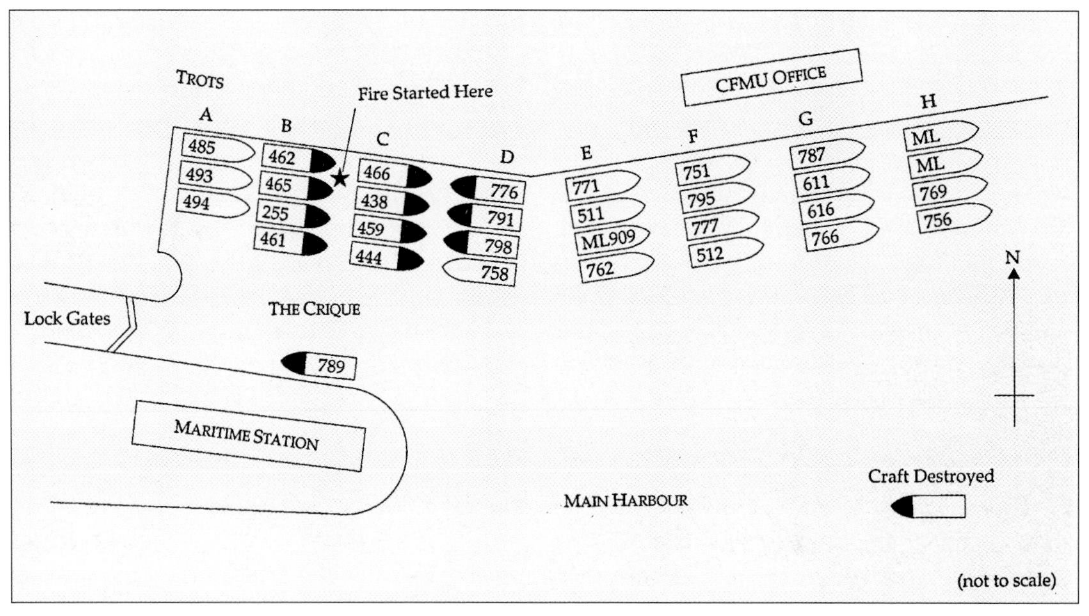

Ostend. Disposition of Coastal Force craft at 1600 on 14 February 1945. (Sketch compiled from an official report and eyewitness information.)

received no help from others who should have shouldered more responsibility.

Among those commended in the Board's Report was Lt I.A.B. Quarrie, the CO of 776, who was said to have been indefatigable in his efforts to save both his own boat and the three outside him in Trot 'D'. Another was Stoker L. Young RCNVR who on his own initiative started the engines of 485 in Trot 'A'; by moving her ahead, together with the two boats outside her, he snapped the shore lines and put enough distance between them and the fire to save all three boats.

Fourteen boats were destroyed: 459, 461, 462, 465 and 466 of the Canadian 29th Flotilla; 255, an independent boat; 438 and 444 of the 3rd; 791, 798, 511 and 512 of the 52nd; 776 of the 63rd; and 789 of the 64th.[9] This catastrophe signalled the end of the Canadian 29th Flotilla, and was a tremendous blow to all the personnel of Coastal Forces as a whole. It was an especially bitter blow because it had happened in the last lap of the long struggle. They mourned those who had lost their lives, and grieved for their families. But they were still at war, and within a week a unit of boats from the 1st and 11th Flotillas was involved with frigates and destroyers in repelling E-boat attacks in considerable numbers. (MO 3027)

These encounters with the constantly active E-boats were to be the main feature of the weeks ahead. The problem was, of course, the very long approach towards the Schelde, which gave the E-boats the opportunity of slipping in to attack the convoys. But it seemed that the control frigates' ability to detect them and despatch a unit of MTBs to tackle them was now enabling most to be intercepted. Time after time the E-boats were engaged at close quarters, and even if not sunk, they were chased away and often damaged. The MTBs, too, suffered damage and occasional

[9] Report of the Board of Enquiry, courtesy J.P. Perkins.

The crew of MTB 447 of the 35th Flotilla prepared for a cold night in the North Sea, wearing fleecy jackets and headgear sent as 'comforts' from Australia, January 1945. (Courtesy R. Wrayton)

casualties. This pattern was precisely that of two interceptions on the night of 28 February/1 March, when HMS *Riou* vectored first 453 and 478 of the 35th and later 489 and 488 of the 1st Flotilla to attack E-boats.

Similarly on 9/10 March the 30th and 1st were vectored by *Seymour* and *Retalick* to two groups of E-boats, and both engaged in gun battles. It seemed that the E-boats now had orders to be more aggressive and their gunnery was consequently fiercer and more accurate than in the past, when their policy had been to avoid close action and thus ensure they were undamaged for their attacks on larger targets. When they met 431 and 483 of the 1st Flotilla, there was an exchange of fire at very close range. One E-boat and 431 both suffered damage, and 431 had one man killed and three wounded. (MO 3494)

The enemy, perhaps in desperation, were still sending out EMBs and human torpedoes, and newer versions of each, despite their earlier lack of success. On 21/22 March a *Seehund* (midget submarine) collided with 394, one of the 73ft Vospers of the 21st Flotilla, and was forced to scuttle; the two occupants were taken prisoner. (MO 3127)

On the same night the plot showed that no fewer than twenty-four E-boats were out. Aircraft were deployed to track them and sank one, and also gave good early warning to the convoy escorts, ensuring that they could be beaten off. (MO 4133)

It was clear that the E-boats were continuing the battle with tremendous spirit,

MTB 383, a 73ft Vosper, the SO's boat of the 31st Flotilla, with Type 970 radar, February 1945. (Courtesy T.H. Stewart)

trying to delay the inevitable end as the Allied armies moved towards the final stages of the battle for the heartland of Germany; simultaneously the Russians were moving inexorably westward. With the German infrastructure of communications and supplies fragmented by heavy air raids, the Kriegsmarine saw its duty as disruption of the supply convoys pouring into Antwerp. But it was a losing battle, and more and more E-boats were being sunk or damaged. 475 (Peter Magnus) and 476 of the 30th Flotilla were credited with an E-boat possibly sunk on 25/26 March, and the Dog Boats as well as the frigates and destroyers were enjoying increasing success.

Early in April, on 6/7th and 7/8th, there were three battles which were later recognized as the climax to the extraordinarily gallant efforts of the E-boats in this final stage. On 6 April six E-boats of the 2nd S-boat Flotilla left Den Helder to carry out a mining operation off the Humber. On their way in they were attacked by destroyers, and later encountered MTBs 5001 and 781. In this action 5001 took a hit in the engine room and sank. The E-boats then set off at speed to return to Den Helder. They had not gone far when they were suddenly intercepted by three 71ft 6in boats of the 22nd Flotilla near Harty Knoll, off the coast of Norfolk. It was an extremely dark night and the MTB unit, comprising 494 (John May), 493 (Alec Foster) and 497 (A.T.J. Harrington), was being directed by a Wellington aircraft which was shadowing the E-boats.

After a pause to await further position reports, John May set off at 30 knots in what was clearly a final intercepting attack. At

0202 he sent the R/T signal 'Nan 255' (meaning 'enemy in sight on bearing 255 degrees'), and three minutes later 'Preparative Flag 5' (meaning 'prepare to open fire'). Within a few seconds Foster saw a wake close ahead, and also realized that 494 had opened fire. In almost the same instant he suddenly saw an E-boat very close and crossing his bow. He had no alternative but to ram, and his bow hit the boat at speed on the port quarter. The two boats separated and 493 crossed the E-boat's wake, regaining speed and opening fire at a range of about 25 yards. Foster turned to port to pursue, hitting the E-boat with the 6-pounder, when suddenly there was an almighty crash and 493 shuddered to a halt. She had hit the overturned hull of 494. Two survivors from 494 were picked up, but 493, which had lost her bow, was now only able to go astern. There was an E-boat (presumably the one that had been rammed) lying stopped nearby, and 493 was able to illuminate her and then open fire.

At this stage, 497 rejoined and also opened fire until the E-boat, now silenced, fired a Very light, presumably to indicate distress. Foster, unable to manoeuvre, sent in Harry Harrington who hailed the E-boat in his best Schools' Certificate German, advising the Captain that he intended to board. The German CO shouted urgently 'I have seriously wounded men: take

MTB 494 of the 22nd Flotilla 'shipping it green' on exercises, March 1945. She was sunk in action shortly afterwards. (Courtesy W.J.R. Howard)

MTB 493 of the 22nd Flotilla at Lowestoft after action in the North Sea, 7/8 April 1945. (Courtesy J. Lake)

us off – we shall sink in seven minutes'. Harrington concluded from this precise figure that scuttling charges had been set, and hastily abandoned the idea of boarding; instead he decided to tell the E-boat captain that he would take him in tow – reasoning that he was unlikely to blow himself up! The CO cooperated, and first 497 and then a Dog Boat (775) which had just arrived, took the E-boat (S 176) in tow. Sadly she sank, but the survivors were picked up by 775 and 497.

493 was towed stern-first to Lowestoft, arriving by 0520. The 22nd had suffered grievously with the loss of 494 and most of her crew – there were only two survivors – and 493 was never repaired. Intelligence later revealed that one of 497's targets (S 177) had sunk before reaching the Dutch coast.

As John May had perished with his boat, the Action Report was written by Alec Foster, and this forms the basis for much of this description.[10] But the author is also greatly indebted to Foster's former first lieutenant, John Lake, who undertook detailed research in 1990 which led to meetings in Germany with the COs of the leading E-boat, S 174 (Lt Stohwasser) and of S 176 (Lt Stockfleth). He was extremely well received, and from Friedrich Stockfleth received much fascinating information.

The E-boats had no radar and the sudden attack by the 22nd was totally unexpected. Stockfleth remembered every detail of the action – being rammed and totally disabled, towed, and finally having to abandon ship. He told an amusing story about his rescue. When he was pulled aboard 775 and lay

[10] MO 4597; ROP from A.D. Foster.

The E-boat S 176 later sunk in action on 7/8 April 1945. (Courtesy J. Lake)

panting on the deck, he was very shaken to find a rating standing over him, apparently holding a knife to his throat. This seemed to be in direct contravention of the Hague Convention for prisoners of war! Then his tie was cut and the British sailor said 'now you'll be able to breathe better, sir!' He was given a large whisky in the wardroom which rapidly restored his morale. Both the COs that Lake met had been regular naval officers who had joined in 1937, and they said all their COs were regulars.

It was also established that 493 had rammed the *second* boat (not the third) in line and it was this boat, S 176, that eventually sank after further gunfire from 493 and 497. Alec Foster, whose first command had been in the Mediterranean in June 1942 and who had fought off North Africa in the Tunisian campaign until he was wounded in the Strait of Messina in 1943, was at last awarded a DSC. (Appendix 1, Note 21)

The 2nd S-boat Flotilla, besides losing two boats, suffered a further tragedy. When S 209 (which had been fourth in line) tied up in Den Helder next morning, the CO lost his footing when alighting from the bridge; his fall caused a gun to fire and he received injuries from which he died.

On the following night, 7/8 April, Dudley Dixon's 35th Flotilla, after many weeks of countless patrols and inconclusive actions, had a resounding success. Aircraft had plotted two groups of E-boats aiming for the convoy route. The first group, with five boats, was intercepted by 482 (Dixon) and 454 (Irvine), vectored by their control frigate HMS *Rutherford*. They fired rocket flares beyond the targets, in the light of which they saw the five E-boats fine on the port bow at 3,000 yards. Dixon could see that the fourth and fifth in line were lagging astern and decided to 'box them out'.

He opened fire on the leading boat at 1,000 yards, and then altered course to attack his two main targets at 700 yards. Within a very short time a large explosion was observed on the fourth in the line, and the E-boat was seen to disintegrate. Both MTBs then concentrated their fire on the fifth,

MTB 496, with the crew of 493 about a week after the action on 7/8 April 1945. (Courtesy W.J.R. Howard)

which was hard hit by Oerlikons and 454's 6-pounder. 482 fired rockets to illuminate the scene and the target was shown to be stopping. Dixon ordered Irvine to go in and finish her off, and himself set off in pursuit of the other three in case any had been slowed by the earlier gunfire. But the range steadily increased and the frigate ordered 482 to discontinue the chase. The MTBs then searched the area for survivors and picked up 3 officers and 37 ratings from the E-boats; they were transferred to HMS *Rutherford*.

In forwarding Dixon's report to C-in-C Nore, the CO of HMS *Beehive* commended the skill and efficiency of all involved in the attack, remarking: 'An action such as this, basically simple, rapid in execution, and fought without loss to our forces, bears the hallmark of class.' The flotilla and all at *Beehive* were highly gratified to receive a signal from C-in-C:

> I heartily congratulate CF Direction Officers of *Rutherford* and *Torrington* and all ships and Coastal Forces concerned, for their good work last night when the enemy received very rough handling. Especially do I congratulate MTBs 482 (Lt J.D. Dixon DSC RNVR) and 454 (Lt P.G.A. Irvine RNVR) on their brilliantly successful action in which two E-boats were so swiftly destroyed in bad weather conditions and at a range never less than 700 yards. Their shooting must have been magnificent and shows what good gunnery can achieve.

The two E-boats sunk were S 202 and S 703. S 223 (in a different group) also sank after hitting a mine off Ostend, and thus these two nights had proved very expensive for the S-boat flotillas.

This was the last action for the 35th, which had fought so hard throughout Operation Neptune, and it was fitting that Dudley Dixon should be awarded a second Bar to his DSC, together with a DSC for Peter Irvine.[11]

The last recorded action by the home waters 'short' boats took place on 25/26 April off Terschelling. The boats

[11] MO 4432; ROP from A. Banger; *Seedie's List of Coastal Forces Awards.*

MTB 391, a 73ft Vosper of the 31st Flotilla, March 1945. (Courtesy T.H. Stewart)

involved were 458 (4th Flotilla) and 380 and 382 (31st) as Division 1, and 383 and 381 (31st) as Division 2. They were guided to the convoy by aircraft reports and flares, and decided that it was probably evacuating the more southerly ports. Both divisions fired zones of torpedoes; the second division fired at 1,700 yards and hit a gun coaster which was considered sunk.[12]

From the Royal Navy's viewpoint, the war in the North Sea came to an end with the 'Instrument of Surrender' signed on 4 May on

[12] MO 4855; Summary of Actions.

MTBs 469, 456 and 492 of the 4th Flotilla in Hamilton Dock, Lowestoft, dressed overall on VE Day. (Courtesy T.H. Stewart)

Adm Brauning of the Kriegsmarine arrives at Felixstowe with charts showing minefields and to confer with C-in-C Nore, 13 May 1945. (Collection G.M. Hudson)

S 204 and S 205, two surrendered E-boats in Felixstowe, 13 May 1945. (Courtesy R. Coventry)

Luneburg Heath, to take effect at 0800 on 5 May 1945. The surrender of all German armed forces included all naval ships in the area – 'these forces are to lay down their arms and surrender unconditionally'. For the men of the boats of Coastal Forces in home waters – the MLs, the 'long' MTBs and the 'short' MTBs – it was the end of an unrelenting struggle in which many hundreds had given their lives. The symbolic end of the conflict in the North Sea was marked by the arrival on 13 May of two E-boats wearing the white flag of surrender; they were escorted into Felixstowe by ten MTBs representing the flotillas based on the east coast.

Aboard the boats were the Senior Officers of these flotillas, who in turn were representing all their crews. The E-boats were carrying a German admiral who was bringing charts of all the minefields, but the huge crowd which watched the E-boats come alongside did not see it in such a pragmatic way. For them, this was the final act of victory – and who could blame them?

EPILOGUE

This trilogy has covered the operations of almost 800 MTBs and MGBs of many different classes in various theatres throughout the six years of the Second World War. It is surely appropriate here not only to attempt an assessment of the achievements of the 'short' boats in home waters, but also to go on to survey the contribution to the war effort of this small branch of the naval service, which was regarded in some quarters as a sort of 'private navy' of somewhat dubious provenance!

There is no doubt that this third volume has described the operations of the largest group of boats and the longest continuous period of operations. It also saw the most important advances in the technical development of the boats, and in the awareness of the special tactical needs of MTB warfare. It is therefore relevant to summarize here the main elements in that progress from their primitive beginning to their sophisticated end.

The early flotillas threw up the first generation of outstanding Senior Officers whose experience and total commitment to take the war to the enemy was inherited by those who followed them. Naturally enough, the initial flotillas and boats were commanded almost entirely by Royal Navy officers, but it was not long before they were replaced by talented RNVR men with established pedigrees in seamanship. Similarly the crews, which were originally composed mainly of long-service RN ratings, were rapidly supplemented and gradually replaced by 'hostilities only' sailors.

The British Power Boats designed by Hubert Scott Paine and the Vosper MTBs designed by Peter Du Cane provided the bulk of the early boats, and developments of these designs remained the predominant classes throughout the war, with variants built in the USA. When the Isotta Fraschini and Rolls-Royce Merlin engines became unavailable, US Packards provided a highly reliable universal replacement, although there was a period in 1941–2 when this change led to problems with overheating shafts and with engine-room layout in the Vospers. It was not until 1943 that greater power and reliability and steadily increasing fire-power began to make these fast torpedo carriers into a more constant threat to any form of target.

Radar improved but not at the rate which would have revolutionized operations, a fact that was bemoaned especially loudly because the US PT boats were very much better equipped in this respect. The alternative eventually employed was to use frigates to control the units of MTBs and vector them to the enemy targets – a technique that was employed very successfully throughout Operation Neptune and thereafter in the Nore.

These improvements were matched in terms of human resources by the increasing experience of officers and men, their skills honed not only by battle but by highly sophisticated training and working-up programmes. Together with an explosion of production throughout 1943 and 1944, these developments created a powerful force of MTBs which succeeded in increasing the 'strike rate' against the enemy – the most obvious mark of success – through to the end of the war in Europe.

The differences between the tasks of the enemy MTBs (E-boats) and those of the Royal Navy were far more clearly demonstrated in home waters than in other areas. It is a commonly held misconception about Coastal Forces warfare that the battle was largely fought between these two groups of boats. In fact, as has already been mentioned, the general policy of the E-boats, certainly until late in 1944, was to avoid direct confrontation with MGBs and MTBs, as their true priority was to torpedo larger targets. Their main hunting grounds were the numerous east coast and Channel convoys, with their large numbers of vulnerable merchant ships often thinly escorted. In contrast the MTBs had to search night after night for the far less frequent enemy convoys creeping along the coasts of the far shore, protected by heavy guns and coastal batteries and very densely escorted by numerous heavily armed and larger vessels such as Torpedo Boats, fleet minesweepers and armed trawlers with their 88mm and 37mm guns. There is no doubt that the arrival in quantity of the much more powerfully armed Fairmile Ds – the Dog Boats – during 1943 was a key factor in the successful confrontation of those escorts.

It is right, in this overview of operations, to acknowledge the very significant contribution of the mining campaign which sank a large number of enemy vessels – naval and mercantile – just as the German mines did. Increasingly, too, the enemy convoys were attacked by the RAF whenever they sought to sail by day. This was a matter of extreme strategic importance, as the pressure on the convoys was never relaxed. The problems for the enemy were by no means from Coastal Forces alone.

Similarly, as part of their duties included defending the home convoys against E-boat attack, the men of the MTBs and MGBs had ample opportunity to see and appreciate the work of the MLs, those unsung vessels which, without great speed and with no powerful armament, performed miracles of reliability and seamanship day in, day out, for months on end.

The work of the two training bases, HMS *St Christopher* at Fort William and HMS *Bee*, first at Weymouth and then at Holyhead, cannot be underestimated. At *St Christopher* thousands of officers and men had their first brief introduction to the boats of Coastal Forces and to the work they could be expected to do. At HMS *Bee* the crews of individual boats and sometimes a whole flotilla could undertake a very intensive programme of working-up, learning the 'best practices', assisted by experienced officers given a break from operations to enable them to pass on their expertise.

There were still perceived weaknesses in equipment which rankled among those at the sharp end of operations. Complaints about the radar, for example, were exacerbated by observation of the great improvements in, for instance, the PT boats of the US Navy. Their SO Radar, with its greater range and PPI screen, was available as early as 1942, although it was found only in a handful of US-built RN boats in the Mediterranean from 1944. (Appendix 1, Note 22)

Similarly the vastly superior CCR pistols in Mark VIII torpedoes would, if introduced earlier, have made an enormous difference to the successful strike rate of the MTBs, particularly since many of their targets were of shallow draft. Another essential aspect of Coastal Forces warfare relied on the ability of a Senior Officer to communicate efficiently and immediately with his COs by voice radio throughout each phase of an attack, a nagging problem that was only really solved when the TCS system became generally available. Some blamed the dilatory attitude in the relevant sections of the Admiralty. Although there were obvious production problems and conflicting priorities for the receipt of equipment, there were many examples in wartime of such difficulties being overcome by dynamic action and advocacy to speed up the supply chain.

In the Epilogues to the previous books, great emphasis was placed on the difficulty of quantifying precise numbers of enemy craft sunk. Obviously reports included certain and probable sinkings, and damage to enemy ships. But the experience of the men of Coastal Forces as they heard the enemy's extravagant and totally inaccurate claims helped to develop a greater caution in the compilation of statistics. Here, there will be no calculation of successful sinkings. 'Claims' are very different from confirmed results, and wherever possible the evidence in support of claims has been reported in the descriptions of actions, with reference to enemy records if available.

A post-war Admiralty press release, presumably prepared after all available evidence had been studied, makes interesting reading fifty years later:

> The Navy's 'Little Ships' – the MTBs, MGBs and MLs of Coastal Forces – fought 780 actions during the war in Europe, and sank more than 500 enemy vessels. They fired 1,169 torpedoes, and their percentage of hits or probables was better even than that of the submarines.
>
> In addition, they shot down 32 enemy aircraft and carried out nearly twice as many minelaying operations as were credited to other minelayers.
>
> All this, it can now be disclosed, was done at a cost of the loss of 170 of these tiny craft, none of which exceeded 120 tons.
>
> When war broke out, there were only two flotillas in commission, but in four years the force had expanded a hundredfold, and by 1944 employed 3,000 officers and 22,000 ratings, over 90 percent of whom were RNVR or 'hostilities only'.
>
> Coastal Forces began their operational career with Dunkirk, when there was so much to be done that they shared minelaying, convoy escort, and air-sea rescue work, together with evacuation duties which included the Belgian Cabinet and Admiral Keyes.
>
> The Navy's contribution to the raid on St Nazaire was exclusively from Coastal Forces, with the exception of the destroyer *Campbeltown* which rammed the dock gates. Of the 18 small craft which went in, only four came back.
>
> MTB operations extended to the Norwegian Fjords in 1942. In the Aegean and Adriatic they developed the technique of boarding enemy vessels after surprise attacks.
>
> In 1944, Coastal Forces averaged more than one action a day, and of 81 midget submarines sunk or captured, Coastal Forces claimed 23.

Examination of the quoted statistics suggests that some are questionable, but the general message confirms that the MTBs and MGBs played a very significant part in the battle of the Narrow Seas. From very early in the war, MTBs or MGBs patrolled off the enemy coasts on almost every night when the weather made it possible to do so. This represented an enormous number of sorties, which were tense and demanding whether or not they led to action.

The only truly quantifiable statistic concerns the number of times they met the enemy. A schedule was compiled of every occasion, derived from the reports passing through Commands, and recorded by the Admiralty under the continuous numbering system

(MO ——) extensively quoted in these three volumes. Sadly, the record is by no means complete, as during very busy times (such as the invasions of Sicily and of Normandy) reports often lumped together multiple operations in narrative form. Similarly there was no strict definition of what constituted 'action': hazardous operations such as minelaying, clandestine landings on the enemy coast and incidents such as destruction by mines were frequently omitted, and indeed the systems of reporting used by different Commands was in itself a hindrance in the compilation of a complete record.

Nevertheless, the existence of this authentic list makes possible an analysis of one aspect of the activities of Coastal Forces, and enables the facts to be broken down into areas, types of boats and types of enemy contact. This follows in tabular form opposite.

Any analysis is only as valuable as the criteria adopted, and therefore I have attempted to separate 'actions' into one of two categories:

A – actual exchange of fire by guns or torpedoes; i.e. the normally accepted 'surface action';

B – attack by or on aircraft, or by shore batteries, and incidents resulting in destruction or damage by mines.

There is no attempt to include clandestine operations, as these are rarely included in the lists. It is accepted that type B actions are also, regrettably, incompletely reported in the lists.

When a comparison is made between these tables and the figures quoted in the Admiralty communiqué referred to earlier, it can be seen that the figure of 780 actions is substantially short of those reported by Commands. The figures given for torpedo firings must be accepted, as these were very closely monitored by the Admiralty Operations Division, and certainly annual statistics set out for all the various torpedo carriers – aircraft, submarines, destroyers, cruisers and MTBs – place the MTBs as the most successful in 1943, 1944 and 1945.

The men of the MTBs were often afforded in the press a 'glamorous' image similar to that of the fighter pilots of the RAF. The situation in practice was very different. There was nothing glamorous about tired, wet crews, buffeted about in their boats whenever the sea was other than calm, facing the enemy at close range. There may have been a sense of exhilaration at the speed and power of their tiny boats and pride in a successful attack – but such feelings were often mirrored by sadness and distress when shipmates were killed or maimed. In one respect, however, this type of press reporting was of value: it caught the imagination of the public and boosted morale in the country at times when there was little to cheer about.

Another special feature of Coastal Forces' life was without doubt the tremendous benefit of an intensive fellowship. Because of the small numbers involved – two officers and a dozen ratings in many of the 'short' boats – and their mutual reliance, this developed beyond the normal 'shipmate' level for which the Navy is renowned. Contact between officers and men was so close and frequent that it often led to a reciprocation of respect and understanding which in a larger group would be impossible to sustain. This has stood the test of time: there are thousands of veterans still in contact with one another, especially through the Coastal Forces Veterans Association and reunion groups whose numbers have remained remarkably constant over the years.

The final point made in each of the two earlier volumes of this history deserves to be repeated. The main justification for the compilation of such a detailed survey of MTB operations is the fact that the major histories

ANALYSIS OF RECORDED ACTIONS

NO. OF BOATS		ACTION TYPES A	B	TOTALS
	Home Waters			
191	Short MTBs	223	14	237
75	Short MGBs	71	0	71
24	Fairmile Cs	21	1	22
141	Fairmile Ds	136	5	141
7	SGBs	17	0	17
NK	Fairmile As & Bs	45	9	54
NK	USN PTs	9	0	9
		522	29	551
	Mediterranean			
109	Short MTBs	135	8	143
40	Fairmile Ds	104	13	117
NK	Fairmile Bs	48	15	63
NK	USN PTs	70	0	70
		357	36	393
	Norway			
2	Short MTBs	2	0	2
23	Fairmile Ds	33	3	36
		35	3	38
	Far East			
9	Short MTBs	1	0	1
NK	Fairmile Bs	9	4	13
		10	4	14
	TOTALS	924	72	996

ANALYSIS OF ACTIONS BY BOAT TYPES AND AREAS

BOATS*	BOAT TYPES	HOME	MED	NORWAY	FAR EAST	TOTALS
302	Short MTBs	237	143	2	1	383
75	Short MGBs	71	–	–	–	71
24	Fairmile Cs	22	–	–	–	22
204	Fairmile Ds	141	117	36	–	294
7	SGBs	17	–	–	–	17
NK	Fairmile Bs	54	63	–	13	130
NK	USN PTs	9	70	–	–	79
		551	393	38	14	996

* NB: Excluded: Boats never in active commission in the war period; flotillas in India and West Indies.

of the naval war have paid virtually no attention to the contributions of Coastal Forces. Of course, it was never to be expected that individual actions would be commented upon, but what is surprising is that there is no acknowledgement at all of the general effectiveness of the special assets the MTBs brought to the war in the Narrow Seas. No other vessels of the fleet were able to operate so close to the enemy coast that they were often inside the minefields, under the guns of the coastal batteries. They alone were comparatively 'expendable', and able to fight their battles at very close range, constantly hampering the passage of supplies and reinforcements to the enemy.

Perhaps most significant of all, their part in the Normandy landings, as the inshore arm of the destroyers and frigates, was arguably crucial to the success of the Second Front by ensuring that the invasion armada and then the supply route remained virtually free from attack by enemy surface craft.

Lord Lewin, in his Foreword to *Dog Boats at War*, made a comment that truly sums up Coastal Force warfare:

> The employment of our Coastal Forces in the Second World War on frustrating convoy escort, the interception of enemy shipping and the brisk and bloody action at close quarters this usually entailed, hazardous clandestine landings on hostile shores – all these operations would have been recognized by the men who manned the brigs and cutters of the Napoleonic wars.

Certainly Nelson's signal 'Engage the enemy more closely' was the precept by which MTBs and MGBs served their nation and earned their proud reputations.

APPENDIX 1

NOTES

The following abbreviations are frequently used in both footnotes and in the end-notes in this Appendix:
PRO: Public Record Office; NHB: Naval Historical Branch; MO numbers are Admiralty references, found at NHB; ROP: Report of Proceedings; ADM: numbers are Admiralty series leading to 'pieces' at PRO; the ADM 199 series refer to operational reports at the PRO; WIR: War Intelligence Reports; NID: Naval Intelligence Division; CFPR: Coastal Forces Periodical Reviews; CFI: Coastal Forces Information Bulletins; CCF: Captain Coastal Forces. 'Summary': references to an Admiralty list of recorded actions, with summaries, held by the author at NHB.

CHAPTER 1

NOTE 1
A general note on sources.
Surprisingly little remains traceable in official records about these early operations. Information is largely derived from personal contacts, particularly with Cdr C.W.S. Dreyer and Capt D. Jermain. Peter Scott in *The Battle of the Narrow Seas* (1945) had the advantage of being able to refer to individuals and to their copies of Reports of Proceedings. Bryan Cooper's *The Battle of the Torpedo Boats* (1970) is also valuable, especially for its additional coverage of the MTBs of other nations.

NOTE 2
MTB 102 is still running in 2000, more than sixty years after she was built by Vosper Ltd. She has been preserved by the 102 Trust, and until recently served as a training ship for the Sea Scouts of Norfolk. Her CO in 1940, C.W.S. Dreyer, has taken her to Dunkirk on several anniversaries of her sterling deeds there in 1940. He retired as a Commander with a DSO and DSC and Bar, all earned in Coastal Forces, having been the Operations Officer for Coastal Forces in Operation Neptune and also a post-war Senior Officer of MTBs at their base, HMS *Hornet*. Later he was an executive with Vosper Thornycroft for many years and is now President of the Coastal Forces Veterans' Association.

Lt J. Cameron RNVR, the CO of MTB 107, had served in destroyers in the First World War, and had already taken silk. He died in 1996 aged ninety-six, having accompanied Cdr Dreyer back to Dunkirk in MTB 102 at the age of ninety. He was Scotland's premier judge and became Lord Cameron.

CHAPTER 3

NOTE 3
The daylight attack on the *Scharnhorst*, *Gneisenau* and *Prinz Eugen* took place on 12 February 1942. The author had the benefit of correspondence with Capt E.N. Pumphrey DSO** DSC RN (Retd) and his notes on the action, similar to those which made the account in Peter Scott's *Battle of the Narrow Seas* so fascinating. Together with the ROP which he loaned to me, these were the prime sources. Further details came from S. Roskill, *The War at Sea*, Vol. 2. It will interest Coastal Forces veterans that in

Correlli Barnett's *History of the Royal Navy in the Second World War, Engage the Enemy More Closely*, his account of this action is the only reference to MTBs in 1,052 pages, despite the book's stirring title which surely fits Coastal Forces more precisely than any other group. At least Correlli Barnett does not blame the MTB personnel for its inability to press home the attack:

> The MTB attack proved another poor advertisement for British technology, this time with regard to the design and manufacture of fast motor boats. . . . For all the determination of their crews, the attempt to press home the attack was thwarted by the E-boat screen and by a well-directed fire from the German destroyers.

He might well have directed his strictures more at the politicians and prewar naval hierarchy than at the manufacturers and designers who had invested their capital in experimental boats unsupported by the Admiralty.

Details of awards are from *Seedie's List of Coastal Forces Awards.*

CHAPTER 4

NOTE 4

George Selman was the chief designer for the British Power Boat Company of Hythe, and for years had been one of the team of gifted designers that Hubert Scott Paine had gathered round him to develop his ideas on building of fast boats. Selman was involved in the production of the 60ft and 70ft boats, and the 71ft 6in development from those earlier designs proved to be his most significant wartime achievement, and of tremendous value to the fleet of MTBs available from 1943 to 1945.

NOTE 5

Throughout the chapters describing the battles fought (and the development of tactical aspects of MTB/MGB warfare) involving Robert Hichens and Peter Dickens, reference is frequently made to the books they wrote which convey a great deal about the philosophy of both men. Hichens was writing *They Fought Them in Gunboats* during 1943, but the account stops abruptly some time before he was killed in April 1943.

Peter Dickens, in retirement taking to the pen like his illustrious grandfather Charles, did not publish *Night Action* until 1974, and he had the enormous advantage of access to enemy records.

Both of these books provide both information and insight into character, invaluable to a researcher.

CHAPTER 5

NOTE 6

The operations of the SGBs and C Class MGBs (including the raids on Dieppe and St Nazaire) are referred to, albeit briefly, in a supplementary chapter in *Dog Boats at War*.

CHAPTER 6

NOTE 7

The description of Bernard Torzynski's correspondence with John Perkins is by no means the only example of contact between the officers and crews of the ships and boats of both sides. The E-boat flotillas have well-established veterans' associations, many of which are in touch with individuals in the Royal Navy's Coastal Forces, and exchange visits are not uncommon. The camaraderie of 'men of the sea', however focused and patriotic in war, bears no malice as the years leave the events behind.

CHAPTER 7

NOTE 8
Lt David Pelham James RNVR was a difficult man to contain in a prisoner-of-war camp, and after one unsuccessful attempt he escaped in February 1944. He was awarded an MBE for that feat, and subsequently a DSC for the action on 27/28 February 1943. He later became a Member of Parliament and in 1947 wrote a successful book (*A Prisoner's Progress*) about his escape.

NOTE 9
Michael Bray DSC served from 1941 to 1943 in MGBs at Lowestoft and Ramsgate, gaining his first command at the age of twenty. He wrote, and published through Square One Publications in 1993, a memoir of his wartime naval service, *One Young Man's War*, which has provided some detailed descriptions of actions, particularly those with Lt G.D.K. Richards, his SO. I acknowledge with gratitude his permission to use material for this book.

NOTE 10
Lt C.A. (Tony) Law RCNVR, who led the unit of Dog Boats from the 31st MTB Flotilla on 22/23 March 1943, was already a veteran of 'short' boat operations. He returned to 'short' boats in October 1943 to become SO of the Canadian-manned 29th MTB Flotilla which distinguished itself during Operation Neptune. He was a widely acclaimed artist.

CHAPTER 8

NOTE 11
In 1974 Peter Dickens, who had retired as a captain, wrote his splendid book *Night Action, MTB Flotilla at War*, published by Peter Davies, which is dedicated 'to all who fought with the 21st MTB Flotilla, and to the dead and wounded on both sides'. It is probably the most valuable document ever written on Coastal Forces operations, and was crafted by a thinker of deep intellect and sensitivity to the demands of command. Making full use of enemy reports, he analysed each operation thoroughly and presented his tactical and strategic conclusions with great humility. He displayed to the full the vision and professional skills acquired in a distinguished naval career.

CHAPTER 9

NOTE 12
Much of the information on the planning and execution of the part played by Coastal Forces in Operation Overlord – and particularly in the naval aspects, code-named Operation Neptune – was derived from two documents made available to the author. These were the report on the operation by Captain Coastal Forces (Channel), made to C-in-C Portsmouth by his staff, and the similar report written for C-in-C Plymouth. These reports are enhanced by information from two other people: Cdr C.W.S. Dreyer DSO DSC RN, who played a very significant part during the whole period, and Lt Cdr P.M. Scott MBE DSC RNVR, another Operating Staff Officer, who was able to describe many facets of the operation in his book *The Battle of the Narrow Seas*.

NOTE 13
More information about the service of these officers is to be found in *Dog Boats at War* and *Mediterranean MTBs at War*. Although Cdr Dreyer's name appears quite frequently in this third volume, he gained his DSO in operations in the Strait of Messina during the Sicily campaign. Having spent virtually the whole of the war in Coastal Forces, he returned to HMS *Hornet* and also held Staff appointments in the Admiralty during the post-war period when it seemed that there

was some chance of fast boats having a place in the Royal Navy of the future.

Peter Scott served for over two years as Senior Officer of the 1st Steam Gun Boat Flotilla before joining Christopher Dreyer on CCF (Channel)'s team for Operation Overlord. The multi-talented Scott is remembered as an artist, a record-breaking glider pilot and a world-renowned naturalist.

NOTE 14

The history of the Free French 23rd MTB Flotilla is recorded in several ways. There is a useful booklet (in French) published as a supplement to a French naval journal Numero Special of *Forces Sous-Marines* – la 23e Flotille de Vedettes Rapides FNFL. Secondly, the author received notes from John Hatfield, a British liaison officer with the flotilla, and from J.R. Fletcher, a radar officer who served with the French boats at one time. Thirdly, there exists Paper 6 of the Dartmouth History Research Group, written by Tony Higgins and published in association with the Dartmouth Museum, 1993. All these sources are gratefully acknowledged.

CHAPTER 10

NOTE 15

One of the HDMLs involved was ML 1387 (*Medusa*), which is still (in 2000) afloat and running, having been preserved by a dedicated group of volunteers. It is currently in the care of the Coastal Forces Heritage Trust. In 1994 she led the armada of ships that sailed across the Channel to celebrate the fiftieth Anniversary of D-Day, being the only Royal Navy ship of that fleet which was actually present on 5/6 June 1944.

NOTE 16

For much of the remainder of Chapter 10, the sources are similar, since individual actions rarely featured in the ROPs of the ADM 199 series now in bound volumes at the PRO. Many of the ROPs are held by the author, supplied by (for example) Lt Cdr J.D. Dixon of the 35th Flotilla and Lt P. Magnus of the 30th Flotilla. Others are paraphrased in books, largely derived from CCF (Channel)'s Report which is the main source, or from the summary list of all Coastal Force actions compiled at the Admiralty from reports. For this reason, instead of having a footnote, MO numbers are given to distinguish an individual operation.

NOTE 17

The majority of the 21in torpedoes used by MTBs in 1941–1943 were Mark IVs which demanded great accuracy to hit. When used against shallow-draft vessels, they could miss by passing below the target's keel. In 1944 Mark VIII torpedoes with CCR pistols became available. These pistols enabled the warhead to be detonated from any position within the magnetic field of the target, rather than requiring actual contact with the hull. This increased the rate of successful firings.

Lt D.E.J. Hunt DSC* was later SO of the 31st Flotilla, and a distinguished officer. He is renowned throughout Coastal Forces as the founder of the MTB/MGB Officers' Association, organizing reunions, maintaining records and corresponding with hundreds of his contemporaries for over fifty years.

NOTE 18

Apart from CCF (Channel)'s Report, ROPs in ADM 199 collections at the PRO Kew, extensive notes in the Summary of CF actions, and ROPs held by the author, some details are available in the main reference books, and are extremely valuable. Peter Scott was intimately involved in all aspects of the planning of Operation Neptune and therefore had immediate access to first-hand descriptions from individuals, which he used in his *Battle of the Narrow Seas* (1945).

C.A. Law, also a distinguished artist, led the Canadian 29th Flotilla throughout the operation and his *White Plumes Astern* is an intensely personal account of the major contribution made by his boats.

CHAPTER 11

NOTE 19
Principal sources of information on the military situation affecting the naval war in the region are:
a) Churchill, W.S., *The Second World War, Volume 6, Triumph and Tragedy*, Chapter XIII, Cassell, 1954.
b) Wilmot, C., *The Second World War: The Struggle for Europe*, Chapter XXVIII, Collins, 1952.

NOTE 20
The author is indebted to Brian Hetherington, who has been very active in attending reunions of S-boat flotillas and has maintained correspondence with several German COs, who kindly sent the letter from the CO of S 199, and also to a local research group who sent me the letter from the former CO of the Tongue Fort.

NOTE 21
This fascinating description of human reactions to war situations, especially in a manner so warmly and courteously conveyed to John Lake by Herr Stockleth, the former CO of S 199, is gratefully acknowledged. It is a fine example of how chivalry prevails in war, and illustrates the lack of bitterness towards former 'enemies'.

EPILOGUE

NOTE 22
Radar. Type 286 MU sets began to be fitted in most boats by November 1941 but with little effect. A set with improved aerial (286 PU) was fitted from mid-1942. Then 291 U – more powerful – in early 1943, although not universal for many months. But all these sets had considerable drawbacks: hand-rotated aerials, poor accuracy and range, giving only bearings relative to ship's head, and a display that was very difficult to read and subject to false echoes (known as 'gremlins' to all in Coastal Forces). These shortcomings led to a lack of confidence, although skilled operators got good results in favourable conditions. Compared with the USN PT boats' 10cm type SO sets with PPI display and power-rotation aerials, they were primitive. British naval radar design and production facilities were so hard pressed that in 1943 Canada was asked to help in producing a centimetric set for Coastal Forces. Although early design work went well, production difficulties meant that they became available too late to make any impact on operations.

APPENDIX 2

TABLES

TABLE 1: AWARDS OF DECORATIONS

(from *Seedie's List of Coastal Forces Awards*)

DISTINGUISHED SERVICE ORDER

MTB	212	Lt M. Arnold-Forster
	221	Lt Cdr E.N. Pumphrey RN
	234	Lt P.G.C. Dickens RN
		Lt G.J. Macdonald RNZNVR
MGB	67	Lt Cdr G.E. Bailey
	110	Lt G.D.K. Richards RN
HMS *Beehive*		Lt Cdr R.P. Hichens

BAR TO DISTINGUISHED SERVICE ORDER

8th MGB Flotilla	Lt Cdr R.P. Hichens

DISTINGUISHED SERVICE CROSS

MTB	22	Lt Cdr A.B. Cole RN
	24	Lt V.F.W. Clarkson
	31	Lt D. Jermain RN
	31	Sub Lt G.J. Macdonald RNZNVR
		Sub Lt J. Weeden
	32	Lt D.G.H. Wright
	34	Lt I.C. Trelawny
	35	Lt Cdr E.N. Pumphrey RN
	38	Sub Lt P.T.E. Nicholson RNR
		Lt M. Arnold-Forster
		Sub Lt G.H. Bradley
	44	Sub Lt R.F. Saunders RANVR
	45	Lt L.J.H. Gamble RN
	47	Lt W.I.C. Ewart RN
	54	Lt P.E. Danielsen RNorN
	56	Lt S.N. Ostervold RNorN
	70	Sub Lt T. Neill
		Sub Lt J.H. Saunders
	74	Sub Lt R.C.M.V. Wynn

MTB	83	Lt J.D.C. Coombs
	88	Lt A.T.J. Harrington
	98	L de V R.L.E. Lagersie FN
	102	Lt C.W.S. Dreyer RN
	201	Lt G.L. Cotton
	203	Lt E.H. Larive RNethN
	204	Lt W.A. De Looze RNethN
		Lt H.C. Jorissen RNethN
	209	Sub Lt J. Ferguson RANVR
	210	Lt P.R. Everett
	211	Lt N.W.G. Taylor
	212	Lt Cdr F.H. Dunlop RN
	218	Lt C.E. Bonnell RCNVR
		Sub Lt H. Teckman RCNVR
	219	Sub Lt P.A. Berthon
	221	Sub Lt B. Easton
	224	Sub Lt A.J. Lee
	225	Sub Lt D.G. Gill
	227	L de V De Casanove FN
	230	Lt J.P. Perkins
	232	Sub Lt V. Ohlenschlager
		Lt J.A. Wolfe
	234	Lt P.G.C. Dickens RN
	236	Sub Lt R.Q. Drayson
	238	Lt R.G. Eburah
	245	Lt D.E.J. Hunt
	250	Lt G.H. Baker
	254	Lt D. Rigg
	255	Lt P. Aspinall
	256	Sub Lt J.A. Peters
	344	Sub Lt F.W.P. Bourne
	350	Sub Lt H.G. Franklin
	352	Lt J.M. Moore
	354	Lt R.F. Plugge RN
	386	Lt P.J. Liddell
	417	Sub Lt T.G. Hughes
	418	Sub Lt L.N. Benthall
		Lt L.E. Thompson
	430	Lt T.J. Mathias
	431	Sub Lt C.C. Gough
	439	Lt C.A. Burk RCNVR
	440	Lt W.L. Fesq RANVR
	444	Sub Lt P.R. Davis
	447	Lt E.C. Glennie
	448	Lt R.T. Sykes

MTB	450	Lt Cdr J.D. Dixon
	452	Lt L.E. Yock RANVR
	453	Lt N. Watson RNZNVR
	454	Sub Lt G.K. Natusch RNZNVR
		Lt P.G.A. Irvine
	455	Lt M.V. Rout RNZNVR
		Sub Lt E.H.R. Womersley
	459	Lt Cdr C.A. Law RCNVR
	464	Lt L.C. Bishop RCNVR
	467	Lt R.R. Crosley
	468	Lt B.L. Bazeley
	471	Lt F.P. Standley
	473	Lt J.J.F. Aimers
	475	Lt P. Magnus
	480	Lt R.C. Campbell RCNVR
	493	Lt A.D. Foster
23rd MTB Flotilla		L de V P.L. Iele
HMS *Beehive*		Lt B.M. MacGinty
		Lt P.W.T. Warren
HMS *Hornet*		Lt J.A. Eardley-Wilmot RN
HMS *Mantis*		Sub Lt (Sp) P. Knowles
MGB	6	Sub Lt R.M. Barge
		Sub Lt P.S. Marshall
	10	Sub Lt P.G. Lee
	13	Lt T.G. Fuller RCNVR
		Lt G.D.K. Richards RN
	20	Lt G.R. Dale
	21	Lt J.E. Dyer RN
		Lt J.S. Price
	41	Lt R. King RN
	43	Lt P.F.S. Gould RN
	46	Lt J.A. Schreuder RNethN
	61	Sub Lt E.D.W. Leaf
	67	Lt L.G.R. Campbell
	78	Lt G.F. Duncan RCNVR
		Lt R.M. Eggleston
	79	Lt D.P. James
	87	Lt S.B. Bennett
	88	Lt J.B. Horne RN
	91	Lt P.A.R. Thompson RCNVR
	110	Sub Lt W. Waterman
	113	Lt F.A.M. Bray
	117	Lt A.W. Cotton
MA/SB	24	Lt W.E.A. Blount

MA/SB	25	Lt R.R.G. Gallichan
	26	Lt R.L. Foster
6 MGB Flotilla		Lt P.N. Howes RN
1 MA/SB Flotilla		Lt Cdr E.C.D. Custance
HMS *Beehive*		Sub Lt F.J. Head
HMS *Fervent*		Lt Cdr W.R. Szuster PolN
HMS *Wasp*		Lt R.B. Rooper RN
HMS *Hornet*		Lt R.G. Fison
(Frigate Control Officers)		Lt R.G.O. Hudson
USN PTs		
35 PT Sqn		Lt G.E. Fowler USNR
		Lt W.J. Ryan USNR
		Lt S.I. Saltsman USNR

BAR TO DISTINGUISHED SERVICE CROSS

MTB	25	Lt B.C. Ward RN
	44	Lt C.W.S. Dreyer RN
	56	Lt P.E. Danielsen RNorN
	202	Lt E.H. Larive RNethN
	224	Sub Lt A.J. Lee
	232	Lt J.A. Wolfe
	234	Lt H.A.J. Hollings RN
	241	Lt G.J. Macdonald RNZNVR
	245	Lt D.E.J. Hunt
	252	Lt D.A. Shaw RN
	350	Lt H.G. Franklin
	355	Lt I.C. Trelawny
	444	Lt E.D.W. Leaf
	450	Lt Cdr J.D. Dixon
	455	Lt J.S. Price
	461	Lt C.A. Burk RCNVR
	464	Lt L.C. Bishop RCNVR
	467	Lt R.R. Crosley
	475	Lt The Hon F.M.S. Shore
		Lt P. Magnus
	495	Lt R.G. Eburah
HMS *Mantis*		Lt D.G.H. Wright
MGB	43	Lt P.F.S. Gould RN
	64	Lt Cdr R.P. Hichens
	76	Lt L.G.R. Campbell
	112	Lt D.C. Sidebottom
	118	Lt P.G. Lee

SECOND BAR TO DISTINGUISHED SERVICE CROSS

MTB	454	Lt Cdr J.D. Dixon
	458	Lt D.G.H. Wright
		Lt J.S. Price
	461	Lt C.A. Burk RCNVR
MGB	77	Lt Cdr R.P. Hichens
HMS *Beehive*		Lt G.J. Macdonald RNZNVR
Frigate Control Officer		Lt P.G. Lee

MEMBER OF THE ORDER OF THE BRITISH EMPIRE

MGB	79	Lt D.P. James

CROIX DE GUERRE

23 MTB Flotilla		Lt P.F. Flynn

CONSPICUOUS GALLANTRY MEDAL

MTB	74	CMM W.H. Lovegrove
	201	Sto R.J. Spinks
MGB	8	AB J. Booth
	9	LMM F.N. Dowson
	43	AB L.D. Lanfear
	77	AB J.R. Barnes

DISTINGUISHED SERVICE MEDAL

MTB	24	CMM A. Fox
	31	PO E.W. Matthew RNR
		O Tel J.A. Hirst
		PO H. Unsworth
	32	L Sto N.R.A. Fowle
		POMM E.R. Rowe
		PO R. Walker
	35	AB J. Carruthers
		CMM T.C. Gordon
		POMM W. Abram
		PO W. Stead
	38	PO J.W. Hadley
		L Sto S. Johnson
	43	AB E. Fletcher
	43	Sto A.F. Pearce
	44	L Sto K.E. Marshall
	47	Sto M. Beason
	56	Sto K. Hals RNorN
		PO I. Sorensen RNorN
	69	Sto J.C.E. Parry
	70	PO T.S. Pennington

MTB	70	CMM G.A. Williams
	83	POMM D. Welsh
		PO L.W. Pratt
	93	PO M. Murray
	98	QM L. Prufer FN
	102	ERA G.W. Hymas
		AB A.R.C. Stephens
	201	L Sea A.E. Collins
	202	PO Tel G.A. Dekker RNethN
	204	PO C. Van Kruiningen RNethN
	208	AB D.M. Collin
		CMM P. Dundas
		L Sea L.S.D. Stapley
	210	L Sea A.W. Armitage
		LMM J.H.A. Carter
	212	AB A. Macdonell
	218	L Tel P. Phillips
	221	AB W.J. Wyborn
		CMM J.M. Henderson
	223	L Sea R.A. Chappell
	224	L Sto W. Greenland
		L Sea H.G. Haylock
		AB G. Oliver
	225	PO P. Edwards
	226	LMM W.J. Donovan
	232	L Sea J.T. Valentine
		POMM A.I. Redwood
	233	PO R.A. Henry
		Tel J.C. Dargie
		AB A.A. Craig
	234	POMM R.J.E. Cuthbert
		L Sea J.R. Saunders
	238	AB A.E. Metheringham
		L Tel C. Tatham
	241	PO E.J. White
		CMM E. Waite
	244	PO W.A. Cooke
	245	LMM H.C. Carty
		Tel H. Morrey
		PO D.G. Smith
	257	CMM E.J.F. Fullard
	344	L Sea T. Hannah
	347	L Sea J.F. Hunter
		Sto G. Sykes
	350	CMM E.J. Cartwright

MTB	350	POMM E. Bannister
		AB D.T. Ashton
	352	AB J. England
	353	AB J. Gilchrist
	355	PO C.C. Keem
	359	CMM F. Blain
	413	AB E.T. Bishop
	415	AB E.A. Bradshaw
	418	AB J.D. Wilson
	431	AB T.W. Simpson
	434	AB D. Falk
		POMM J.R. Pacey
	437	POMM R.D. Hanks
	438	AB P. Henry
		POMM R. Sharman
	440	AB D. McIntosh
		L Tel A.F. Johnson
	441	AB C.G. Townsend
		POMM S.T. Campbell
	442	AB H.E. Danks
		O Sea T.H. Taylor
	444	Sig J.A. Bussey
		Tel S.J. Downey
		LMM T.F. Lunnon
	446	AB H.L. Bray
		Sto R.B. Finch
	447	L Sea T.O. Oliver
		AB W.A.S. Dodd
	448	L Sea P.H. Joyce
	450	AB E. Hall
		CMM G. Poffley
		PO C.S. Young
	451	L Sea J. Brown
		AB J. Wolstenholme
	453	LMM R.J. Constable
		AB J. Johnston
		AB J.B. Prescott
	454	AB A.R.R. Banger
	455	PO F. Atkinson
		AB R. Allan
	458	AB S. Allman
		PO C.W.A. Parham
		L Tel W. Healey
	459	AB W. Bushfield RCNVR
		O Sea W. Dublack RCNVR

MTB	459	L Sea W. Reid RCNVR
	461	L Sea A.G. Stubbins RCNVR
	466	AB J. Wright RCNVR
	467	PO J. Summers
		POMM F.W. Wilton
		Tel A.C. Habben
	468	AB D.G. Campbell
		L Tel S. Mercer
		CMM J.E.W. Snoswell
	469	POMM R.W. Southcombe
	471	CMM B.E. Holmes
		O Sea K. Morgan
		AB E. Carter
		POMM D.E. Biddiscombe
	473	Sto G.H. Spilstead
	473	L Sea H.F.W. Davey
	474	AB G.J. Boatman
		AB E.G. Hall
		L Sea J. Wilkinson
	475	PO G.A.C. Stevens
		AB J. Close
	476	AB W.F. Greatbatch
	477	AB E. Dresser
		O Sea H.E. Jones
		L Sea A.G. Ellis
	482	AB J. Gillespie
	493	AB G.E. Rives
	495	L Sea D.H. Wade
	497	Tel S.G. Rose
		L Sto S. Dean
		AB F. Ibbotson
MGB	6	O Sea H.D. Weeks
		L Sto J.W. Wood
	7	AB G.W. Wetherall
	10	L Sto R. Mackenzie
		LMM J.E. Wibrin
	13	AB A. Horsfall
	17	POMM C. Dobson
	21	O Tel G.W. Slater
	42	AB R.G. Guest
		Sto PO C. Harper
	43	AB J. Tate RNR
		PO I.W.H. Stevens
	46	ERA 2 P.F. De Loos RNethN
		ERA 2 P. Haringa RNethN

MGB	52	AB A.W.D. Bontoft
	59	MM R.C. Broughton
		AB J.W. Dickson
	64	L Sea H.G. Curtis
	65	PO E.S. Stacey
	67	PO S.R. Whistler
		AB L. Fletcher
		CMM R.H. White
		PO W.A.J. Wollage
	70	AB R.C. McGregor
	75	L Sea L.S. Nicholl
	76	PO A.A. Hartland
	77	CMM V.G. Stay
	78	CMM B. Heron
	83	AB E.W. Surridge
	86	AB G. Murray
	87	POMM G.G. Biddlecombe
	88	AB G.E. Green
		Tel C. Lowe
		AB R.T. Smith
		Tel D.G. Robertson
		PO D.J. Ross
	89	L Sto F.T. Newport
	91	Sto J. Richards
		O Tel D.R. Terry
		L Sea R.W. Tate
	108	L Sea J.J. Billings
		AB J.R. Caleb
	110	PO C.F. Checklin
		L Tel W. Lovell
		AB K.W. Drage
		AB W. Grainger
	112	AB L.D. Conroy
	113	AB J. Sanlon
	118	O Sea D.J. Francis
		AB A.W. Carrington

BAR TO DISTINGUISHED SERVICE MEDAL

MTB	32	L Sto J.C.E. Parry
MGB	110	POMM J.E. Wibrin
HMS *Hornet*		AB T. Lamont

BRITISH EMPIRE MEDAL

MTB	465	O Sea R.V. McNally
14 MTB Flotilla		AB A. Nunn RCN

3 MGB Flotilla		CPO C. Olesinski PolN

NORWEGIAN WAR MEDAL

MTB	54	Tel E.J.W. Slater

CROIX DE GUERRE

MTB	90	Tel F.E. Jones
		Tel F.J. Wardell
	91	Tel F.N. Tyldesley
		Tel P.S. Walsh
	92	Tel A.S. Trenwith
	94	Tel G.M. Morrow
	96	Tel K. Butler
	98	Tel S.J. Bennett
	227	Tel J.A. Knight
	459	O Sea G. Belliveau RCNVR
	461	AB G. Workman RCNVR
23 MTB Flotilla		Tel E. Peters

TABLE 2: WAR LOSSES

(NB: CTL = 'Constructive Total Loss' – beyond economic repair)

MOTOR TORPEDO BOATS

MTB	Flotilla	Date	
05	1st	26.12.40	Mined off Gunfleet as MAC 5.
N5	11th	1. 7.41	(RNorN) Destroyed by explosion in Ferry Dock, Dover.
N6	11th	26. 9.40	(RNorN) Abandoned after springing a leak in heavy weather off Beachy Head.
15	1st	24. 9.40	Mined in Thames estuary.
16	1st	31.10.40	Mined in Thames estuary.
17	1st	21.10.40	Sunk in action off Ostend.
28	3rd	7. 3.41	Destroyed by fire and explosion at HMS *Hornet*, Gosport.
29	4th	5.10.42	Sunk after being rammed by MTB 30 during action with E-boats.
30	4th	18.12.42	Mined in North Sea.
33	–	26. 9.40	Destroyed by explosion while fuelling for trials at Vosper, Portsmouth.
37	–	11. 1.41	Destroyed by fire while under construction, when Vosper's Camber Yard was bombed.
39	–	11. 1.41	Destroyed by fire while under construction, when Vosper's Camber Yard was bombed.

40	-	11. 1.41	Destroyed by fire while under construction, when Vosper's Camber Yard was bombed.
41	5th	14. 2.41	Mined in North Sea.
43	5th	18. 8.42	Sunk in action off Gravelines.
44	5th	7. 8.42	Sunk in action in Dover Strait.
47	5th	17. 1.42	Sunk in action off Cap Gris-Nez.
74(i)	-	11. 1.41	Destroyed by fire while under construction when Vosper's Camber Yard was bombed.
74(ii)	Ind.	28. 3.42	Sunk in action after leaving St Nazaire.
75(i)	-	11. 1.41	Destroyed by fire while under construction, when Vosper's Camber Yard was bombed.
80	24th	2. 3.43	CTL. Severely damaged when ran aground while working-up at Weymouth.
87	22nd	31.10.42	Mined in North Sea.
93	22nd	18. 8.44	Sunk in collision with MTB 729 off Harwich.
105	Ind.	1. 1.43	(Tender to HMS *Fidelity*) Sunk by HMCS *Woodstock* 200 miles north of Azores.
106	10th	16.10.40	Sunk by mine off Sheerness.
108(ii)	-	11. 1.41	Destroyed by fire while under construction, when Vosper's Camber Yard was bombed.
201	9th	15. 6.42	Sunk in tow after action damage off Boulogne.
203	9th	18. 5.44	Mined off Etaples while minelaying.
218	6th	18. 8.42	Sunk by enemy action and mine, Dover Strait.
220	6th	13. 5.42	Abandoned after action off Ambleteuse, NE France.
222	22nd	10.11.43	Sunk in tow after collision with MTB 230 off the Dutch coast.
230	22nd	10.11.43	Rammed by MTB 222 and sank off the Dutch coast.
237	21st	7. 8.42	Sunk in action off Barfleur.
241	21st	31. 3.44	Sunk in tow after action damage off Ymuiden.
248	14th	6. 6.44	Rammed by MTB 249 and 251 and sank off Normandy.
255	Ind	14. 2.45	Lost in fire and explosion at Ostend.
345	att'd 30th(Ds)	28. 7.43	(RNorN) Captured by Germans while lying up at Aspoy, north of Bergen.
347	11th	1.10.44	Sunk in action off Ymuiden.
352	11th	26. 3.44	Sank after being rammed by MTB 351 on patrol, Dutch coast.
356	11th	16.10.43	Scuttled after disabled in action off Scheveningen.
357	5th	24.12.43	CTL after serious damage in action off Dunkirk.
360	11th	1.10.44	Sunk in action off Ymuiden.
412	1st(2)	27. 7.44	Collided with E-boat and blew up in action off Cap d'Antifer.
417	2nd(2)	16. 3.44	Sunk in action off Calais.
430	1st(2)	27. 7.44	Rammed by E-boat and blew up in action off Cap d'Antifer.
434	1st(2)	9. 7.44	Sunk in action off Le Havre.
438	3rd(2)	14. 2.45	Destroyed in fire and explosion, Ostend.
441	3rd(2)	23.10.44	CTL. Hit by gunfire from Allied merchant ship, flooded and beached.
444	3rd(2)	14. 2.45	Destroyed in fire and explosion, Ostend.

448	35th	11. 6.44	Sunk by gunfire from MTB 453, following heavy damage in action with E-boats off Barfleur.
459	29th	14. 2.44	Destroyed in fire and explosion, Ostend.
460	29th	3. 7.44	Mined off Normandy.
461	29th	14. 2.44	Destroyed in fire and explosion, Ostend.
462	29th	14. 2.44	Destroyed in fire and explosion, Ostend.
463	29th	8. 7.44	Mined off Normandy.
464	29th	14. 2.44	CTL after fire and explosion, Ostend. Towed to England and paid off.
465	29th	14. 2.44	Destroyed in fire and explosion, Ostend.
466	29th	14. 2.44	Destroyed in fire and explosion, Ostend.
493	22nd	7. 4.45	CTL. Severely damaged after ramming E-boat in action, North Sea.
494	22nd	7. 4.45	Rammed by E-boat in action and sank, North Sea.

MOTOR GUNBOATS

MGB	Flotilla	Date	
9	2nd	15.10.42	CTL. Boat not repairable, following broken back and earlier damage in action.
11	2nd	30. 1.42	CTL. Damaged in heavy weather. (Used as target, 1943.)
12	2nd	6. 2.41	Sunk in tow after mined on 3.2.41 at Milford Haven.
14	5th	11. 7.42	CTL. Damaged in air raid on Lowestoft. (Used as target, 1943.)
15	5th	11. 7.42	CTL. Damaged in air raid on Lowestoft. (Used as target, 1943.)
17	ex-5th	10. 6.44	Mined off Normandy.
18	5th	30. 9.42	Sunk in action off Terschelling.
19	5th	6.11.42	Bombed and wrecked while on slip at Oulton Broad.
25	MA/SB-ASR	17. 1.44	CTL. Grounded on Goodwin Sands. Sunk as target.
30	MA/SB	14.12.41	Lost in collision with boom, Humber.
62	6th	9. 8.41	Lost in collision with MGB 67 in action off Ymuiden.
64	6th	8. 8.43	Foundered in heavy weather returning from patrol off Ostend.
76	8th	6.10.42	Blew up and sank while returning after action off Flushing.
78	8th	3.10.42	Beached and abandoned after being heavily hit in action off Dutch coast.
79	8th	28. 2.43	Sunk in action off the Hook.
90	7th	16. 7.41	Destroyed by fire after explosion on MGB 92 at Portland.
92	7th	16. 7.41	Destroyed by fire after explosion at Portland.
98	Ind	11. 3.41	Lost by bombing at HMS *Hornet*, Gosport.
99	Ind	4.45	CTL.
109	9th	25. 2.43	Mined and severely damaged on 7.2.43 off South Foreland and formally paid off 25.2.43.
110	9th	29. 5.43	Sunk in action off Dunkirk.

TABLE 3: THE SHORT MTB AND MGB FLOTILLAS IN HOME WATERS

(*with acknowledgements to G.M. Hudson*)

(NB: 'BPB': British Power Boat)

A note on flotilla numbers not listed here will be found at the end of this Table, to help with an understanding of the complete MTB/MGB flotilla allocations.

THE MTB FLOTILLAS

1st MTB Flotilla (1) 1939–1942

Arrived at Portsmouth in December 1939 on return from Mediterranean. MTBs 01 to 05, 14 to 19 (60ft BPBs). In October 1940 01–05 and 19 redesignated Motor Attendant Craft (MAC) 1–6. 14–18 operated from Felixstowe/Harwich. Losses reduced to two boats by November 1940. MTBs 14, 18, 100 (60ft BPBs), 71 and 72 (60ft Vospers) operated from Felixstowe until disbanded in August 1942.

SO1: Lt Cdr C.M. Donner RN
SO2: Lt J.T. Mannooch RN
SO3: Lt I.C. Trelawny

1st MTB Flotilla (2) October 1943–1945

MTBs 412–416, 430, 431, 434 (71ft 6in BPB Mark V, ex-8th MGB Flotilla); later MTBs 483, 487–490 (71ft 6in BPB Mark VI) added.

Dartmouth, Ramsgate, Portsmouth, Lowestoft, Felixstowe.
SO1: Lt F.N. Stephenson RN
SO2: Lt T.J. Mathias
SO3: Lt J.A. Bennett RCNVR
SO4: Lt C.E.M. Thornycroft RN

2nd MTB Flotilla (2) October 1943–1944

MTBs 417, 418, 432 (Polish S4), 433 (RNethN), 435, 436, 437 (71ft 6in BPB Mark V, ex-9th MGB Flot); by April 1944 all boats were manned by Dutch personnel.

Dover, Ramsgate.
SO1: Lt R.B. Rooper RN
SO2: Lt R.M. Barge
SO3: Lt W.A. de Looze RNethN

3rd MTB Flotilla (2) 1940–1941

Training Flotilla

MTB 102 (68ft Vosper), 100 (60ft BPB); later, MTBs 24, 25, 28 (72ft Thornycroft), from 4th MTBs.

Portsmouth, Dover.
SO1: Lt C.W.S. Dreyer RN
SO2: Lt Cdr C.S.D. Noakes RN

3rd MTB Flotilla (3) 1943–1945
MTBs 438–445 (71ft 6in BPB Mark V); later, 485, 486, 491 (Mark VI).
Lowestoft, Ramsgate, Felixstowe.
SO1: Lt E.D.W. Leaf
SO2: Lt J.S. Price
SO3: Lt G.R. Dale RNVR

4th MTB Flotilla (1) 1940–1943
MTBs 22, 29, 30 (70ft Vosper 1938 class); 24, 25, 28 (72ft Thornycroft 1938 class); 31, 32, 34 (71ft Vosper 1939 class); later 69, 70 (70ft Vosper, ex-Greek); 71, 72 (60ft Vosper, ex-Norwegian).
Blyth, Dover, Felixstowe.
SO1: Lt Cdr A.B. Cole RN
SO2: Lt C.A. James RN
SO3: Lt H.L. Lloyd RN
SO4: Lt I.C. Trelawny

4th MTB Flotilla (2) 1944–1945
MTBs 455–457 (71ft 6in BPB Mark V); 458, 467–470 (Mark VI)
Lowestoft.
SO1: Lt D.G.H. Wright
SO2: Lt Cdr J.S. Price

5th MTB Flotilla 1940–1943
MTBs 41–48 (72ft White 1939 class). In spring 1942 merged with 6th Flotilla; 35, 38, 218–221, then 24 and 25 (ex-3rd).
Felixstowe, Dover.
SO1: Lt Cdr J.C. Cole RN
SO2: Lt L.G.H. Gamble RN
SO3: Lt C.W.S. Dreyer RN
SO4: Lt B.C. Ward RN
1943–1944 By the end of 1943, only 24 and 25 remained; joined by 353, 354, 357–359, 361, 362 (71ft Vosper 1942 class).
Dover.
SO1: Lt B.C. Ward RN
SO2: Lt R.F. Plugge RN

6th MTB Flotilla 1941–1942 (merged with 5th)
MTBs 35, 39 (71ft Vosper 1939 class); 218–221 (71ft Vosper, ex-Greek).
Dover.
SO: Lt E.N. Pumphrey RN

8th MTB Flotilla (2) 1944–1945
MTBs 424–429 (Polish S5–10) (71ft 6in White 1943 class).
Dover, Felixstowe, Portsmouth.
SO: Lt Cdr W.R. Szuster Polish Navy

9th MTB Flotilla 1942–1943
MTBs 201–204 (71ft White 1940 class, Vosper design); MTBs 229, 231, 235, 236, 240 (71ft Vosper 1941 class).

Dover, Dartmouth.
Manned by British and Dutch personnel:
SO: Lt C. Philpotts RN
From 1943 all boats manned by Dutch personnel:
SO: Lt E.H. Larive RNethN

11th MTB Flotilla (1) 1940–1941
MTBs 69, 70 (70ft Vosper, ex-Greek), 71, 72 (60ft Vosper, ex-Norwegian), N5, N6 (60ft Vosper) RNorN.

Dover.
SO: Lt J.B. King-Church RN
SO2: Lt R.A.M. Hennessy RN

11th MTB Flotilla (2) 1941–1942
MTBs 49–56 (74ft Thornycroft 1939 class); also 102 (68ft Vosper); 105 (45ft Thornycroft).

Dover, Portland, Portsmouth.
SO1: Lt K.A. Cradock-Hartopp RN
SO2: Lt J.A. Eardley-Wilmot RN

11th MTB Flotilla (3) 1943–1945
MTBs 348–352, 355, 356, 360; later, 347 (71ft Vosper 1942 class).

Felixstowe, Lowestoft, Ostend.
SO1: Lt I.C. Trelawny
SO2: Lt H.A.J. Hollings RN
SO3: Lt J. Dyer RN
SO4: Lt C.E.M. Thornycroft RN
SO5: Lt F.W. Bourne

12th MTB Flotilla 1941–1942
MTBs 327–331 (55ft Thornycroft, ex-Philippines); 345 (55ft Thornycroft).

Portsmouth, Dartmouth.
SO: Lt Keyworth RN

13th MTB Flotilla 1942–1944
MTBs 205–212 (71ft White 1940 class, Vosper design).

Portland, Dover, Newhaven, Portsmouth.
SO1: Lt A.S. Hughes
SO2: Lt/Lt Cdr M. Arnold-Forster

14th MTB Flotilla 1942–1944

MTBs 246–251 (71ft White 1941 class, Vosper design); 252–257 (71ft 6in White 1942 class, White design).

Portland, Newhaven.
SO1: Lt F.E. MacVie RN
SO2: Lt D.G. Shaw RN

21st MTB Flotilla 1942–1944

MTBs 223–225, 232–234, 237, 241, 244 (71ft Vosper 1941 class).

Lowestoft, Felixstowe, Harwich.
SO1: Lt P.G.C. Dickens RN
SO2: Lt H.A.J. Hollings RN
SO3: Lt G.J. Macdonald RNZNVR

1944–1945 Replacement boats: MTBs 385, 387–390, 393–395 (73ft Vosper 1943 class).
Lowestoft.
SO: Lt Cdr G.J. Macdonald RNZNVR

22nd MTB Flotilla 1942–1944

MTBs 83, 87, 88, 93, 222, 230, 238, 245 (71ft Vosper 1940–41 class); 347 (71ft Vosper 1942 class). Later, 25 (72ft Thornycroft 1938 class).

Lowestoft and Felixstowe.
SO1: Lt D. Long RN
SO2: Lt D.G.H. Wright
SO3: Lt R.G. Eburah

1944–45 Replacement boats: MTBs 446, 484, 493–497 (71ft 6in BPB Mark VI).
Lowestoft.
SO: Lt R.G. Eburah

23rd MTB Flotilla 1942–1945

MTBs 90–94, 96, 98, 227, 239 (71ft Vosper 1940–41 class). Manned by Free French Navy personnel.

Dartmouth, Newhaven.
SO1: Lt Cdr E. Meurville
SO2: Lt P. Iehle

29th MTB Flotilla 1944–1945

MTBs 459–466; later, 484–486, 491, to replace losses (71ft 6in BPB Mark VI). Manned by Royal Canadian Navy personnel.

Ramsgate, Dover, Portsmouth, Felixstowe, Ostend.
SO: Lt Cdr C.A. Law RCNVR

30th MTB Flotilla (2) 1944–1945

MTBs 471–477, 479, 480 (71ft 6in BPB Mark VI).

Lowestoft, Dover, Ramsgate, Portsmouth, Ostend.
SO: Lt P. Magnus

31st MTB Flotilla (2) 1944–1945
MTBs 380–384, 386, 391, 392 (73ft Vosper 1943 class).
Lowestoft, Portland.
SO1: Lt Cdr Moseley RN
SO2: Lt D.A. Shaw RN
SO3: Lt D.E.J. Hunt

35th MTB Flotilla 1943–1945
MTBs 447–454 (71ft 6in BPB Mark V). Later, 478, 481, 482 (71ft 6in BPB Mark VI).
Felixstowe, Newhaven, Portsmouth.
SO: Lt/Lt Cdr J.D. Dixon

36th MTB Flotilla 1945
MTBs 499–506 (71ft 6in BPB Mark VI).
Felixstowe, Portland.
SO: Lt R.F. Plugge RN

THE MGB FLOTILLAS

1st MGB Flotilla 1941–1942
MGBs 69–73, 100–106 (69ft Higgins, ex-USA)
Grimsby, Lowestoft.
SO1: Lt A.A.T. Seymour-Hayden RN
SO2: Lt J.G. Llewellyn

2nd MGB Flotilla 1941–1943
MGBs 6–13 (70ft BPB, former MA/SBS).
Dover, Ramsgate, Dartmouth, Portland.
SO1: Lt G.D.K. Richards RN
SO2: Lt W.B.G. Leith

3rd MGB Flotilla 1941–1943
MGBs 40–43, 44 (Polish S2), 45 (Polish S3) (63ft BPB, ex-Swedish and Norwegian), 46 (70ft BPB, ex-Dutch), 47, 48 (Polish S1) (75ft White, ex-Polish). All former MA/SBs.
Fowey, Dartmouth, Dover.
SO1: Lt Cdr A.A. Fitzroy-Talbot RN
SO2: Lt R.G.H.G. Eyre RN
SO3: Lt T. Dorrien-Smith RN
SO4: Lt P.F.S. Gould RN
SO5: Lt R. King RN
SO6: Lt Cdr W.R. Szuster Polish Navy

4th MGB Flotilla 1941–1943
MGBs 50–57 (70ft BPB, ex-French). Former MA/SBs.
Fowey, Portland.

SO1: Lt H.R.A. Kidston RN
SO2: Lt E.M. Thorpe RN
SO3: Lt D.F. Johnson RN

5th MGB Flotilla 1941–1943
MGBs 14–21 (70ft BPB). Former MA/SBs.
Lowestoft.
SO1: Lt W.F. Willett RN
SO2: Lt J.E. Dyer RN
SO3: Lt A.N. Macpherson RN

6th MGB Flotilla 1941–1943
MGBs 58–65, 67 (70ft BPB, ex-French). Former MA/SBs.
Fowey, Felixstowe.
SO1: Lt P. Howes RN
SO2: Lt Cdr R.P. Hichens
SO3: Lt G.E. Bailey
SO4: Lt J.E. Colville
SO5: Lt H.A.J. Hollings RN

7th MGB Flotilla 1941–1944
MGBs 82–92 (70ft Elco, ex-USN PTs 1–11).
Portland, Dover, Lowestoft.
SO1: Lt J.B.R. Horne RN
SO2: Lt J.E. Dyer RN
SO3: Lt A.N. Macpherson RN
SO4: Lt J.A.C. Findlay
SO5: Lt F.N. Thomson

8th MGB Flotilla 1942–1943
MGBs 74–81; later, 111, 112, 115 (71ft 6in BPB Mark V).
Felixstowe, Dartmouth.
Surviving boats became 1st MTB Flotilla (2) in October 1943.
SO1: Lt Cdr R.P. Hichens
SO2: Lt T.J. Mathias
SO3: Lt F.N. Stephenson RN

9th MGB Flotilla 1942–1943
MGBs 107–110, 113 (S4 Polish), 114 (RNethN), 116, 117; later, 118 (71ft 6in BPB Mark 5).
Dover, Ramsgate.
Surviving boats became 2nd MTB Flotilla (2) in October 1943.
SO1: Lt G.D.K. Richards RN
SO2: Lt R. King RN

10th MGB Flotilla 1943
MGBs 119–122, 124–127 (71ft 6in BPB Mark V).
Lowestoft.
Became 3rd MTB Flotilla (3) in October 1943.
SO: Lt E.D.W. Leaf

TRAINING BOATS

At HMS *St Christopher*, Fort William, 1941–44.

MTBs – New boats: MTB 36 (71ft Vosper 1939 class), 66 (Extension class), 228 (1941 class); 346 (45ft Thornycroft).
– Old boats: 42, 45, 46, 48 (72ft White 1939 class).

MGBs – New boats: MGB 68 (81ft Higgins); 66 (70ft BPB); 93 (70ft Elco).
– Old boats: 47 (75ft White); 51, 52, 54 (70ft BPB).

At HMS *Attack*, Portland, 1943–44.
Engine room training and despatch boats.

MGBs – Old boats: 72, 100 (69ft Higgins); 6, 7, 8, 10, 13, 46, 50, 53, 55, 56, 57; 16, 17, 20, 21 (all 70ft BPB MGBs).

THE MISSING FLOTILLAS
The flotilla numbers missing from this list will be found elsewhere in the Trilogy. See *Mediterranean MTBs at War* for: 1st (1), 2nd (1), 7th, 8th (1), 10th, 15th–17th, 19th (1), 20th, 24th, 27th and 28th Flotillas (pp. 193–195); 3rd (1) (p. 5), 19th (2) (p. 101). See *Dog Boats at War* for Fairmile D Flotillas: 30th (1), 31st (1), 32nd–34th Flotillas (pp. 274–278).

18th: Due to losses in shipment from the USA, this flotilla was never formed. The remaining boats joined the 16th and 17th MTB Flotillas.
25th: MTBs 363–370. Vospers built in the USA and intended for this flotilla were transferred to the USSR in 1944.
26th: MTBs 371–378. Vospers built in the USA and intended for this flotilla became the 19th MTB Flotilla (2) – see above.

APPENDIX 3

BIBLIOGRAPHY

PUBLISHED SOURCES

Agar, Captain Augustus, VC DSO RN. *Baltic Episode*, Conway Maritime Press, 1983

Anderson, Rear Admiral Courtney C., CB. *Seagulls in my Belfry*, The Pentland Press Ltd, 1997

Barnett, Correlli. *Engage the Enemy More Closely*, Hodder & Stoughton, 1991

Beaver, Paul. *E-boats and Coastal Craft* (Second World War Photo Albums), Patrick Stephens, 1980

Bray, Michael DSC. *One Young Man's War (1939–46)*, Square One Publications, 1993

Chatterton Dickson, Captain W., RN (Retd) ('Seedie'). *Seedie's List of Coastal Forces Awards for World War 2*, Ripley Registers, 1992

Churchill, Winston S. *The Second World War*, Vols 1–6, Cassell, 1948–1954

Cooper, Bryan. *The Battle of the Torpedo Boats*, Macdonald, 1970

—— *The Buccaneers*, Macdonald, 1970

—— *The E-boat Threat*, Macdonald & Jane's, 1976

Dawson, Christopher. *A Quest for Speed at Sea*, Hutchinson, 1972

Dickens, Captain Peter, DSO MBE DSC RN. *Night Action: MTB Flotilla at War*, Peter Davies, 1974

Forsyth-Grant, Michael. *Courage in Adversity*, The Pentland Press Ltd, 1990

Hichens, Lt Cdr Robert Peverell, DSO DSC RNVR. *We Fought Them in Gunboats*, Michael Joseph, 1944

Holman, Gordon. *The Little Ships*, Hodder & Stoughton, 1943

Jefferson, David. *Coastal Forces at War*, Patrick Stephens Ltd, 1996

Lambert, John & Ross, Al. *Allied Coastal Forces of WW2, Volume 2, Vosper MTBs and US Elcos*, Conway Maritime Press, 1993

Law, Commander C. Anthony DSC CD RCN (Retd). *White Plumes Astern*, Nimbus Publishing Ltd, Halifax, Nova Scotia, 1989

Lawrence, Hal. *Victory at Sea: Tales of His Majesty's Coastal Forces*, McClelland & Stewart Inc., Toronto, 1989

Lenton H.T. & Colledge, J.J., *Warships of World War 2*, Ian Allan, 1964

Nolan, Brian & Street, Jeffrey. *Champagne Navy – Canada's Small Boat Raiders of the Second World War*, Random House, Toronto, 1991

North, A.J.D. *Royal Naval Coastal Forces 1939–1945*, Almark Publishing Co., 1972

Phelan, Keiren, & Brice, Martin H. *Fast Attack Craft*, Macdonald & Jane's, 1977

Rance, Adrian. *Fast Boats and Flying Boats* (a biography of Hubert Scott Paine), Ensign Publications, 1989

Reynolds, Leonard C. OBE DSC. *Gunboat 658*, William Kimber, 1955

—— *Dog Boats at War*, Sutton Publishing, 1998

—— & Cooper, H.F. *Mediterranean MTBs at War*, Sutton Publishing, 1999

Rohwer J. & Hummelchen, G. *Chronology of the War at Sea 1939–45* Vols 1 and 2, The Military Book Society, by arrangement with Ian Allan Ltd, 1972

Roskill, Captain S.W. DSC RN. *History of the Second World War: the War at Sea 1939–1945*; Vol. 1: *The Defensive*, HMSO, 1954; Vol. 2: *The Period of Balance*, HMSO 1957; Vol. 3: *The Offensive*, Parts 1 and 2, HMSO, 1960

Ryder, Commander R.E.R, VC RN. *The Attack on St Nazaire*, John Murray, 1947

Scott, Lt Cdr Peter, MBE DSC RNVR. *The Battle of the Narrow Seas; a History of the Light Coastal Forces in the Channel and North Sea 1939–1945*, Country Life Ltd, 1945

Whitley, M.J. *German Coastal Forces of World War 2*, Arms & Armour Press, 1992

Wilmot, Chester. *The Struggle for Europe*, Collins, 1952

PRIVATELY PRINTED AND DISTRIBUTED BOOKS, BOOKLETS, MANUSCRIPTS

Borthwick, J.B., CD RCN. *History of the 29th Canadian MTB Flotilla.*

Bradford, Donald Gould DSO DSC. *Day In, Night Out.*

Coombes, F.B., DSM. *Reminiscences of World War 2.*

de Casenoze, Paul de G. 'La 23 Flotille de Vedettes Lance – Torpilles de FNFR 1942 – 1945', en *Forces Sous – Marines* No. 6/7.

Higgins, Tony. *The Free French 23rd MTB Flotilla in Kingswear*, Dartmouth History Research Group, Paper 6.

Jea, Tom. *MTB 102.*

Lake, John. *The 13th MTB Flotilla.*

NAVAL RECORDS

At the Naval Historical Branch (NHB)

ADM 199/2327, RACF's Information Reports (CFIs).

ADM 208, Red Lists – weekly lists of movements of minor war vessels in home waters.

Card Index of all MTBs and MGBs.

Coastal Forces Monograph, 1952.

Coastal Forces Periodical Reviews (CFPRs).

List of Recorded Coastal Forces actions with summaries.

Navy Lists.

NHB Search Documents.

War Diary.

War Intelligence Reports.

At the Public Record Office, Kew

ADM 199/261	Coastal Forces actions	1943–4
262	"	1944
263	"	1944
264	"	1943–4
265	"	1944–5
266	"	1944
267	"	1944–5
536	Coastal Forces Operations	1942–3
537	"	1943
680	Coastal Forces Actions	1942–3
782	"	1942
784	Operations against E-boats	1942
1036	Coastal Forces actions in Channel	1943

ADM 116/5493 and 6077 Ostend Explosion

OTHER SOURCES

Article 1, 'Narrow Waters in War', by Capt P.G.C. Dickens DSO MBE DSC RN (Rtd), in the *Journal of the Royal United Services Institute.*

Report of CCF (Channel) on Operation Overlord.

Report of CCF (Plymouth) on Operation Overlord.

Newsletters of the Coastal Forces Veterans' Association.

Questionnaires from veterans.

INDEX

IN HOME WATERS

THE MTB FLOTILLAS

THE MGB FLOTILLAS

PERSONNEL